Across the Waters
of Remembrance

Across the Waters of Remembrance

A Handbook for Liberal and Progressive Clergy

HERBERT E. HUDSON IV

Foreword by Richard Agler

RESOURCE *Publications* · Eugene, Oregon

ACROSS THE WATERS OF REMEMBRANCE
A Handbook for Liberal and Progressive Clergy

Copyright © 2020 Herbert E. Hudson IV. All rights reserved. Except for brief quotations in critical publications or reviews, no part of this book may be reproduced in any manner without prior written permission from the publisher. Write: Permissions, Wipf and Stock Publishers, 199 W. 8th Ave., Suite 3, Eugene, OR 97401.

Resource Publications
An Imprint of Wipf and Stock Publishers
199 W. 8th Ave., Suite 3
Eugene, OR 97401

www.wipfandstock.com

PAPERBACK ISBN: 978-1-5326-9540-7
HARDCOVER ISBN: 978-1-5326-9541-4
EBOOK ISBN: 978-1-5326-9542-1

Manufactured in the U.S.A.　　　　　　　　　　　　　　06/10/24

To my favorite PKs
Debbie, Wendy, and Sean

Contents

Foreword by Richard Agler | xi

Preface | xiii

Acknowledgements | xv

Part I: The Dawning of Awareness | 1

1. A Free Faith | 3
2. Of Reason and Hope | 9
3. And the Greatest of These | 15
4. Billy Budd: Adam or Christ? | 20
5. The Paradox of Theodore Parker | 27
6. Do We Have Two Selves? | 38
7. Earth's the Right Place for Love | 42
8. Gotama Buddha | 48
9. If Jesus Were Alive Today | 54
10. Jesus, Son of Man | 59
11. Life Has Loveliness to Sell | 63
12. No Greater Love Hath Any Man | 67
13. Out of the Stars | 72
14. Palm Sunday | 76
15. The Last Teachings of Jesus | 82
16. The Prophets | 87
17. The Story of a Diabetic | 93
18. Where Rivers Begin | 96

Part II: A Soul in Transition | 101

19. 75th Birthday of Church | 103
20. Christmas 1988 | 106

21. Christmas 1990 | 108
22. Christmas 1991 | 110
23. Crossing the River | 112
24. Easter 1987 | 115
25. Francis | 119
26. Road to Emmaus | 121
27. The Sunday After Easter | 125
28. Thy Will, Not Mine | 129
29. Wings Like Eagles | 132

Part III: A Seasoned Spirit | 135

30. A Better Love | 137
31. Celebration of Life for H. E. Hudson, Jr. | 140
32. Dark Night of the Soul (*Kenosis*) | 143
33. Earth's the Right Place for Love | 147
34. Endings and Beginnings | 151
35. Feeding of the 5,000 | 155
36. God Is Nigh | 159
37. Happiness in an Imperfect World | 163
38. Hospitality | 166
39. The Keys of the Kingdom | 169
40. The Kingdom of God | 173
41. Prayer | 177
42. Spirituality | 182
43. The Least of These | 186
44. The Meaning of Pain | 190
45. The Sun Also Rises (*Koinonia*) | 194
46. This Side of Eden | 197
47. Where Is God? | 201
48. Wings Like a Dove | 205
49. A Cure for Tocharianism | 210

Part IV: Prayers and Readings | 215

50. Invocations and Opening Words | 217
51. Readings and Songs | 239
52. Prayers and Meditations | 252
53. Benedictions and Closing Words | 263

Part V: Special Services | 271

54. Membership | 273
55. Weddings and Commitments | 278
56. Christenings and Dedications | 284
57. Funerals and Memorials | 288
58. Albert Schweitzer Service | 324

Appendix A: Online Videos of Sermons | 335

Appendix B: List of Unitarian Universalist Meditation Manuals | 337

Bibliography | 343

Foreword

THE ESSENTIAL TASK FACING the minister, priest, rabbi, or imam is as challenging as any in the professional canon. In addition to the endless pastoral, administrative, and executive duties that devolve upon a religious leader, the preacher needs to stand before a congregation on a weekly basis and offer insight in a confusing world, grounding in a tumultuous world, and comfort in an oft-times brutal world. All the while remaining fresh, insightful, and relevant to an audience consisting largely of "regulars" who have been there many times before.

Rev. Herbert "Terry" Hudson not only faced this challenge, he met it, consistently, over the course of a career that spanned six decades—and counting.

His discourses on faith transcend every religious and political boundary and are a witness to the human experience that we all share. Whether you are a member of his Unitarian Universalist denomination or not, this collection of readings, prayers, and sermons will reach you intellectually and spiritually.

Writing with gentle eloquence, comprehensive knowledge, and above all, caring, the good pastor uplifts as he informs, inspires us as he teaches, and opens us to affirming, loving, and embracing perspectives on life's great questions. His writing would be a gift in any age—it is especially welcome in our own.

The compilation is remarkable for its steady tone. Beginning before the 1960's got "hot," and continuing through the second decade of the twenty-first century, across very different historical times and circumstances, Rev. Hudson continually finds ways to impart transcendent wisdom.

As the book takes us through decades' worth of "issues of the day," he finds, and amplifies, the prophetic voices of decency and justice. We know that such issues are often muddled and distorted by the passions of political discourse. Rev. Hudson cuts through them and places the larger questions before us. What is Right here? How do we best honor our shared humanity? What does the living God want from us? Our own perspectives clarify as we listen.

The "Prayers and Readings" section could serve as a book of daily inspiration by itself. It offers a lifetime's worth of opportunity for reflection, insight, and uplift. Even contemplating one per day—because who among us can fully digest and make even that much wisdom our own?—will leave us the better for having done so.

Writers are often told to "Write what you know." There is better advice, I believe, and that is to "Write what you want to know." Rev. Hudson often takes the latter course. He navigates complex issues through the lens of spiritual quest. He is constantly seeking, uncovering, and growing. It is all here for us to appreciate and incorporate into our lives.

Scholarship informs Rev. Hudson's work but never overwhelms it. His congregants may have felt on occasion that they were in a university seminar—but they would have never gotten lost in it. Through careful use of personal story and everyday language, his talent brings the eternal questions of the human condition into manageable relief. With a thoughtful balance between the emotional and the rational, never veering too far in the direction of either, his writing educates as it edifies.

While he is far too wise to give simple answers to unsolvable conundrums, Rev. Hudson does make them more accessible. Viewing life through the lens of Scripture's timeless perspective, he extracts the verities of love, knowledge, and truth. The principles of honesty, justice, and spiritual integrity come to life in ways that reach heart and mind alike.

From the international to the local, from the familial to the individual, from sources ancient and modern, Rev. Hudson leads with wisdom, clarity, and above all, hope. Start at the beginning of the book or open it to any page. Explore, take your time, and prepare to be strengthened. This collection from his life's work is a gift to us all.

Rabbi Richard Agler, DD
Rabbi Emeritus of Congregation B'nai Israel
in Boca Raton, Florida and Resident Scholar
of the Keys Jewish Community Center
in Tavernier, Florida
January 2020

Preface

MY FIRST SERMON WAS given when I was a ministerial student at Harvard Divinity School in 1959. This was a time when Paul Tillich was on the faculty, completing the writing of his *Systematic Theology* (Tillich 1967). After later graduating from the Starr King School in Berkeley, I was called to be the pastor of the Unitarian Universalist Church in Utica, New York, from 1961 to 1966. I then became a professor at the State University of New York in Cortland and served as a part-time minister of the First Universalist Church of Central Square from 1967 to 1983. Subsequently, I moved to Key Largo, Florida, where I became an adjunct professor at the Miami campus of Trinity International University and regularly filled the pulpit of the Coral Isles United Church of Christ. I earned my DMin degree from Trinity Evangelical Divinity School.

This book is the capstone of my ministry from 1959 to 2020—literally a span of six decades. The sermons are grouped into three periods. Sermons given in Utica tend to be more academic and are termed "The Dawning of Awareness." Sermons given at Central Square, a time of personal growth and change, are considered as "A Soul in Transition." Finally, sermons in Key Largo reflect more certainty and trust in life and are referred to as "A Seasoned Spirit." (Videos of some Key Largo sermons are available on YouTube under Terry Hudson.) The balance of this handbook includes readings, prayers, invocations, benedictions, and special services for weddings, christenings, and memorials that I have accumulated and used during my spiritual odyssey in the pre-COVID era. Those written by me are cited simply as "Author."

It is my hope that this compilation will serve as a resource for liberal and progressive clergy, and it is my prayer that you will find life to be as blessed and fulfilling as I have.

Herbert E. Hudson IV

Acknowledgements

I AM INDEBTED TO Rabbi Richard Agler, author of *The Tragedy Test* (Agler 2018), who wrote the Foreword to this book. I am grateful to Will King, Michael Delgado, and Eric Anderson for their computer help—and to Richard Knowles and Jeffrey Cale for their photography. Thanks to Matthew Wimer at Wipf and Stock Publishers, and particularly to Rachel Saunders for her patience and typesetting skills. I am appreciative to Charlotte Twine Caria for her expertise in proofreading. I am beholden to Arnold Crompton who once shared with me the words that inspired the title of this volume, words which may have originated with the writings of Michael Fairless (Fairless 1905, 24). And special appreciation goes to my life partner, Maria Teresa Kwalick, for her encouragement and support.

PART I

The Dawning of Awareness
Sermons in Utica, New York

— 1 —

A Free Faith[1]

SOMEONE ONCE SAID, "THE world is made up of two kinds of people—those who try to divide the world into two kinds of people and those who don't."

In a similar form it could be said that, "In the world there are those who divide history into different periods and those who don't." One such "periodizer," a man not well known today, was a Christian scholar of the Middle Ages by the name of Joachim of Flora. It was this man's interpretation, and for some reason this has stuck with me from Harvard Divinity School days, that Christian Church history distributes itself into three eras, that of the Father, the Son, and the Holy Spirit. The Old Testament period was that in which emphasis was placed upon the action of God in history. With the advent of Jesus, the periods rapidly shifted into that in which we are now participating, that over-shadowed by the Son. And somewhere perhaps in the not too distant future, when Christianity will no longer depend upon such overt expressions, we will enter the era of pure Spirit.

It is the view of Unitarians and Universalists, of course, that we have already arrived at this third era. The only trouble is that the remainder of the Christian world does not agree. In a prophetic mood that equals Joachim of Flora's only in part, I am suggesting in this series of three sermons that what has been the "Trinity" of Unitarianism for some time, the qualities of freedom, reason, and tolerance may be conceived as emphases of three different periods of Unitarianism and Universalism. It should

1. Sermon delivered by the author at the Church of the Reconciliation Unitarian Universalist, Utica, New York, on October 29, 1961.

be underscored, however, that these elements are by no means exclusive, but during a period when one is considered dominant, the others overlap and reinforce each other.

We begin, then, with freedom. Without freedom of belief Unitarianism and Universalism would not have begun; only because of freedom of belief is our denomination what it is today. Unitarianism and Universalism as they originally appeared, however, were quite different than we know them now. They were, and we should continually bear this in mind, but sects of Christianity that dared dissent on a point or two of doctrine. In every other respect early liberals remained faithful Christians.

As a quick survey of church history would tell us, it was not really until the fourth century that the Christian Church found it necessary to promulgate a doctrine of the Trinity. It is a curious commentary upon the millions of Christians who have believed in the divinity of Jesus that this doctrine had its origin in a church council over 1600 years ago, was proposed by a minority, and was accepted only because Constantine threw his weight into the balance due to reasons as much political as spiritual. Another participating group called the Arians exercised freedom of belief, rejected this doctrine and thereby became one of the first forerunners of Unitarianism. Just think what the implications would have been for the history of Christianity as well as our denomination had Constantine decided on the side of the Arians at this first summit meeting!

Throughout the following centuries there are innumerable examples of freedom of belief, but one of the most dramatic is that of Michael Servetus. Servetus, who excelled in geography and medicine as well as religion, came to oppose the doctrine of the Trinity from his own reading and study of the Bible. When his book, *On the Errors of the Trinity*, appeared there were many attempts to convert him, notably by John Calvin. But Servetus stood fast and became such a frustrating and offensive opponent that he was soon branded a heretic and was sought for trial by the Inquisition. It was only a matter of time until he was recognized while traveling through Geneva, imprisoned, and burned alive on October 27, 1553. Michael Servetus is sometimes called the first Unitarian, but it is important to remember that he lived and died a devout Christian, differing on but a single point of doctrine.

There were others, and there were other movements, but perhaps not another so prominent until Faustus Socinus. Where Servetus failed, Socinus in Poland succeeded. Socinus established a following and a church that persists to the present day. Socinus also exercised freedom of belief on the issue of the Trinity, but on other matters such as the divine birth and resurrection of Jesus, he remained quite orthodox. An additional emphasis we find in Socinus is that of the goodness of man.

From Socinus and his emphasis on the goodness of men to the rise of Universalism in America is a big step, but it is one we must make if we are to give attention to our whole denomination. Where Unitarians distinguished themselves by their insistence upon the humanity of Jesus, the Universalists were originally defined by their denial of the doctrine of election and their claim of universal salvation. Of early Universalists and their exercise of freedom of belief there are three who were particularly distinguished: George de Benneville, John Murray, and Hosea Ballou.

"The Father of American Universalism" was George de Benneville, who was responsible for bringing Universalism to this continent. Persecuted in France and educated in England, he came to America as a doctor and preacher. A humane man, de Benneville placed emphasis upon the primacy of persons, their intrinsic worth and possible high destiny. Again, it is significant to note that although this founder of our faith believed in universal salvation, he was faithful to such Christian presuppositions as the divine inspiration of the Bible, and invariably used it in arguing with opponents.

John Murray, an excommunicated Wesleyan evangelist, established the First Universalist Church at Gloucester, Massachusetts, and is the man most often associated with the rise of organized Universalism in this country. Murray, who was heavily influenced by James Relly, took his stand unequivocally against Puritanism's doctrines of election and predestination. Although Murray exercised freedom of belief on this point, his mode of proof was to argue a thoroughly orthodox position on the vicarious atonement of all men through Christ's sacrifice.

It was not until Hosea Ballou, the giant of Universalism, published his *Treatise on Atonement* that less emphasis came to be placed on supernatural atonement and more upon the goodness of God and the adequacy of man that warrant his redemption. An interesting example of the freedom that characterized early Universalists was the Restorationist controversy between those who felt there must be some punishment after death before the soul can go to heaven and those who felt that sin brought its own punishment. Under the diplomatic leadership of Ballou this controversy raged, lost its course, and passed into insignificance.

This, then, has been something of Unitarianism and Universalism historically. In their initial stages it would have been hard to imagine them without freedom of belief, but freedom only to question certain dogmas such as the Trinity or Salvation. A freedom that never questioned the spiritual dominance of Jesus, the divine inspiration of the Bible, the reality of heaven, and the sovereignty of God.

This took place over a period of almost 1900 years. Then less than 100 years ago, something very different, something entirely unprecedented began to happen. The attitude of freedom of belief, the spirit of critical inquiry previously reserved for a particular aspect of Christianity began to question the very foundations of Christianity itself.

This tendency began gradually with the insight and scholarship of Theodore Parker and Emerson who we will consider in detail next week. Parker, who remained in what we could call the Christian church, emphasized the critical study of the Bible, the complete humanization of Jesus, and the primacy of social reform. Emerson was one of the first to break with the Church in his stress upon the accessibility of God in nature and the soul of man, and upon the significance of other world religions, notably Hinduism. James Freeman Clark carried this tendency to its natural conclusion in the last part of the nineteenth century with his work on comparative religions.

Another age had been ushered in, the Age of Enlightenment. Everywhere humanity was beginning to see new horizons of truth—in the sciences, in psychology, in world literature, etc. Truth was not dead, embalmed and entombed in glass cases to be reverently but uncritically viewed. Truth was alive, growing, ever enlarging and changing in multiple patterns.

Unitarians and Universalists saw no reason to believe that religion was an exception. Religion was no longer a matter of working out salvation within a given historical faith; religion had become for us a quest for the living truth, wherever it may lead. The only faith fit for such a conception of truth was a free faith. Only through complete freedom of belief can the growing truth be comprehended, can man realize his destiny.

A new Unitarianism and Universalism had been born. The concept Unitarian came to refer to the oneness of life, the unity of experience; while Universalism came to reference all truth, even that of different world religions. Our denomination came to rely on the scriptures of all the world, and we added the symbols of all major religions to our houses of worship. We supplemented prayers with meditations.

Much as such an attitude characterizes most of Unitarianism and Universalism and should characterize the forward thrust of our denomination, we are haunted by recurring questions: What is, or should be, our relationship as religious liberals to Christianity? Can we dismiss Christianity as just another imperfect formulation of truth in our search, or is this too abrupt for a faith that has been so much a part of our tradition and even, in some instances, of our earlier lives?

I think the answer lies in each of our hearts. If Christianity truly has no special meaning in your background, if you had minimal contact with it in youth and secular channels of truth or world religions have come to mean more to you, then we do not need to belabor the point, although we could always wonder whether one could help be raised in this culture with its literature and morals and Christmas, and not find that Christianity has a special meaning.

And if Christianity occupied a prominently unpleasant part of our background, I think we could view with suspicion the claim that now it doesn't mean anything to us. It does—it means something to be forgotten, and what is good will be forgotten along with what was unpleasant, and this is not freedom. One of the poorest grounds for liberalism is an incomplete resolution of one's orthodox past.

What I am suggesting is that there should also be room in this freedom of ours to come to terms with Christianity, and to be free to accept that which is good. For example, the idea of prayer can still have a meaning for liberals. In the words of a colleague, "Prayer doesn't change things. Prayer changes people—and people change things." So, too, can a sensitive, carefully prepared worship service have a place in speaking to our deepest needs. We all have feelings: we do not need to be ashamed of them; they are a part of life and truth; worship should be a place where our feelings as well as our ideas find expression.

Let me say a word about hymns. Many of us will pass up the words that are disagreeable; some will sit them out. There is a point here: we need to continually write new hymns that are an expression of a free faith. But I also think this tendency to be so intent upon the intellectual meaning that we cannot accept a hymn for what it is—an artistic unity that is not a statement of a creed but an expression of beauty—suggests that perhaps we have not completely worked our way through our relationship to Christianity.

As for Jesus, I find myself strangely warmed by this heroic figure. A man to be sure, but what a man. Would he be alive today few of us would waste a minute to rent him the city auditorium or invite him to our discussion group. The fact that he lived long ago, that so many people have muddled the issues since, should not render him any less potent. As a bold and loving leader of men, he has much to say to us today.

So also, can the prophets of the other world religions, although one could wonder whether we can identify ourselves culturally as well with them. Surely, we must learn to do this if we are to become one world, and there are some who do now.

Many of us consider ourselves agnostics and atheists. Certainly, we are atheist about the traditional God conceived as anthropomorphic mover and judge of history. I wonder how many of us can remain agnostic about life. Can life be lived without decision, commitment, not as to the imponderables, but as to the attitudes and assumptions necessary to live each day? Of course it can't. We have all made assumptions about what is for us primary in being, about how we should live and why. It remains only to recognize what this basic reality is that works in our lives and try to enhance and nurture it. This is for us the equivalent of what other men have called God, and if we are free enough to see its parallels or even consider it a dimension of life special enough to be known as divine, we can learn a great deal from the insights of centuries past.

But we can also learn from every other source of human good today—from the sciences, the arts, the philosophies, the psychologies. For centuries will pass and Christianity will be forgotten, but our faith in the living truth will not. The cause of a free faith will never die. It is a faith that takes account of the grandeur of man; it is a faith fashioned to the character of truth.

And it is a faith, make no mistake about it. Not faith in what the many believe and in what now exists, but faith in what does not yet exist, in the unseen, in tomorrow.

— 2 —

Of Reason and Hope[1]

THE ATTEMPT TO COVER the subject of "Unitarian Universalism—Yesterday, Today and Tomorrow," even in a series of three sermons, makes me feel akin to an ant who was scampering down a jungle path. "See that black spot on the horizon?" the ant puffed breathlessly to a friend without slowing down. "That's an elephant. The other day the big lug almost stepped on me. Ever since I've been chasing him. At night when he lies down, I catch up. Then I attack!"

Although I may be no more effective than the ant in the pursuit of his objective, I trust that I will be as persistent. If you will remember last week, we considered the classical Unitarian and Universalist positions as expressions chiefly of freedom. We spoke in detail of European and early American developments, mentioned the role of freedom in the Age of Enlightenment, and suggested how this characteristic is sustained today, notably in our relationship to Christianity, as an expression of a free faith.

You may recall also that when we touched upon the Age of Enlightenment our discussion became sketchy, and that was because I felt that a characteristic other than freedom best describes that period, and that characteristic is reason. Indeed, the Age of Enlightenment is known synonymously as the Age of Reason. It is our purpose this morning to consider the rise of reason and the attending attitude of hope, as an emphasis of Unitarianism and Universalism, that has come to occupy a prominent position in our church today.

---

1. Sermon delivered by the author at the Church of the Reconciliation Unitarian Universalist, Utica, New York, on November 5, 1961.

Part I: The Dawning of Awareness

We begin this second sermon with reason. Before the Age of Enlightenment reason was not totally absent, but neither was it dominant or it would have carried our forefathers beyond their supernaturalism. Since that time reason has become so basic that we have not always been free to deviate from its demands.

The spirit of the early 1800s was one that despaired of man and his destiny. Man was held to be totally depraved and eternally damned. Man was estranged from God not only because he himself was unworthy but because such a wrathful, vengeful God was one man would just as soon keep at a distance. There was little, if any, hope.

Then came a new spirit striding boldly across the century. With the dawning of the Age of Reason man was touched by a new sense of his capability. Everywhere man turned there was a new sense of hope—in the sciences and the doctrine of evolution which spoke not only of beginnings but of an onward process of development, in political science and Lockean thought, and in philosophy, notably German idealism.

The spirit was contagious, and religion soon became infected through the person of William Ellery Channing, the father of American Unitarianism. Where Calvinism posited the alienation of man from God, we find in Channing the tendency to progressively reconcile and identify man with God.

Channing drew his insight directly from the English philosopher John Locke. Channing preached of the goodness of God and the perfectibility of man; in Channing we find the first strains of social reform with his concern about slavery. With the need for hope in combatting Calvinism, it was no coincidence that the school of Unitarianism founded by Channing placed great emphasis upon the miracles of Jesus. Although there was still reliance upon a mediating figure and the Bible was still held to be divinely inspired, in Channing's method we have an unprecedented reliance upon rational process.

With the transcendentalists, use of reason and the identification of man with God went a step further. The Bible was no longer necessary as the sole source of revelation, nor was emphasis placed on Jesus as mediator. In Ralph Waldo Emerson we have one of the most significant figures in Unitarianism, significant because of the scope of the transition he effected and the new hope he brought to man. It his pantheism, Emerson held that God was no longer distant and impersonal. God was in every tree and sunset. Man knew God as the sciences increasingly familiarized him with nature. God also spoke directly to men through reason. It should be stressed, however, that for Emerson reason was not just rational process, but referred to the intuitive sense that today we call conscience.

Theodore Parker was, of course, one of the greatest scholars our denomination has known, and he stressed intelligence as equal to any situation. The hope that Parker brought was largely social, however. Although Parker had a foot in the theological tradition of Emerson, he had another planted firmly in the social concern of his century. Parker summoned every resource of the heart and mind in his struggle not only against slavery, but every other injustice of his day—capital punishment, women's rights, labor conditions, prison reform, and war.

With the popularization of Darwin's theory of evolution by Huxley not only were all religions behooved to make accommodations, but within Unitarianism and Universalism a new school of liberalism was born called naturalism. This school, which is popular today, argued that all values are founded in natural process rather than historic tradition. God was brought even closer. For Emerson, he is revealed in nature of which we are a conscious part. One of the leading proponents of this view was the minister of the Universalist Meeting House in Boston, Kenneth Patton.

The attitude of hope reached its fullest expression in the optimistic view prominent in the early 1900s of the progressive development of society—onward and upward forever. If a man did not yet approximate the ultimate, he soon would. Evil was not something to be lived with, but to be overcome. Thus followed the great pacifism of John Haynes Holmes and the social gospel which finds current expression in our Los Angeles Unitarian minister, Stephen Fritchman.

Finally, we have the most recent and influential expression of reason, Humanism, led by John Dietrich and Curtis Reese. The "Humanist Manifesto" was signed in 1933, and this orientation represents a large segment of our denomination today, particularly among younger members in the Fellowship movement. In the perspective we have been considering of the identification of man with God, this view is the complete assimilation of anything we might have called divine into the character of man.

The best illustration of the effect of reason upon our denomination is the transition in our view of the relationship between God and man. With Channing and earlier forerunners, man was quite apart from God, requiring Scripture for revelation and belief in an exemplary mediator. With Emerson and Parker God came closer, the importance of a mediator lessened. God spoke directly to man in nature and within his heart. And now, with the Humanists, all truth, goodness, and power previously attributed to the divine is seen as a part of man that through education and the right conditions can be realized.

A manifestation of this view of man has been an optimistic attitude towards society and life in general, namely the conviction of the progressive defeat of evil and establishment of the good life. Thus, we have great emphasis on social action, unparalleled in any other denomination except perhaps the Quakers. This emphasis began with Channing, reached classical expression in Parker and is perpetuated through the Social Gospel to the present day, where it occupies a dominant role in the approach of men such as Fritchman.

Confidence in man, optimism about society. In a word, hope. It was a new sense of hope, born out of the despair of New England Calvinism, upheld and given substance by reason. Our denomination has been said to promote "Salvation by character;" it could be more correctly characterized as "Salvation by reason." This is the hope of our free faith.

It is this grand, bold spirit that we must never lose. Particularly the stress on social reform occupies a permanent and unique position in liberal religion. If we ever cease to be alive to social wrongs and active on their behalf, we are not truly liberals.

And yet, we cannot help but be uneasy about some of the conclusions that reason has led us to. Last Sunday we accepted the spirit of a free faith but qualified some of the results of that freedom. This morning while rejoicing in the spirit of hope, we should be critical of some of the findings of reason in this last century. Where the issues last week were of our relationship to Christianity, this week they are on the problem of evil and the relationship of man to God.

In the early 1900s liberals thought they had dispensed with the problem of evil. Our nation had consolidated after the Civil War; we had just passed through one of the greatest centuries known to man. The sciences were booming; the industrial revolution was upon us. All that was needed was education and social action, and we would go onward and upward forever.

Two world wars, a Great Depression, and prolonged international tension under the shadow of nuclear holocaust have changed that view. For practical purposes, the problem of evil is with us; for the foreseeable future it will be one of the conditions of existence. Liberals seem as slow to adapt to the realities of today, however, as we accused the orthodox of being in relation to science a century ago. One of the weaknesses of our liberal faith has been the inability to deal with recurring problems of evil such as the meaning of pain, death, crime, and war. Not to be preoccupied with them, but to be able to cope with them in a way other than superficial optimism.

So, too, has our view of man changed through the insights of psychology and of existentialist philosophy. With the advent of Freud and his revelation of unconscious and almost uncontrollable emotions, the nineteenth century view of the glorified man of reason had to be modified. And the rise of existentialism with its emphasis upon the limitations of existence could not help but have an impact.

I am not suggesting that we be oppressed by these views, but illuminated by them. Many would argue from them that man has no right to claim that which is primary is within us, as some Humanists do. On the other hand, many Humanists argue that they really have no conception of God, or even of what is primary in being.

My own position would be somewhere in between. I believe that there is that which is absolute. The problem for me is not whether there is a God or not, but where it is and by what name it shall be called. Yet I am enough of a Humanist to know that whatever its reality, it must be a part of what we already are. Many of us have an understanding about what this something is that for us is absolute. It functions as quite a natural part of our being.

But for others there is no such reality. I believe there must be, even in the context of the search for truth, something to which we are ultimately committed in the present. This is one of the shortcomings of internalizing what is primary in being. It is too easy to relegate it to the ordinary, to take it for granted, to forget that it places a special demand on us.

It is to this extent that I believe what is primary in being must be considered separate from man. My grounds are as much pragmatic as theological. There is surely no such reality aside from men, but I'm enough of a mystic to feel that the extent to which its assimilation reduces its sovereignty and diminishes its effectiveness is the extent to which we should formulate it as an entity in itself. This need not be because we think the less of man, but because we think the more of this reality.

I think there is a general observation we could make about reason, and that is although it has brought us hope, it has not always left us faith. Our religion has come to be one dominated by the intellect. Our church has been accused of not having warmth. We have glorified reason almost to the point that the Old Testament prophets would call idolatry. Our religion must never do violence to our reason and it must always challenge our intelligence, but we should also draw from other resources of the human spirit.

So where are we to go beyond reason? Where are we to go to restore freedom? What is the absolute of which I speak? We have faith and hope. Now, what is the greatest of these? What will be the emphasis of Unitarianism and Universalism that I prophesy for tomorrow? That, my friends, is to be the subject of next week's sermon.

— 3 —

And the Greatest of These[1]

IT HAS BEEN MY design in this series of three sermons to suggest that the qualities of freedom, reason, and tolerance, which Earl Morse Wilbur identifies in his *History of Unitarianism* (Wilbur 1952), are representative emphases of different periods of Unitarianism and Universalism. We begin by asserting that freedom was indispensable to the rise of Unitarian thought on the continent and Universalist faith in the colonies. Last week we posited the dominance of reason in our denomination from the nineteenth century to the present day. This morning it remains for us to see something akin to tolerance is indicated as the central emphasis of Unitarian Universalism in the years ahead. Tolerance of different opinions always has been and remains a need of our denomination. Yet that which assures us of the truest freedom and that to which reason points is something greater than tolerance.

We begin with tolerance. Our denomination has never really been conspicuous for its tolerance of diverging opinion, much as we would like to think to the contrary. At the time Wilbur's book was published, one of the chief criticisms that appeared in reviews was that he neglected to establish tolerance as historically characteristic of our church. In European Unitarianism, freedom referred more to that of dissent than to that of upholding the church's position. A side of Servetus that is seldom displayed, for example, is the side that could spurn John Calvin as "impudent, ignorant, know-nothing, ridiculous, sophist, crazy, sycophant, rascal, beast, monster, criminal, murderer" (Wilbur 1952, 174). At least

1. Sermon delivered by the author at the Church of the Reconciliation Unitarian Universalist, Utica, New York, on November 12, 1961.

Servetus was correct on the last count! Nor once into the context of American liberalism did our faith become completely tolerant. One of the most remarkable demonstrations of intolerance in any denomination was the way in which Theodore Parker was ostracized, and the way in which he denounced his opponents. A contemporary example in our Church is the growing suspicion with which Humanists regard theists or Unitarian Christians, and the way in which conservatives view agnostics and atheists.

If ever an emphasis upon tolerance was indicated, it is today. Yet I believe that the emphasis needed should be broader than Wilbur's concept of tolerance. I have long felt that the concept of tolerance is limited and unsatisfactory. Strictly speaking, it means the lack of negativism. What I feel is indicated is more than passive acquiescence to existing opinion, of letting the other hold his view. What is needed is the affirmation that not only is it alright for him to hold a different view, but on the basis of understanding him, it may be the best position for him to take. Moreover, it could be an even better position for me than the one I now hold. This kind of attitude is predicated upon a security in what one is that transcends the position held and enables one to support another's difference without being threatened.

It is clear that in carrying the idea of tolerance to its ultimate expression, we have come up with something categorically different from freedom and reason. What we have considered in the first two sermons are for the most part not ends but ways at arriving at truth. This third quality that we are concerned with this morning is one such truth itself. It is a kind of faith; it is the ground of hope. It is the greatest of these. It is a profound sense of charity, of love. Two theologians on the contemporary scene that I feel make a signal contribution to our understanding of love are Martin Buber and Paul Tillich.

Buber's small volume, *I and Thou*, is a classic and I recommend it to you without reservation (Buber 1958). Buber's point is that our only significant relationships are those wherein we can think of the other as a person with needs and potentials of his own, rather than as an object to be manipulated to our own ends. True relationship, however, is not self-sacrificing, but in a paradoxical way, fulfilling. The real problem, then, becomes the ability to transcend oneself in order to fulfill oneself.

Paul Tillich gives a more or less traditional solution, although his existentialist analysis of the conditions of life I commend to your deepest consideration. Tillich's answer is that this ability to love another comes from beyond ourselves and includes self-acceptance so that we can forget ourselves in loving others. This love is "agape," a Greek term, in contrast to self-seeking or lustful love.

There are many other sources we could draw upon for the nature of love, such as Erich Fromm, but one other I would mention is contemporary thinking on creativity, notably Brewster Ghiselin's volume on *The Creative Process* (Ghiselin 1954). The creative act, the reaching beyond oneself in something more than what previously existed, is possible only when our inner needs are met, and we lose all sense of self-consciousness. As long as there is preoccupation with self the creative act is imperiled. When such distractions are overcome and the artist can concentrate solely upon the note to be sung, for example, there is a moment when he reaches for it and all else fades into nothing, and the next moment it is there, filling the room with splendor. So, too, is love. The absorption and empathy necessary, require an integrated, secure self.

So it is that when in the presence of acceptance and affection from another we can reflect similar compassion. To return love for love is not difficult. But what of the many times when we are not in the immediate presence of love? Often, we are not equal to the situation, but sometimes we are able to initiate goodwill. This is an extraordinary thing. Unlike other creatures, our response does not depend solely upon immediate and direct provocations. Somehow, we are conscious of our broader experience; the love we had known before forms the basis of security that tides us through; we have reserves of support that we can draw upon; we are compensated in ways that transcend the particular moment and are the accumulative result of past positive associations.

This is nothing more than the result of human experience, yet it transcends particular instances of human affection. We are able to respond in a given case as fully as if it were present, yet it isn't. This miracle of a presence that isn't yet is, that is far away and yet immediate enough to produce every bit of the response it originally inspired, is worthy of being called divine.

In each of the previous two sermons we said something about the concept of God, each one going a little further until now I am in a position to say what for me is primary in being, what may be called God.

In my first sermon I emphasized that although we may reject the traditional God of Christianity, we cannot be agnostic about life. It is on this point of human concern and care that I cannot be agnostic. In last week's sermon I suggested that the idea of the absolute often has more significance when considered as an entity apart from man. And here, apart from men's immediate influence, we have a force operating that is so remarkable that it merits the name of the highest we know. For me, then, God is the power of remembered love.

Search for a conception of God confronts us with reassurance and demand. There is reassurance in the memory that we are loved; there is a demand remembering love is the course we too must follow. This is the only authority that I have found acceptable to religious liberals, the authority of love. As we outgrow the authority of our parents, we are able to accept the authority inherent in being married and establishing families of our own. We are able to accept it in all of life. "When I was a child, I spake as a child, I understood as a child, I thought as a child: but when I became a man, I put away childish things" (1 Cor 13:11 KJV).

Just as man has relations other than with his fellows so I would say that this principle has other implications. The other major area in which men are related is to the natural world. This is an aspect found in Eastern religions and in transcendentalism, but not so much in Unitarian Universalism today. We are part of all that is. One member of the congregation put it to me recently as the "oneness of being and the joy of life." I think I'd go still further and say it is a sense of belonging in the world, of at-homeness in the universe.

Just as there are times when love is remembered, so there are occasions of suffering, illness, natural violence, and death when we must be sustained as living creatures by remembering the basic fact of our acceptance into the universe. God, then, is the power of remembered love.

Yet we have still to know what is "the greatest of these." Just as earlier we distinguished freedom and reason by saying they were both ways of arriving at truth and not a truth themselves, all we have done so far this morning is to present our conception or formulation of this reality of acceptance and peace. But the "greatest of these" is not our formulation of the truth—it is the truth itself.

This is one of the most important distinctions that I can make as a minister. There are formulations of truth, and there is the truth itself. The formulation is not the truth, it is but an expression and representation of it. In Plato's terms, we have been dealing with but shadows of truth. Or, to return to Joachim of Flora, the promised era is not that of such forms as Father and Son, but that of Spirit.

It is the truth itself that is basic to religion. The formulation of it is secondary and is justified only to the extent to which it enhances and promotes the truth. The task of religion is to get people to live and to be the truth, rather than to utter it. In this respect our preoccupation with intellectualizing truth is potentially little better than the orthodox repetitions of dogma and prayer.

It is the primacy of truth rather than its formulation that is characteristic of the great religions and prophets of all times. Jesus, for example, never wrote anything and spoke almost entirely in parables that conveyed the spirit rather than the literal truth he lived. Lao-Tse, the Chinese sage, never found it necessary to write anything until he was about to leave his country and the gatekeeper required that he write a book before departing. Indeed, this anti-intellectualism is prominent in Eastern religions. If you interrupt a Zen Buddhist who is deep in contemplation by asking, "What is the truth?" he will allegedly throw you through the window, not in contempt, but so you will have some experience of what is real. Then, too, we have the silent worship of Quakers, and we have a man like Albert Schweitzer leaving a life of study and writing for a life of devotion to what he believes is true.

So, too, what is the greatest of these lies beyond anything we could say here today. It will always be so, that here in this hour we can try only to formulate what is true; it remains for us the rest of the week to find the real truth in our lives. As Gibran has said, "If you would know God be not therefore a solver of riddles. Rather look about you and you shall see Him playing with your children" (Gibran 1942, 89). We will often speak as if what we say here is the truth, but at least once at the beginning of this ministry we have acknowledged that we know better.

So, I commend each of you to the silence of this other realm. I commend each of you to the experience of what is the greatest of these. The truth awaits. Nay, it is about us already. And as you venture forth, one last word: Do not be troubled if there is that which you cannot explain. There will be that which is so inscrutable that it must remain as you find it, a mystery.

> ... whether there be prophecies, they shall fail; whether there be tongues, they shall cease; whether there be knowledge, it shall vanish away. For we know in part, and we prophesy in part.... For now we see through a glass, darkly; but then face to face. (1 Cor 13:8–12 KJV)

– 4 –

Billy Budd: Adam or Christ?[1]

MELVILLE'S IMMORTAL *MOBY DICK* ends with the destruction of the whaler *Pequod* and the loss of all hands save one, Ishmael. His lesser-known novel, *Billy Budd*, concludes its main action with the sacrifice of only one and the survival of all others. This significant difference has suggested a new, more hopeful aspect of Herman Melville. *Billy Budd* has therefore been enjoying a re-discovery, or properly speaking a process of discovery since it was not published in America until 1928. The Ustinov film production, released in the Fall of 1962, is most successful and impressive.

The unmistakable religious symbolism in *Billy Budd* suggests the need for a study of its theological themes and the meanings that they hold for religious liberals. Melville's character, Billy Budd, represents both the mythological Adam and the figure of the Christ. Before taking up these themes it will be helpful to recount briefly the history of the story and to summarize its contents.

I

Almost all of Melville's prose fiction was written between 1845 and 1857, a period of only twelve years. From 1857 to 1888 Melville devoted himself almost exclusively to poetry. Then, on November 16, 1888, he began *Billy Budd*. Although much shorter than his early novels *Billy Budd* took

---

1. Sermon delivered by the author at the Church of the Reconciliation Unitarian Universalist, Utica, New York. Printed in *The Crane Review* (Winter 1965), pp. 62–67. Reprinted in the following: Walter K. Gordon (ed.), *Literature in Critical Perspectives: An Anthology*, 1968, New York: Appleton-Century-Crofts, pp. 753–57.

three years in the writing. It was finished on April 19, 1891. Five months later Melville died.

Thus, *Billy Budd* occupies a singular position in Melville's writings. It is the last and apparently most carefully written of his works. As Ronald Mason says in his book, *The Spirit Above the Dust,* Melville "seems to have taken far more pains with the detailed construction of this story than he ever did with any of his previous writings. . . ." (Mason 1951, 246). It was almost as if he had something very important to say.

In 1949 *Billy Budd* became the basis of the play "Uniform of Flesh," written by Louis O. Coxe and Robert Chapman. This play ran for seven performances at the Lenox Hill Playhouse. The play was then re-written and opened at the Biltmore Theatre under the title "Billy Budd." Here it narrowly missed the Drama Critics Award for the best play in the 1950–1951 season.

II

Such is the history of *Billy Budd*. Before proceeding with an interpretation of its themes, it might be best to summarize the contents of the novel. The action takes place in 1798 on the high seas when England and France are at war. This is the year of the naval mutinies at Spithead and Nore when English sailors, infected by the spirit of revolution, protest such abuses as impressment, flogging, and capital punishment.

Billy Budd, a slim, handsome boy of nineteen is impressed from the merchantman, *The Rights of Man,* to serve on the man-of-war, H.M.S. *Indomitable,* commanded by Captain Vere. Of a cheerful, cooperative nature, Budd quickly adapts to navy life. His frank, trusting disposition makes him well-liked by his shipmates.

His very presence seems to create a sense of goodwill and confidence—with all except one, the ship's Master-at-Arms, John Claggart. The spiritual antithesis of Budd, Claggart's nature is sinister and evil. As Melville wrote: "[In Claggart was] an evil nature, not engendered by vicious training or corrupting books or licentious living, but born with him and innate, in short "a depravity according to nature" (Melville 1952, 843).

Claggart becomes obsessed by the need to hurt Billy Budd. He plots with his assistant, Squeak, to discredit Budd by sabotaging his gear. He insults him and tries to provoke him, but to no avail. Soon it becomes clear that Claggart will not rest until he has destroyed Budd. One night he has Squeak try to tempt Budd into mutinous behavior by offering the young seaman two gold guineas. When this fails, Claggart executes his masterstroke. He goes to Captain Vere and accuses Budd of mutiny. Captain Vere knows Budd is not guilty and has long suspected Claggart of improprieties, so he sees this as an opportunity to catch Claggart on a perjury charge, which is a capital offense.

Summoning Billy to his cabin Vere has Claggart repeat the charges. Standing falsely accused, Billy is shocked, tongue-tied, enraged. Although he had been known to stammer when under stress, this is the first time he completely loses control of himself. Billy is choked with anger, his face twisted, his body almost convulsed. Not able to answer in any other way, his arm strikes out and catches Claggart squarely on the temple. There is a groan and Claggart topples over dead.

Suddenly the plot turns, violently the roles are reversed. Now Budd is guilty of deed if not of intent. A court martial ensues and we cannot believe that Budd will be convicted. But there is no choice for the tormented Captain Vere: Budd has killed a ship's officer; it is time of war; he must hang. Before we can fully grasp what has happened, the crew is summoned to witness punishment, Budd is marched forward and executed. The crew stands by, fixed in horror. Just before Billy is lifted from the deck he shouts—for he has trusted Captain Vere implicitly and bears him no malice—"God bless Captain Vere!"

The story then follows the history of the H.M.S. *Indomitable* and Captain Vere, who is soon killed in a naval engagement, but concludes shortly thereafter.

III

Throughout the story certain themes and religious symbolism emerge which we are now in a position to interpret. Two minor images suggested are David felling Goliath and Abraham being called upon to sacrifice his son. The relationship of trust and affection between Vere and Budd is much like that of father and son. As Vere says in the play, "If I had a son, I'd hope for one like Budd" (Gassner 1952, 381). Since Budd is illegitimate yet of noble bearing, the possibility is never dismissed that Vere could in fact be his father.

By far, however, the dominant images which Budd embodies are those of the mythological Adam before the Fall, and the Christ figure.

Billy Budd clearly embodies the qualities of Adam. Budd, as he arrives from *The Rights of Man*, is simple, completely natural. His innocence, carried almost to the point of naivete, make this association with Adam inescapable. In this handsome young sailor there is only one flaw, an impediment of speech which proves his undoing, as did the fatal flaw of Adam, curiosity. Melville himself calls attention to this similarity at several points in the text of the novel. Melville describes Billy as "a sort of upright barbarian, much such perhaps as Adam presumably might have been ere the urbane Serpent wriggled himself into his company" (Melville 1952, 817).

Yet the serpent does find his way into Budd's company: in the form of Claggart and his false accusations Budd is tempted to the limit of his endurance and commits an act of anger and violence. In striking Claggart, Budd has finally recognized the evil in the Master-at-Arms and found the potential for it in himself, and in this knowledge he falls from the state of innocence that he previously held.

So, the Adam theme is completed. This would be story enough. For the first time the character of Budd is believable, but Melville is not content to leave him as the Fallen Adam. It would have been enough to affect the Fall if Budd simply struck Claggart out of hatred and anger, but through a quirk of fate Melville has Budd kill him. Nor is Melville going to let him off at the court martial to live as Fallen Man. Captain Vere asserts the need to fulfill the law, and Budd, because of his human failing, is condemned and sacrificed.

Thus, Melville sets into motion yet another theme, that of the Christ. Budd's character is still one somewhat of innocence, but it is described by one critic as a "dynamic pervasive innocence credited to Jesus" (Mason 1951, 250). Throughout the entire story, as with the Adam theme, there are frequent parallels between Budd and Jesus. Budd is confronted with the temptation of the two gold guineas, as Jesus is said to have been tempted by Satan. Both Budd and Jesus were falsely accused of the same crime—treason. Both were equally innocent. One was convicted under Mosaic law and the other under the Mutiny Act. Neither, when accused, uttered a word in his own defense. The friends of both stood by helplessly while they were killed. When the chaplain saw Billy before the execution, he stooped and kissed him on the cheek, reminiscent of the act of Judas. Budd's cry as he was being executed, "God Bless Captain Vere!" echoes that other cry of compassion, "Forgive them! For they know not what they do!" Melville's own description of Budd's execution and the appearance of the early morning sky cannot be ignored:

> ... it chanced that the vapory fleece hanging low in the East, was shot through with a soft glory as of the fleece of the Lamb of God seen in mystical vision and simultaneously therewith, watched by the wedged mass of upturned faces, Billy ascended; and, ascending, took the full rose of the dawn. (Melville 1952, 894)

Following his death Melville reports that sailors followed the spar from which Budd was hanged "from ship to dock-yard and again from dock-yard to ship, still pursuing it even when at last reduced to a mere dock-yard boom. To them a chip of it was as a piece of the Cross" (Melville 1952, 902).

In Billy Budd, then, we have a figure who was admired by his fellows for his strength and goodness and who was revered after his tragic death. Throughout his time aboard the *Indomitable,* his spirit was one that transformed the circumstances of hardship and suffering into joy and hope. There is even reason to believe that death was for him something that could be accepted with trust, something that did not vanquish his sense of goodwill and serenity. Thus, his final words were unmarked by a trace of stammer.

Our interpretation, then, is that Billy Budd represents both Adam and Christ. He is not completely either, yet a curious combination of both. By character he is very much Adam; by circumstances he is forced to play out the role of the Christ. As Milton Stern said in his excellent work, *The Fine Hammered Steel of Herman Melville*: ". . . in *Billy Budd* Melville tells his history of humanity in a reworking of the Adam-Christ story, placing prelapsarian Adam and the Christ on a man-of-war, and demonstrating the inevitability of the Fall and the necessity of the Crucifixion" (Stern 1957, 211).

IV

This being our interpretation, what does it mean to Melville, and to us? If the Adam-Christ interpretation of *Billy Budd* is as Melville intended, it is clear that this final work is categorically different from his earlier novels. In the earlier works man is locked in deadly combat with the inscrutable forces of evil. In Ahab's defiance and Pierre's despair there is no reconciliation to life, only struggle and crushing defeat. In *Billy Budd*, however, Melville suggests a degree of resolution and transcendence over the forces of evil not hitherto expressed. Billy Budd rises above the annihilating circumstances of life and death, and asserts his spirit of goodness and acceptance.

If this is the meaning Melville intended, the consequences are far-reaching. It means that Melville underwent a transition not only in literary outlook but in his own convictions about life. "Towards the end," said Auden in his poem on Melville, "he sailed into an extraordinary mildness" (Mason 1951, 246). Ronald Mason remarked, "[*Billy Budd*] is a calm and authoritative revelation; the doubts which had tormented [Melville's]... most vigorous and productive moments have by years and years of unrecorded wrestling, both of intellect and imagination, been resolved" (Mason 1951, 245).

If this is so, it means that *Billy Budd* is one of Melville's most important novels, that it cannot be ignored as a natural sequel to the greatest of the earlier works such as *Moby Dick*. Some scholars are skeptical, however, whether Melville intended *Billy Budd* to be taken seriously, or whether instead the work is a misleading effort at ironic, satiric comedy. They suggest that since Melville was negative about religion and Christianity throughout his life it is too much to expect that he could make such a transition; they feel that a deathbed recantation is somehow too pat. Lawrance Thompson, a chief spokesman of this point of view, states in his book, *Melville's Quarrel With God*:

> My suggestion is that Billy Budd should be viewed as Melville's most subtle triumph in triple-talk; that it was designed to conceal and reveal much the same notions as expressed years earlier in Moby Dick and Pierre and The Confidence-Man; that Melville came to the end of his life still harping on the notion that the world was put together wrong and that God was to blame. (Thompson 1952, 332)

We could understand such skepticism if *Billy Budd* were something Melville dashed off in a few months. We could imagine him spending no more time on a satiric comedy. But it is improbable that Melville would take longer than he ever had taken on works many times the size, that he would summon the last of his strength and occupy his final moments simply restating what had earlier received classic form.

What Melville intended is perhaps something we shall never know. What the story means to us, however, is another matter. We are free to accept it at face value, as this writer is inclined to, as a positive treatment of the Adam and Christ themes and for the meaning these symbols hold. As such the story becomes a commentary on man's epic struggle for goodness. The struggle takes place in a world of imperfection and human failings—but it is not without hope. Man has resources of compassion, joy, and courage upon which he may draw. In *Billy Budd* we have the promise that even in the stark world of Herman Melville the goodness in man's heart cannot be vanquished.

— 5 —

The Paradox of Theodore Parker[1]

To be human is to be paradoxical. To be human is to contain many forces, any one of which may appear ambiguously weak or strong, beautiful or ugly, creative or destructive. In relation to each other these forces may appear the same yet different, similar yet opposite, complementary yet contradictory. The tension between such forces may be resolved by the dominance of one that is unexpected and perhaps undesired. These paradoxical tendencies of ambiguity, contradiction, and ironic resolution characterize human personality.

The quality of Theodore Parker as a human being, therefore, is best expressed as the paradox of Theodore Parker. The paradox of Theodore Parker emerges in three dimensions: first, Parker as an individual; second, Parker in his relations to others; and, third, Parker's courage that underlies his greatness.

First, the paradox of Theodore Parker is conspicuous in his individual intellectual and physical powers. Parker's intellectual powers participate in the paradox. At an early age young Theodore distinguished himself as a scholar. Before he was eight Parker read Homer, Plutarch, and Rollin's *Ancient History*; while he was nine the ambitious student read widely in Pope, Milton, Cowley, and Dryden; at ten he began to study Latin, translating Virgil and Cicero's *Select Orations*; he tackled

---

1. Sermon delivered by the author at the Church of the Reconciliation Unitarian Universalist, Utica, New York; the Unitarian Church of Cortland, New York; the Unitarian Fellowship of Gainesville, Florida; the First Unitarian Universalist Church of Detroit, Michigan; and the First Unitarian Church of Los Angeles, California. Reprinted as "The Paradox of Theodore Parker," *The Crane Review* (Spring 1959), 111–20.

Greek at eleven and, as he casually announced, "I took to metaphysics about eleven or twelve" (Weiss 1864, I:43).

The record of such study is doubly impressive considering that Parker was for the most part self-educated. Languages and the classics particularly, Parker said, "I learned ... almost wholly alone without help" (Weiss 1864, I:368). He continues, "Natural Philosophy, Astronomy, Chemistry and Rhetoric I studied by myself" (Weiss 1864, I:44). Such remarkable scholarship was possible because of Parker's power of retention: he had a photographic memory. He remembered a poem of 500 to 1,000 lines after a single reading, memorized hymns in church while the minister read them through before singing, retained the table of contents of a book not seen in twenty years, and recited a comic song of more than a dozen verses after having heard it once thirty years earlier.

Into manhood Theodore Parker remained an accomplished scholar. He registered for work at Harvard but reported to the college only to take examinations. He mastered over twenty languages. His constantly growing library of over 11,000 volumes and 2,500 pamphlets caused Emerson to say of him, "It looked as if he was some president of council to whom a score of telegraphs were ever bringing in reports" (Emerson 1860, 14–15). Parker translated and added a definitive commentary to De Wette's *Introduction to the Books of the Old Testament*. His *Defence,* written on the occasion of his indictment before the Grand Jury for aiding a fugitive slave, has been hailed as "the best account extant of judicial and legal tyranny from the reign of James I to the period of his own indictment" (Weiss 1864, II:150).

Parker belonged to the "true race of the giants of learning" (Higginson 1899, 38). Men that grow into giants, however, sometimes have faults in their organic development. In almost a compulsive way Parker seized upon everything there was to learn and know. Even his great mind could not possibly assimilate the endless deluge of material. The overflowing information in letters, sermons, and lectures reflects a want of discrimination. The preoccupation with study and learning interfered with more imaginative applications.

It is a paradox that in rushing to quench his insatiable thirst at the fountain of knowledge, Parker bloated his mind full of information and thus was not always capable of complete assimilation, fine discrimination, and imagination. Such criticism, however, does not reduce but only qualifies the intellectual stature of Theodore Parker: "It is only the loftiest trees of which it occurs to us to remark that they do not touch the sky" (Higginson 1899, 57–58).

Parker's physical, as well as intellectual, powers participate in the paradox. From his mother and from the spongy meadows of his farm home Parker inherited a basic source of weakness, consumption. Yet, paradoxically, he possessed great strength and endurance. As a young man Parker could carry a full barrel of cider in his arms. On the farm he had occasionally worked twenty hours a day for several days at a time.

As a man it was not uncommon for Parker to work from twelve to seventeen hours a day in his study. He once walked from New York to Boston, averaging thirty miles a day. When convalescing from a serious illness Parker drove about London with an old friend, Charles Sumner. After six hours of riding Parker decided to go about on foot for more exercise. Sumner went home to rest.

Yet, no man has so much strength that with the burden of hereditary disease he can continually tax himself without injury and eventual destruction. So, it is a further paradox that with all he had to offer the world intellectually, Parker virtually destroyed himself physically. He went too far. He sustained a voluminous correspondence, writing thousands of letters a year. During 1856 he consented to preach twice a week, riding to Watertown every Sunday afternoon regardless of the weather.

It was the lecturing, however, that most deeply taxed Parker's endurance. Appointing himself a "home missionary for lectures," Parker went about in every Northern state east of the Mississippi lecturing eighty or a hundred times a year (Weiss 1864, II:479). He took pride in signing himself as "Theodore Parker of everywhere, and no place in particular" (Frothingham 1874, 301). The lecture tour to central New York State was typical. On this trip Parker slept in the railroad cars or between the "damp sheets" of a tavern, had few meals except what fruit he carried in his wallet, and contracted a sharp pain in his side and the chills of an incipient fever. Parker continues to describe the tour:

> I lectured, took the cars at 2 or 3 A.M. having waited for them three or four hours in the depot, and reached Albany in time for the 4 P.M. train, Friday, and got to Boston about 2 A.M. on Saturday, having had no reasonable meal since noon, Thursday. Sunday I preached at Boston and Watertown, as my custom was. The next week I was ill, but lectured four times; so the next, and the next, until in March I broke down utterly, and could do no more. Then I had a regular fever, which kept me long in the

house; but soon as I could stand on my feet an hour, I began to preach. (Weiss 1864, II:246)

When Parker preached on this occasion, he tells of the effort: "I spread out my feet as far apart as I could... to make a wide basis, and kept my hand always on the desk, so that I need not fall over" (Frothingham 1874, 492). The strain of lecture tour and sermon resulted in pleurisy and an effusion of water on the lungs that lasted eight months. Parker had an operation, lost twenty pounds, admitted that it was all a nuisance, but said, "It did not much interfere with my work" (Commager 1936, 273).

How can such a man hope to recover? On Sunday, January 9, 1859, Parker wrote to his congregation, "I shall not speak to you to-day; for this morning, a little after four o'clock, I had a slight attack of bleeding in the lungs or throat" (Frothingham 1874, 504). The "slight attack of bleeding" proved to be a serious hemorrhage of the lungs. Parker scurried to the West Indies and Europe attempting to recover lost health, but it was too late, and on May 10, 1860, he expired in Italy.

Theodore Parker presents a paradox, then, as an individual in his intellectual and physical being. He also presents a paradox in his relations to others. John Weiss, one of Parker's first biographers, identified the basis of this paradox: "For he would be loved by men, as well as love and worship truth" (Weiss 1864, I:51). It is one of the most tragic paradoxes of Theodore Parker that, although he desperately wanted the affection and approval of others, his relentless search for religious truth made him bitterly hated.

Theodore Parker was a man hungry for affection. Born on August 24, 1810, Theodore was the last of eleven children; the next youngest child was five years older. Thus, as the baby of the family young Theodore was the favorite; the little fellow in his brown home-spun petticoats would eagerly dash from one member of the family to another for a pat on the head and a word of approval. Young Parker received great care and love and hence learned to need great love. He later wrote, "I remember often to have heard neighbors say, 'Why Miss Parker, you're spilin' your boy! He never can take care of himself when he grows up.' To which she replied 'she hoped not,' and kissed my flaxen curls anew" (Weiss 1864, I:24).

Throughout his life, Parker was an extremely sensitive person. J. H. Morrison, who sat near him each time Parker preached, said:

> More than half the time, in his prayer, I could see the tears run down his face before he was done. Two years, on attempting to

read on Easter Sunday the story of the trial and crucifixion of Jesus, he could not get through, but, overcome by his emotions, had to sit down, and give way to his tears. (Morrison 1875, 251)

His need for human closeness and affection continued. As he declared, "I want someone always in the arms of my heart, to caress and comfort; unless I have this, I mourn and weep" (Weiss 1864, I:51). With this great need for someone to lie in his arms and comfort, it is a paradox that Parker and his wife, Lydia, were not able to have children. Instead, Parker treated the children of his friends as if they were his own. They climbed the long flights to have a chat with "Mr. Parkie," and it warmed his heart to have them call him that. He opened the top drawer of a secretary and out tumbled a store of carts and jumping-jacks. The floor became a playground and Parker on his hands and knees was the biggest child of them all.

This is the same man who was to write President Fillmore, "No man out of the political arena is so much hated in Massachusetts as myself" (Weiss 1864, II:100). Because of his religious conviction, this man with such an intense need for affection was destined to become bitterly despised.

Parker's quest for religious truth resulted in an early rejection of Calvinism and a serious qualification of Unitarianism of the time. Parker's earliest recorded protest against traditional religious forms was at the age of two and a half. It was the occasion of his christening, and a larger concourse of friends than usual made the event impressive. As the water was sprinkled on his head, however, little Theodore vigorously fought off the dismayed clergyman and lustily shouted, "Oh, don't!"

Of more serious character was the effect of the doctrine of eternal damnation. Having heard the doctrine expounded from a nearby pulpit, little Parker lay in bed for hours weeping in terror and praying until sleep gave him repose. As a young man, Parker attended meetings of the famous Calvinist preacher, Lyman Beecher. "The better I understood [Beecher's theology]," said Parker, "the more self-contradictory, unnatural and hateful did it seem. A year of his preaching about finished all my respect for the Calvinist scheme of theology" (Weiss 1864, I:57).

So, Parker, confirmed in his Unitarianism, went to Harvard Divinity School and entered the Unitarian ministry. To understand Parker's qualification of Unitarianism we should place it in the perspective of Unitarian history. Under the influence of William Ellery Channing and his famous "Baltimore Sermon" Unitarianism had abandoned the major dogmas of Calvinism such as the Trinity, a wrathful God, total depravity, and predestination but still held that the Scriptures were the final authority. Although interpreted by reason, the Scriptures were considered a source of revelation external to man.

After the initial thrust by Channing, Unitarians had little interest in going further. They had achieved a degree of respectability that felt good. They fell to defending a new orthodoxy based on the authority of the Scriptures. The creative period had passed. Parker characterized the situation this way:

> Alas! After many a venturous and profitable cruise, while in sight of port, the winds all fair, the little Unitarian bark, o'ermastered by its doubts and fears, reverses its course, and sails into dark, stormy seas, where no such craft can live. (Weiss 1864, II:483)

Then, on July 15, 1838, Ralph Waldo Emerson delivered his "Divinity School Address" to an astonished convocation of Harvard Divinity School students and faculty. Emerson disputed the final authority of the Scriptures since they were a source of revelation external to man and insisted that all knowledge of truth must come from within each man through intuition. A year later Andrews Norton answered Emerson in his speech before the alumni of the Divinity School, "The Latest Form of Infidelity." And, on May 19, 1841, a day of infamy for orthodox Unitarians, Parker with transcendentalist sympathies responded with his well-known sermon at the ordination of Charles C. Shackford, "The Transient and the Permanent in Christianity."

Parker was now a marked man. Fellow Unitarians cancelled and avoided pulpit exchanges because of "ill health," "home engagements," and "frequent absence from their desks" (Frothingham 1874, 152). Other ministers refused to serve with him on committees, to attend the same funeral or wedding, to sit on the same bench at public meetings, to remain in the same public apartment, to trade at the same bookstore, to reply to his letters, or even to return his salutation on the street. Parker sadly said, "I see men stare at me in the street, and point, and say, 'That is Theodore Parker,' and look at me as if I were a *murderer*" (Frothingham 1874, 345).

In 1842 Parker published his *Discourse of Matters Pertaining to Religion*, the most thorough statement of his transcendentalist qualification of Unitarianism. He believed that man has the ability to perceive truth directly, that God is in the soul of man and man in the soul of God, that

The Paradox of Theodore Parker

the term "sin" is tainted and of little value, that the Bible should be read as Plato, Seneca, or any other book, and that Jesus was human, a religious genius as Homer was a poetical genius.

This was too much for the Unitarians, and they summoned Parker before the Boston Association of Ministers, of which he was a member. With few exceptions, members of the Association criticized Parker, exhibiting the orthodoxy and disregard for freedom of speech that then characterized Unitarianism. Some attacked his works as "vehemently deistical," others as "subversive of Christianity." Chandler Robbins asked that Parker withdraw from the Association. The Unitarians, however, failed to intimidate him, for despite the criticism of that meeting and the abuse to follow for the rest of Parker's life, he refused to withdraw or retreat. A typical sentiment about Parker was voiced by a Boston layman:

> I would rather see every Unitarian congregation in our land dissolved and every one of our churches occupied by other denominations or razed to the ground than to assist in placing a man entertaining the sentiments of Theodore Parker in one of our pulpits. (Angoff 1927, 85)

Disapproval was most desperate, however, from clergymen of even more orthodox persuasions, who publicly prayed against him:

> O Lord! Send confusion and distraction into his study this afternoon, and prevent his finishing his labor for tomorrow . . . confound him, so that he shall not be able to speak. O Lord! Put a hook in this man's jaws. . . . O Lord! If this man will persist in speaking in public, induce the people to leave him, and come up and fill this house. . . . Lord, we know that we cannot argue him down; and, the more we say against him, the more will the people flock after him, and the more will they love and revere him. O Lord! What shall be done for Boston if thou dost not take this and some other matters in hand? (Frothingham 1874, 495)

The Liberator once called Parker "more of the hyena than the jackal" (*Liberator,* July 18, 1856) and a Rev. Mr. Burnham said, "Hell never vomited forth a more wicked and blasphemous monster than Theodore Parker" (Frothingham 1874, 495).

All this hatred and abuse for a man so much needing approval and acceptance simply because of a difference in theological belief—a paradox, indeed! We are not to assume, however, that Theodore Parker stood passive before such an affront. He returned the fire. It is a further paradox that this man who was so gentle with the children became such a terrible opponent. It is a paradox that, despite his sensitivity to abuse from others, Parker was sometimes insensitive to his sarcastic and bitter denunciations of them. More often, however, the sensitivity of Parker succumbed to melancholy. O. B. Frothingham, perhaps Parker's best biographer, wrote:

> Parker was brave; but, as has been said already, he was tender, with an immense capacity for suffering. He could battle long and well; but to battle alone cost him dear. He wanted love; and they from whom he had the best right to expect it failed him. (Frothingham 1874, 175)

When he preached the Thursday lecture in 1840 and was accosted afterwards by an abusive colleague, Parker "left him, not in anger, but in sorrow, and went weeping through the street" (Weiss 1864, I:142). Suddenly Parker realized, "I am alone—ALL ALONE!" (Frothingham 1874, 172). His loneliness sometimes gave way to depression. His periods of depression were almost never evident to others, but were occasionally expressed in letters, as in this one to his friend, S. P. Andrews: "You detected something in my bearing which argued that there was unhappiness, at least discontent of some sort, in the wind. I admit its existence in a greater extent than you imagine; but of the cause, *not a word*" (Frothingham 1874, 94–95). Usually, however, his feelings of depression were poured into his mighty journals, of which many a line were "blotted with his manly tears" (Chadwick 1900, 208). At places his prose becomes poetry:

> I know not why, but heavy is my heart;
> The sun all day may shine, the birds may sing,
> And men and women blithely play their part;
> Yet still my heart is sad. . . . (Commager 1936, 34)

So, the greatest paradox of all: despite the difficulty, discouragement, and even depression that were often with him, Theodore Parker was a man of courage. We have seen that Parker represents paradox as an individual and in his relations to others. The third general paradox of Theodore Parker is that adversity served only to summon his courage, which in turn underlies his greatness.

He would lift himself from depths of depression and declare, "What a fool I am to be no happier. . . . I have sterner deeds to do, greater dangers to dare, I must be about my work" (Frothingham 1874, 110, 68). When going to Boston, where he knew he would for the most part stand alone, Parker said, "I feel that I have a great work to do; I think I shall not fail in it" (Frothingham 1874, 217). And when in the midst of controversy with pulpits closed against him, he proclaimed:

> I will go about, and preach and lecture in city and glen, by the roadside and field-side, and wherever men and women can be found. I will go eastward and westward, and southward and northward, and make the land ring. (Weiss 1864, I:184)

Parker's courage is evident in his personal discipline, his fearless scholarship, and his pioneering in Unitarianism, but is perhaps most apparent in his fight against slavery. Slavery was to Parker "the sum of all villainies," and his struggle against it absorbed the last ten years of his life and overshadowed even his activity in Unitarianism.

Parker never forgot his grandfather, Captain John Parker of the Minute Men, who precipitated the Revolution by bravely facing the redcoats on the Lexington Green. Parker needed the same courage to speak against slavery in a Boston that had mobbed Garrison and which greeted the Fugitive Slave Bill with a salute of one hundred guns.

When the Fugitive Slave Bill was passed on September 18, 1850, Parker became chairman of the unpopular Vigilance Committee, dedicated to protecting fugitive slaves. In this position Parker penned a bold letter to President Fillmore:

> I will do all in my power to rescue any fugitive slave from the hands of any officer who attempts to return him to bondage. I will resist him as gently as I know how, but with such strength as I can command; I will ring the bells and alarm the town; I will serve as head, as foot, or as hand to any body of serious and earnest men who will go with me.... (Weiss 1864, II:102)

This was no idle boast. Parker's courage was not reserved for speaking and writing against the Fugitive Slave Bill: he armed himself and took a dramatic part in the rescues of Shadrach and the Crafts, as well as the attempted rescues of Thomas Simms and Anthony Burns. "I have had to arm myself," he said, "I have written my sermons with a pistol in my desk, loaded, a cap on the nipple, and ready for action. Yea, with a drawn sword within reach of my right hand" (Parrington 1927, II:415).

The greatness of Parker grows from his courage as a man. Curious and sympathetic throngs came from everywhere to hear the brave prophet. While lecturing Parker spoke to sixty or a hundred thousand people a year. When preaching in the great Music Hall of Boston, butchers, bakers, small-tradesmen and farmers came from hundreds of miles in such garments as they had, sat in such seats as were vacant, and listened attentively to sermons that were seldom less than an hour and sometimes as long as three hours. These were the people he wanted, for Parker had said, "My chosen walk will be with the humble" (Weiss 1864, II:211). He consistently commanded weekly audiences of 3,000, and there were 7,000 names on his parish register! Nor was this all. Parker achieved national, even international, fame. Little did he exaggerate one Sunday when he remarked:

> I know well the responsibility of the place I occupy this morning. Tomorrow's sun shall carry my words to all America. They will be read on both sides of the continent. They will cross the ocean. (Parker 1867, II:86)

Parker's fearless adherence to principle brought congressmen, governors, and even presidents to rely on him. William Seward, who came to Boston and canvassed the political situation with Parker, remembered his "restless and sagacious and vigorous ability" (Commager 1936, 258). Henry Wilson could not come immediately to Boston, but wrote, "I want to see you some day when you can give me an hour or two, for the purpose of consultation in regard to affairs" (McCall 1936, 28). Charles Sumner affectionately wrote, "I shall always be glad to hear from you, and shall value your counsels" (McCall 1936, 28). Parker's picture occupied a prominent position in the home of Ohio's Governor Chase, who wrote Parker, "I always like to read your heroic utterances" (Commager 1936, 258).

The most dramatic instance of Parker's influence, however, was on Lincoln. Parker sent Lincoln's junior law partner, William Herndon, a copy of his sermon, "The Effect of Slavery on the American People." Henry Steele Commager describes the effect:

> ... Herndron read it eagerly. "Democracy is direct self-government, over all the people, for all the people, by all the people," Parker said. It was a good definition, thought Herndon, and he underscored that passage. It might interest Mr. Lincoln. (Commager 1936, 266)

The paradox of Theodore Parker, then, is seen in three spheres: Parker's individual intellectual and physical being, his relation to others and religious truth, and the courage underlying his greatness as a response to adversity. When Parker was dying in Florence, Italy, he summoned his friend, Frances P. Cobbe, to his bedside and gathering breath uttered a final paradox:

I have something to tell you—there are two Theodore Parkers now. One is dying here in Italy, the other I have planted in America. He will live there, and finish my work. (Weiss 1864, II:438)

The Theodore Parker planted in America has taken root and grown. Slavery has disappeared, although racial discrimination continues. Unitarianism has unfolded in freedom and tolerance, although many religions still cling to the past. The significance of Theodore Parker, however, is not just in what he did, as our significance does not lie only in what we accomplish. The significance of Theodore Parker is in his quality as a human being: in his strength and weakness, in his personality and life of paradox, and in the triumph of what was great in him.

– 6 –

Do We Have Two Selves?[1]

IN 1886 WHEN ROBERT Louis Stevenson wrote his novel *The Strange Case of Dr. Jekyll and Mr. Hyde* (Stevenson 1886) he had no medical or psychiatric aspirations, yet his fictional account has been found to have surprising insight into psychic and personality phenomena and has been a classic precursor of such contemporary studies as *The Three Faces of Eve* (Thigpen and Cleckley 1983). Stevenson's story depicts in extreme and violent form the emergence of a second personality in the mild Dr. Jekyll—it took me a good while to connect the name of Jekyll with the good side of the personality. The second personality, Mr. Hyde, is released or induced by a drug and takes complete charge of Jekyll's body. In Stevenson's account, not only does personality change occur, but a physical transformation reportedly takes place.

I have sometimes wondered how much truth there is in the story. Do we have two selves, even if they do not emerge in such a dramatic and literal form? When the question is put to psychology, as I recently put it to an editor of a psychiatric journal, the answer was, "Yes, at least two!" I have long been under the impression that split personality was what is referred to as schizophrenia. Upon exploration, however, I found that schizophrenia refers less to the emergence of additional selves, and more to the split within a single personality of emotional from rational functions. Although it is characterized by delusions and hallucinations, schizophrenia is usually in the form of inappropriate or irrational behavior on the part of the subject, rather than the manifestation of another self.

---

1. Sermon delivered by the author at the Church of the Reconciliation Unitarian Universalist, Utica, New York, on February 3, 1963.

The proper psychological term for the existence of more than one personality is double or multiple personality, or dissociation of personality. There are a number of studies of such phenomena, among which are the *The Dissociation of a Personality*, a study of Christine L. Beauchamp by Morton Prince (Prince 1906); and as already mentioned, *The Three Faces of Eve* by Corbett H. Thigpen and Harvey M. Cleckley. *The Three Faces of Eve* is one of the most widely known—both the book and its sequel, *The Final Face of Eve*, written by Eve herself, are incomparable (Lancaster 1958). The story is about a woman who alternates between two distinct personalities, Eve White and Eve Black. Unlike Jekyll and Hyde, neither Eve has memory of the other. The most striking thing about the story is the point during psychiatric treatment when a third personality emerges, Jane. For me, there is something awesome in this event. Perhaps it's because personalities just do not happen all at once, but develop over time. Suddenly during an interview with her therapist, Eve changes stance, voice, manner, and the doctor asked her who she is, expecting her to say either Eve Black or Eve White. Her reply is "Jane!"

In addition to psychology, Christian theology has something to say about whether we have more than one self. Theology has long been based upon the symbolic description of the nature of humanity as possessing two aspects or selves, the sinful and the saved. Thus, the nature of humanity and reality for Christian theology is a dual one. We possess a sinful nature caused or represented by the fall of the mythological first man, Adam. Our nature is subject to redemption through the sacrifice and the example of Jesus. Although Calvinism separated people into groups of the elect and the damned, recent Christian theology has been prone to divide each person into that which makes for sin or salvation. In the tradition of existentialism, Paul Tillich expresses this as the difference between humankind in existence as we are and in essence as we would be.

What about us as religious liberals, and presumably as normal psychological specimens? Do we have two selves? It is my thesis that we may think of ourselves symbolically as having two selves, that person which we are and that person which we would become. I think this view is basic for religion, which is concerned with what we are and what we should be and helping us bridge the gap between the two.

The consciousness of these two selves begins early in childhood. Harry Stack Sullivan refers to them as the "good-me" and the "bad-me" (Evans 1996, 86–89). As he suggests, the child learns that approved behaviors are what the "good-me" is, reinforced by acceptance and tenderness of the "mothering one." Likewise, the "bad-me" is learned by the level of anxiety associated with disapproved action. For the child these feelings of tenderness and anxiety must be immense. It must seem as if the "good-me" and the "bad-me" that they define are very real. This is why the "bad-me" qualities are sometimes projected and blamed on imaginary companions, which is a rudimentary form of multiple personality.

As we grow older, however, this dichotomy becomes more abstract and symbolic. We see ourselves as we are, and we think of ourselves as we would like to be. There is a continual tension in the life of the religious person between the polarities of the real and the ideal. In essence, it is an intellectual distinction. But from time to time, something peculiar occurs: when we find ourselves doing something degrading, we are overcome by the sensation that it is not really us doing it. It is almost as if another person is doing it. At the times we find ourselves doing something wonderful, we are surprised and ponder if this can really be us. So, although we really know that this division into two selves is symbolic, there are times in our consciousness when it borders on the literal.

Given the fact that symbolically speaking we have two selves, what we are and what we strive to be, what are the implications for ourselves and for religion? One of the most important things about such a division of personality is that the two selves should not be conceived as being too far apart, and that we should be able to realize our ideal from time to time. There is bound to be some gap between what we are and would like to be unless we happen to be perfect, or unless we do not set our ideals so they challenge us. On the other hand, it is unhealthy to set our goal so high or allow ourselves to slip so low that they cannot be reconciled.

The second application follows closely on the first. When we are not able to realize the ideal and we contain the two selves of what we are and what we would be, we should not lose sight of the fact that both are parts of ourselves. We must never cease being able to affirm and accept either. Religion is deeply concerned that we always be able to affirm our ideals. Religion should be equally concerned that we always be able to accept ourselves as we are. In sacrificing ideals, the inevitable result would be a sense of guilt. On the other hand, rejecting ourselves would be at the cost of our self-respect. Regardless of what depths of despair or dishonor we fall, we must be able to affirm ourselves. When people cannot accept their ideals, they cease to be religious; but when they cannot accept themselves, they may become psychotic.

We have referred to the implications for religion. The most important thing for religion, and this is the final implication I would touch upon, is that religion should help us bridge the gap between the real and the ideal, religion should serve people in the process of becoming. The job of religion is not finished with the presentation of the ideal. The task of religion is concerned with how the ideal is realized and actualized. When someone moves from a limited to a fuller self, if only for a moment and if only in a small way, what takes place? How does this happen? This is what we need to discover, this is what religion has to cultivate. This is what has to be expressed in poetic and compelling ways in our services of worship, in symbols and forms that have meaning for us.

Let us despair of neither our ideals, nor ourselves. As we accept and believe in what we are, let us seek together ways to the greater selves that we may yet be.

− 7 −

Earth's the Right Place for Love[1]

WITH THE FAMILIAR STRAINS of "O come, O come, Emmanuel," we are reminded that Christmas is just around the corner. Christmas is many different things. It is not just a Christian holiday; it is a festival, a midwinter festival, of many religions.

Yet, in our culture, it is a time of year that should have something to do with Jesus. For us as Unitarian Universalists, it is a time of year when the teachings of Jesus have particular import. As the manger scenes appear about our city, and angels and magic stars materialize around us, we think not of the supernatural Jesus—divinely conceived, supernaturally resurrected. We think about the miracle of how anyone could be born as such an innocent, helpless baby, and through the nurture and care of his parents and friends, become such a great man as Jesus was. It is a time of the year when we should pause amidst the commercialism of the season and wonder at the wisdom and simplicity of his teachings:

> You have heard that it was said, "An eye for an eye and a tooth for a tooth." But I say to you, do not resist one who is evil. But if anyone strikes you on the right cheek, turn to him the other also.... (Matt 5:38–39 RSV)

> Love your enemies, do good to those who hate you, bless those who curse you, pray for those who abuse you.... Judge not and you will not be judged; condemn not, and you will not be condemned; forgive, and you will be forgiven; give, and it will be given to you. (Luke 6:27–38 RSV)

---

1. Sermon delivered by the author at the Church of the Reconciliation Unitarian Universalist, Utica, New York, on December 15, 1963.

A new commandment I give to you that you love one another; even as I have loved you, that you also love one another. (John 13:34 RSV)

Yet, wonderful as the teachings of Jesus are, we are sometimes forced to ask the question, "Are they really applicable to twentieth century America? Are they practical?" What place does love have in a land torn by racial hatred and strife? How can we turn the other cheek, when literally, it would mean submitting to communism? We ask is this the time, is this the place for such love? In Robert Frost's phrase, "Is earth the right place for love" (Frost 1969, 122)?

As we approach another Christmas season, it seems to me that is vital that we reaffirm that such love is possible, that earth is the right place for love. We must not despair of our ideals. Perhaps when the evidence is most overwhelming that we lack values, is the time we need them the most. Albert Schweitzer once said, "Truth has no special time of its own. Its hour is now—always, and indeed then most truly when it seems most unsuitable to actual circumstances" (Schweitzer 1947, 30). At this Christmas season, then, we reaffirm our belief in the value of love.

What is love? There is no word so misused or misunderstood. What are we talking about? For a definition of the kind of love we are talking about I turned to the psychologist and author Erich Fromm: "Love is the productive form of relatedness to others and to oneself. It implies responsibility, care, respect, and knowledge, and the wish for the other person to grow and develop" (Fromm 1947, 110). Such love is not an easy thing. We do not always want the other person to grow and change. Change can be threatening. We sometimes want others to remain the same passive or aggressive selves (as the case may be) that we feel more comfortable with—or if they are to change, we want it to be in the direction we choose. The kind of love we are talking about, the kind of love I think Fromm is referring to, is the kind that is concerned with what is best for the other person, what is really best and not just what we prefer. And this may mean accepting a change in others that may be uncomfortable for us. By discomfort, I'm not speaking about the sacrifices that really give us satisfaction, I'm talking about a major shift in the other person in the relationship which may require change and growth on our part as well. And this is always difficult. We say we want to change and improve, but we really believe we are pretty good as we are. It is hard to change, and it is an insecure and anxiety-producing process.

This is all a little abstract. Let us be more concrete and talk about the forms of love that are open to us. One of the most immediate types of love is that for our own family. It is a kind of love for which we give our all. And it is a situation in which making sacrifices that satisfy us may be confused for the real love that permits the other person to become who and what they want to be. We pride ourselves so much about giving up things so our children can have what we didn't, that we sometimes refuse to respect the kind of things they really need and want. We sometimes refuse to accept the kind of person they are becoming.

It is only long after they have grown up that we recognize the fact, and then we are amazed that "we no longer know them." Yet, we do not realize that by keeping them as our children, we are restricting ourselves as well as them. By acknowledging their personhood, we not only give them a gift, but give ourselves a whole new lease on our relationship to them, the relationship of person to person, not just parent to child. It is a wonderful thing for a parent and for the child, suddenly realizing that they can relate as persons.

Such love in our family means bringing out the best in each other. The great magician, Houdini, felt this kind of faith in his family. When his father was dying, Houdini recalled, "His eyes were turned to the door as I hurried in. When he saw me, he lifted his hand feebly and reached out toward my mother. 'Dear wife,' he said, 'Never worry. Harry will pour gold in your apron.' Those were his last words." The incident made such a great impression upon young Houdini that he later testified that the greatest thrill of his life was not any of the dramatic escapes for which he was so famous—not being thrown into the sea chained and locked in a box, not escaping from a straitjacket while suspended from a tall building. He tells of the greatest thrill of his life:

> I received a cable from the old Palace theater in New York. The cable offered me a week's engagement at a thousand dollars. I sent my answer: "Yes, if you will pay my salary in gold."
> On the payday of my first week at the palace I received a handful of golden coins. I carried them, tight in my hands up to my mother's flat, where I found her in her rocking chair and I swallowed hard as I said to her: "Hold out your apron, mother." And I let the golden shower fall. That was the greatest thrill I ever knew. (Mullin 2007, 78–79)

A second kind of love is that of the deepest friendships. This is part of what the marriage relationship should be (although of course it is more). This is the kind of relationship that in our heterosexual culture we are usually only free to develop with someone of the same sex. It is not always understood that it is possible to have a genuine friendship with someone of the opposite sex—but it is and should be.

What is such a friendship? What does love in this sense mean? It usually means that throughout our lives we are able to find only a very few such friends. These are the few we consider "real people," who we know and who know us better than anyone else, who will do anything for us, with whom we feel utterly comfortable and can be our true selves. George Eliot expressed it this way:

> Oh, the comfort the inexpressible comfort of feeling safe with a person; having neither to weigh thoughts nor measure words, but to pour them all out, just as they are, chaff and grain together, knowing that a faithful hand will take and sift them, keep what is worth keeping, and then, with the breath of kindness, blow the rest away. (Goodman 2001, 35)

This kind of friendship was discussed in an article in *Redbook* magazine by Robert Graves, who said:

> [I have about 20 real friends.] All my life I've been sort of picking these people up and sorting them out and being aware of their existence. . . . They become your friends, and so much so that if they said to you, "Fly to the North Pole tomorrow because I need you there," then you'd go. And you'd know that it wasn't for any wrong reason. (Graves 1989, 59)

All through our lives we are searching for those few people who will be our closest friends. We find one when we marry, but we should feel we need more—and our wives and husbands should encourage us to do so.

We have talked about the kind of love in our families and among friends. There are broader examples of love. Several of the most creative expressions of love in our time include democracy and nonviolence. Democracy is in itself, to my way of thinking, an expression of love. Democracy is based upon the presupposition that we are equally worthy of respect and care. This is love expressed in political terms.

The resurgence of nonviolent resistance is one of the most promising forms of love in our time. We are witnessing a revolution, not so much in any one area such as civil rights or peace, but in the tactics that men are using to win their objectives. Within the past century, for about the first time in history, large blocks of humanity are resorting to nonviolent measures and proving their practicality. This happened in India, it is happening in America, it may yet happen on a global scale. As Gandhi said:

> Hatred ever kills, love never dies. Such is the vast difference between the two. What is obtained by love is retained for all time. What is obtained by hatred proves a burden in reality, for it increases hatred. The duty of a human being is to diminish hatred and to promote love. (Gandhi 1947, 352)

And there is a final kind of love that is not of our families or immediate friends, yet it is more immediate than democratic or nonviolent action. I'm speaking of the kind of love that is represented in kindness and goodwill that we can show those around us who we come in contact with every day. This is the kind of thing that is stressed so much by other churches that we Unitarian Universalists sometimes forget to mention it altogether. It is a simple but powerful truth that we should do something good every day, doing a "Good Turn," as Boy Scouts call it. Our love is proved not just in the big issues and our most intimate relations, but in how we live each day, and how we meet each moment and relate to each person. It is too easy for us to be loving at home or church, but indifferent or rude to those we have business dealings with, or who are driving in front of us. We have a responsibility to all whom we meet. It is said that this is a creedless church, but I think this is one of the chief doctrines of life, the responsibility of circumstance.

An elderly man and his wife entered the lobby of a small hotel in Philadelphia. The couple had no baggage. "All the big places are filled up," said the man, "can you possibly give us a room here?" The clerk replied that there were three conventions in town and that there were no rooms available. "But I can't turn a nice couple like you out at this hour of the morning. Would you like to use my own room?"

The next morning, as he paid the bill, the elderly man said to the clerk, "you're the kind of manager who should be the boss of the best hotel in the United States. Maybe someday I'll build it for you." The clerk laughed. And he laughed again when two years later he received a letter containing a round-trip ticket to New York and a request to call upon his guest of that rainy night.

In the metropolis, the old man led the young hotel clerk to the corner of Fifth Avenue and Thirty-fourth Street and pointed to a vast new building there, a palace of reddish stone, with turrets and watchtowers, like a castle cleaving the New York sky. "That," he declared, "is the hotel that I have just built for you to manage." The young man, George C. Boldt, was stunned. His benefactor was William Waldorf Astor, and the hotel the most famous of its day, the original Waldorf Astoria (Amazing Real Life Experiences 2014, 1).

    Love may not always hold such dramatic or lucrative rewards, but its rewards are sure enough. Through love we find our way to becoming greater persons. If, at times, "life's too much like a pathless wood where your face burns and tickles with the cobwebs broken across it and one eye is weeping from a twig's having lashed across it open," and we think we'd "like to get away from earth a while," let us not forget our conviction that "earth's the right place for love" (Frost 1969, 122).

– 8 –

Gotama Buddha[1]

AND THE BLESSED ONE observed the ways of society and noticed how much misery came from foolish offenses done only to gratify vanity and self-seeking pride. And the Buddha said: "If a man foolishly does me wrong, I will return to him the protection of my unbegrudging love; the more evil comes from him, the more good shall go from me; the fragrance of goodness always comes to me, and the harmful air of evil goes to him."

A foolish man learning that the Buddha observed the principle of great love which commends the return of good for evil, came and abused him. The Buddha was silent, pitying his folly. When the man had finished, the Buddha asked him, "Son, if a man declined to accept a present made to him, to whom would it belong?" And he answered, "in that case it would belong to the man who offered it."

"My son," said the Buddha, "thou hast railed at me, but I decline to accept thy abuse, and request thee to keep it to thyself. Will it not be a source of misery to thee? As the echo belongs to the sound, and the shadow to the substance, so misery will overtake the evil-doer without fail."

The abuser made no reply, and the Buddha continued: "A wicked man who reproaches a virtuous one is like one who looks up and spits at heaven; the spittle soils not the heaven, but comes back and defiles his own person. The slanderer is like one who flings dust at another when the wind is contrary; the dust does but return on him who threw it. The virtuous man cannot be hurt and the misery that the other would inflict comes back on himself." The abuser went away ashamed, then came again

---

1. Sermon delivered by the author at the Church of the Reconciliation Unitarian Universalist, Utica, New York.

and took refuge in the Buddha, the Dharma, and the Sangha (Carus, 1894, 100–101).

There was a woman who had only one child and he died. In her grief she carried the dead child to all her neighbors, asking them for medicine, and the people said: "She has lost her senses. The boy is dead." At length she met a man who replied to her request: "I cannot give you medicine for the child, but I know someone who can." And the woman said: "Pray tell me, sir, who is it?" And the man replied: "Go to the great one, the Buddha." She repaired to the Buddha and cried: "Lord and Master, give me the medicine that will cure my boy."

The Buddha answered: "I want a handful of mustard seed." And when the woman in her joy promised to procure it, the Buddha added: "The mustard seed must be taken from the house where no one has lost a child, husband, parent, or friend." The poor woman then went from house to house, and the people pitied her and said: "Here is mustard seed; take it!" But when she asked, "Did a son or daughter, a father or mother, die in your family?" They answered her: "What is this you say? The living are few, but the dead are many. Do not remind us of our grief." And there was no house but some beloved one had died in it.

The woman became weary and hopeless, and sat down at the wayside, watching the lights of the city, as they flickered up and were extinguished again. At last the darkness of the night reigned everywhere. And she considered the fate of men, that their lives flicker up and are extinguished. And she thought to herself: "How selfish am I in all my grief! Death is common to all." And the woman disposed of the dead body of her son and then came again to the Buddha. He said:

> As all earthen vessels made by the potter end in being broken, so is the life of mortals. . . . So, the world is afflicted with death and decay, therefore the wise do not grieve, knowing the terms of the world. In whatever manner people think the thing will come to pass, it is often different when that happens, and great is the disappointment; see such are the terms of the world. Not from weeping or from grieving will anyone obtain peace of mind; on the contrary, his pain will be the greater and his body will suffer. He will make himself sick and pale, yet the dead are not saved by his lamentation. . . . He who seeks peace should draw out the arrow of lamentation, and complaint, and grief. He who has drawn out the arrow and has become composed will obtain peace of mind; he who has overcome all sorrow will become free from sorrow, and be blessed. (Gangulee 1957, 183–84)

These are two of the many parables of Buddhism about its founder, Gotama Buddha. They portray the understanding, compassion, and wisdom that are said to have been typical of him. Something that is not often realized about Buddha is that he was not thought of as a god during his lifetime, and is not thought of as divine today in any sense in which others cannot also be. Throughout the ages he has successfully withstood the temptation to be deified, an amazing accomplishment considering our failure to do likewise with the central figure in our religious tradition.

Buddha's greatness has always laid rather in his quality as a human being. He was a man of rich human sympathy. His friendliness to all who came to him was unfailing. Yet he was also one of the greatest thinkers the world has known; he has been referred to as one of the giant intellects of human history. Buddhism is one of the few great religions in the world that is deliberately and systematically based on a rational analysis of life. Buddha never claimed to have received a special revelation and discarded appeals to the authority of tradition. His teachings stood as they were conceived, on the basis of common sense and human experience. As such, he has a great deal to say to us and can inspire our devotion as Unitarian Universalists.

To understand the life and teachings of Buddha, it is helpful to have some familiarity with the religious environment into which he was born. It is almost impossible for us to comprehend the religions of the East: they are based upon different geographic and social conditions, even upon different conceptions of reality.

The religion into which Buddha was born and from which Buddhism eventually sprang was Hinduism (also known as Brahmanism), the oldest religion in the world that has survived to the present day as a major faith. Hinduism is a religion greatly concerned with suffering. In a part of the world where famine is common and disease frequent, this is not surprising. Thus, the perspective of reality is different from our own. People are conceived much less romantically; life presents a much less promising prospect. In a land where people lie dead in roadside ditches as leaves lie in our gutters, a concept such as the supreme worth of human personality seems out of place. Life is not always nice, and often hopeless.

Therefore, a task of Hinduism is in part to repudiate life and escape from the world. This is accomplished in several ways: by extreme forms of mysticism, such as the trances of Yogi, in which the self is subjugated. The world and all its inequities are considered unstable, transitory, illusory. A person's final escape through death holds the promise of a literal

Gotama Buddha

reincarnation, the next time as a higher form of life if one is lucky. An elaborate caste system of social strata was established and fervently observed. The idea would be to reach the final state of Nirvana, in which an individual would not have to be born again into the world. Because life was conceived as repetitive, time came to be thought of as circular, which differs radically from the Western idea of linear time that does not repeat itself.

It was into this world and religion that Gotama Buddha was born in the fifth or sixth centuries B.C. As would be expected, he did not reject Hinduism entirely, but it is clear that he reformed and transformed it significantly. Gotama was born a prince of the Sakya clan in what is now Nepal, in northern India. Apparently, his parents completely sheltered him from the harsh realities of life, even from knowing about sickness, death, poverty, and old age. Somehow in his early 20s he suddenly and dramatically confronted the major miseries of existence. He was so troubled by these things, that he fled his father's palace, even his beautiful wife and newborn son, to search for understanding about life and death.

At first, he tried the traditional ways of Hinduism in which he had been raised, ways of self-denial and renunciation of the world. For seven years he struggled and searched. Finally, carrying his fasting to an extreme, he fell into a starving swoon. When he awoke, he was convinced that the traditional ways of withdrawal and renunciation were not right. He started upon a new course of contemplation, in which he observed moderation in all things—the middle way—never again to return to orthodox Hindu practices. Gradually his great mind working with maximum concentration achieved the understanding he sought. His search reached its culmination after a long period of meditation under the sheltering branches of a great Bodhi tree, which became sacred to Buddhists, not far from the present city of Gaya in northeastern India. When he arose, it was with an understanding of the truth he had been seeking, and with a resolve to share that knowledge with others. A remarkable, exciting story!

The truths which Buddha found are expressed in the Sermon at Benares, which could be considered Buddhism's Sermon on the Mount. The doctrine of the Middle Way is expressed in the four Noble truths: 1) Existence is unhappiness; 2) Unhappiness is caused by selfish craving; 3) Selfish craving can be destroyed; 4) It can be destroyed by following the Eightfold Path, whose steps are:

I. Right Understanding

II. Right Purpose (aspiration)

III. Right Speech

IV. Right Conduct

V. Right Vocation

VI. Right Effort

VII. Right Alertness (thought)

VIII. Right Concentration

From these initial realizations and from the underlying break with traditional Hindu ways, Buddha went on to question many aspects of Hindu orthodoxy. He became an active critic of the caste system, Vedic sacrifice, and of the far-fetched cosmological systems priests proposed. He challenged the infallibility of the Hindu scriptures, the Vedas. He saw that Hinduism was falling into orthodoxy and instead of serving human needs was becoming unduly preoccupied with ceremony and dogma.

So, it became the task of his great mind to break through the religion of the past and find new answers and beliefs. As we might expect from Gotama's experience, in his religious thought there is less stress upon withdrawing from the world and more emphasis upon the activity and conduct of a person in life. Instead of extracting oneself from the world, there is insistence upon contemplation and meditation about life. Instead of a changeless soul, the human personality is thought to be dynamic. There is a stress upon moral virtues, friendship towards people, compassion towards animal life. Buddha said: "Hatred does not cease by hatred at any time; hatred ceases by love—this is an eternal law" (Tachibana n.d., 186). And "Not in the sky, not in the midst of the sea, not if we enter into the clefts of the mountains, is there known a spot in the whole world where a man might be freed from an evil deed" (Babbit 1936, 21).

Buddha did carry over many aspects of Hinduism. In Buddha there is still a sense of Brahman, the mystical source of life, but man is perhaps less absorbed in it and retains more of his identity. There is still a suppression of one's longing for material things and one's emotions. But for a man who lived the better part of 3,000 years ago, in Buddha we find an astonishing relevance to our time and a stirring sense of kinship for us as religious liberals.

We began with a story about how Buddha comforted a woman who had felt the hand of death. There is another parable of how Buddha celebrated a wedding with a young couple. There was a man in Jambunada who was to be married the next day, and he thought, "would that the Buddha, the blessed one, might be present at the wedding." And it happened that the Buddha passed by his house and met him, and when he read the silent wish in the heart of the bridegroom, he consented to enter. During the course of the wedding, his host prevailed upon him to speak. Rising, Buddha said:

> The greatest happiness which a mortal man can imagine is the bond of marriage that ties together two loving hearts. But there's a greater happiness still: it is the embrace of truth. Death will separate husband and wife, but death will never affect him who has espoused the truth.
>
> Therefore, be married unto the truth and live with the truth in holy wedlock. The husband who loves his wife and desires for a union that shall be everlasting must be faithful to her so as to be like truth itself, and she will rely upon him and revere him and minister to him. And the wife who loves her husband and desires a union that shall be everlasting must be faithful to him so as to be like truth itself; and he will place his trust in her, he will provide for her. Verily, their children will become like unto their parents and will bear witness to their happiness.
>
> Let no man be single, let everyone be wedded in holy love to the truth. And when Mara, the destroyer, comes to separate the visible forms of your being, you will continue to live in the truth and you will have life everlasting, for the truth is immortal. (Caras 1894, 181–82)

From age to age a great spirit is born as a sign to our troubled world that mankind can achieve goodness and peace. Obscured by the passage of time, buried in the folklore of India, the founder of religion that today is the faith of one-fifth of the world's population, is one such a man: Gotama Buddha.

– 9 –

If Jesus Were Alive Today[1]

THE EASTER SEASON IS upon us. It is a season of failure and triumph, of depression and resurgence in life. Next to Christmas, it is one of the most significant times of the year, not just on the Christian calendar but in our lives. It is a time when our feelings run deep.

Easter, of course, is historically about Jesus—his passion, trial, and crucifixion. Since next Sunday we will be considering some contemporary non-Christian interpretations of the season, it behooves us this morning to focus on the meaning of Jesus, clearly one of the greatest human beings who ever lived. He must have been a warm, loving, courageous, engaging person for people to think so highly of him after his death, and for him to have been revered so long.

It strikes me that one of the best ways of understanding what he meant is by hypothetically transporting Jesus, or his equivalent, across 2,000 years of time from a Middle Eastern country to North America, to this century in American society, and by trying to think of what it would mean if Jesus were alive today. We can best understand this by asking three questions. If Jesus were alive today: 1) What kind of a person would he be in our time and culture? 2) What kind of things would he be saying and what kind of problems would he be addressing? and 3) What would what our reaction be and what would we do?

First, what would he be like? What would he be doing? What kind of a person with he be in America? Judging from the attitude Jesus had toward Judaism, he would be interested in religion, and he would not be

---

1. Sermon delivered by the author at the Church of the Reconciliation Unitarian Universalist, Utica, New York, on April 7, 1963.

trying to work outside of organized religion. He would have probably come from a lower middle-class family: his father would possibly be a construction worker. He would have an undistinguished childhood. He would have gone to a public school or community college, and he would have an interest in religion, going on to theological school, perhaps a Presbyterian or Methodist one.

He would, however, be disillusioned with contemporary Christianity. He would preach reforms without any intent to break off from Christianity or to establish a new religion. He would be displeased with the formalism of churches, with the preoccupation they have on ceremony, and the absence of genuine religious feeling and action. He would condemn people who just go to church on Sunday and give lip service to their principles, while forgetting them during the week.

He would probably decide not to stay in a particular parish, but would travel the country speaking at large meetings, perhaps even revivals. He would attract a good-sized group of friends and followers. They would not be intellectuals, but the equivalent of Jesus' disciples today would be small businessmen or tradesmen. Perhaps one would be a machinist, another a butcher. He would not be rich, but as a result of our culture he would have an organization that would arrange speaking places, public relations, and advertising. There would be rumors that he was able to cure people of cancer and heart disease.

In short, if Jesus were alive today, he would be very much like contemporary evangelists such as Billy Graham or Robert Schuller. If you will remember, in Jesus' time there were other prophets such as John the Baptist traveling around Palestine. Jesus was one of many. At the time it was hard to single him out. So, he would be today. Perhaps he would be distinguished by the quality of what he preached or by his impact, but visibly he would be very much like others.

Second, what kinds of things would he be saying? If Jesus were in twentieth century America, what would his message be, based upon what we know of him in the New Testament? I think it is clear that one of the first things he would protest would be our cultural preoccupation with material things. He would preach against our materialistic standards, our effort to compete for social status through newer cars and designer clothes. He would say that the really valuable things in life have gotten lost. He would say that material things have become more important than people, that we are more concerned about saving money and financial setbacks than we are about values such as love and integrity. He would say that money and material things are vulnerable. We may lose them.

> Do not lay up for yourselves treasures on earth, where moth and rust consume and where thieves break in and steal, but lay up for yourselves treasures in heaven. . . . For where your treasure is, there will your heart be also. (Matt 6:19–21 RSV)

He would say that we need to invest our hearts and find our identity in principles and things of the spirit that cannot be destroyed. If we put our hearts into material things, what will happen when they are lost? Where will we be then? He would even say that it might be necessary to make a choice between wealth and principle. This is how he put it to a man in his own time: "If you would be perfect, go, sell what you possess and give to the poor, and you will have treasure in heaven; and come, follow me" (Matt 19:21–22 RSV).

What this all means to us, I think, is that we have become too intent upon our financial security; our lives are devoted to building earning power. We take jobs that pay the most and do what is necessary to keep those jobs. How many of us are willing, are courageous enough to take the kind of a job we most like, do the kind of thing we really want, even if it isn't the most profitable? How many of us consider leaving our businesses to join the Peace Corps or their equivalent? "When the young man heard this he went away sorrowful; for he had great possessions" (Matt 19:22 RSV).

The Jesus that we know of the New Testament, if he were alive today, would be a strong agitator for civil rights, and he might even get involved in politics! He would not spend his time speaking in large auditoriums, but would probably spend a great deal of his time travelling about. He would spend time in the deep South, not just on special occasions, earning the right to take the African-American's side by living with them. He would have been a Freedom Rider, he would have been at the lunch counters. He would have spent time in Southern jails.

He would regularly be in conflict with civil authority. He would declare that God's laws take precedence over man's laws. He would insist that principle is more important than legality. He would take the lead in the practice of nonviolent resistance, as was practiced by Martin Luther King, Jr. He would say that the principle of love and equality for all men is the most important thing in the world. If he were born in the South and his family believed in segregation, and he had to make a choice between principle and going along with his family (as many young Southerners do today), he would choose principle. One of the hardest things to understand in the New Testament is how Jesus subjugates family ties:

> For I have come to set a man against his father, and a daughter against her mother, and a daughter-in-law against her mother-in-law; and a man's foes will be those of his own household. (Matt 10:35-36 RSV)

Finally, if Jesus were alive today, he would be uncompromising for the cause of world peace, advocating such measures as ending nuclear testing and disarmament. I have no question but if Jesus were alive today, he would be a proponent of pacifism, much in the manner of Gandhi and Bertrand Russell. He would not condone the use of war or force in any form. He would probably argue for unilateral disarmament. "But I say to you, do not resist one who is evil. But if anyone strikes you on the right cheek, turn to him the other also" (Matt 5:39 RSV).

He would consider it inexcusable that a nation with as much potential as ours would waste so much of its resources on preparing for war that could destroy mankind itself. If Jesus were alive today, very much as in his own time, he would preach that the end of the world was coming, that our only hope is the establishment of a new kingdom, a world order of peace.

Third, what would we do? What would our response be to such a Jesus? We would find him an entertaining preacher. A good speaker. An interesting idealist. What he says is fine, we'd say. We'd give him lip service as we do for many other idealists today. But if what we know about the appeal and power of Jesus of Nazareth is correct, slowly he'd gain popular approval and power. There would be growing support for his ideas about materialism and discrimination and peace.

Then do you know what would happen? I think it's very clear. What was previously distant and abstract would be in danger of becoming a reality. It is one thing to give lip service to the ideal. But when it comes down to it, we really do not want to change. We like material standards. We have a need for prejudice. We want our preparations for war, which would contribute to our economic comfort. We would resist such idealistic teachings. If there came to be a chance of changing the way our society is, it would pose a threat to us.

Jesus' ideas on peace and disarmament alone would have serious results. Once people begin to listen to him, they would accept his ideals. If there came to be any question that the people would no longer support a war effort and if there was any possibility that they would not fight, it would pose a threat to our country.

Do you know what would happen then? I think there's no question that even in our society the government would have to take steps to curb his influence and quiet him. If he were really influential, it would only be a matter of time and he would be accused of being—a communist! He'd be taken before a Senate committee, perhaps on Un-American activities. If his influence continued, he would be arrested.

If Jesus were alive today, I think there's no question about what we would do. We'd crucify him!

— 10 —

Jesus, Son of Man[1]

HISTORY TELLS US THAT there was a man born nearly 2,000 years ago who lived in an inconspicuous village, in a subjugated country, which was one of the poorest and smallest nations on earth. By almost all standards his life ended prematurely and a failure. His ministry, which began the age of 30, occupied a period of no more than three years, and may have been as short as six months. He was forsaken by his friends and disciples; he was executed as a criminal between two thieves; and his broken body was sealed in a borrowed tomb.

Yet this man called Jesus has become one of the most influential men in the course of history, and today commands a response from hundreds of millions of people. Who was Jesus and what did he stand for? One of the most important things he stood for from our point of view as Unitarian Universalists was the idea of love. What troubles us most deeply, however, is that Jesus' ethic of love does not always seem practical, does not seem realistic for our time. We should acknowledge, of course, that there never has been a time, including Jesus' own, when his commandment seemed practical.

For the ethic of Jesus is an absolute ethic. There is no room left for compromising and applying it to a greater or lesser degree according to the situation. Jesus is not concerned about adapting it to circumstances. He believes that our acts should conform to the ethic. It is an absolute demand that is placed upon us—not just to love our friends, but our

---

1. Sermon delivered by the author at the Church of the Reconciliation Unitarian Universalist, Utica, New York, on April 22, 1962.

enemies as well; not just to walk one mile, but two. It is all or nothing. In the concrete situation, one either loves or one does not.

Was Jesus a hopeless idealist? To one who reads the New Testament closely, it becomes clear that Jesus was far from being a visionary, or even a perfectionist. He had shortcomings and recognized them. There were occasions when he became violently angry; there were those he found it difficult, if not impossible to love. We can cite his attack upon the money-changers in the Temple, his cursing of the cities of Chorazin, Bethsaida, and Capernaum (Matt 11:20–24), his harsh replies to the Pharisees when they asked for a sign in Matthew 12:39, his invective against his opponents in Matthew 23:13 when he entered the long tirade, "Woe unto you. . . ." Thus, when someone called him "good master" he answered, "There is none good but one, that is, God" (Mark 10:18 KJV).

If Jesus was not oblivious to his own limitations and to those of others, if he knew how difficult it was to follow the unqualified commandment of love—why did he continue to hold it, and expect us to follow it? The answer to this question, and it is perhaps the most important one that we can ask of Jesus, is that he stood for something besides the ethical, something which made love possible.

Indeed, contemporary scholars of the New Testament point out that in comparison to this "something else," love is mentioned relatively seldom by Jesus. Although its use is emphatic, love is confined to a few passages such as the Sermon on the Mount, or the passage where a lawyer asks Jesus what the greatest commandment is. Jesus affirms the commandment of love, but he does not explain it. He simply does not present a detailed ethical system. As Rudolf Bultmann said in his book, *Jesus and the Word*:

> The command of love explains nothing concerning the content of love. What must a man do to love his neighbor or his enemy? It is said simply that he is to do it. What a man must do . . . is not stated. It is assumed that everyone can know that. (Bultmann 1958, 94, 113)

If this is so, what is this "something else" which makes love possible, which Jesus emphasizes and develops? If you read the first three or four books of the New Testament carefully, you will know the answer. It is what almost every one of the parables is devoted to. The something else is what Jesus called the "Kingdom of God."

What did the Kingdom of God mean for Jesus? There are three divergent interpretations. First, the one which we most often associate with him is there would be an eminent and catastrophic end of history and God's new order would be established. Second, and this is an interpretation which has become most popular in our denomination during the past century with social action and belief in human progress, the Kingdom of God could be established within history. A third interpretation is that the Kingdom of God did not depend upon the termination of history or a consummation of it but was a reality of the spirit rather than of the world and it is among us even now.

Which view did Jesus endorse? According to scholars, clearly not the second, which is a product of modern times. For a while perhaps the first, as Albert Schweitzer maintains. But during the latter part of his ministry, as men like Rudolf Bultmann and C.H. Dodd contend, Jesus held to the third, that the Kingdom of God is a reality of the spirit aside from history.

What influence could such a reality have had on moral decision-making? Jesus never fully explains what he means, but I think I have a sense of what he meant. We must remember that for Jesus, God was not only a central teaching but a living reality. In Jesus we have a radical break from the God of Judaism, the unapproachable ruler of the universe. For one of the first times in history, God is considered as a father, from whom support and strength could be expected.

It was precisely this expectancy, this trust and confidence, this security in one's acceptance, that was the spiritual reality that constitutes the Kingdom of God. There is no good reason why this sense of acceptance and trust of life cannot be ours also. It doesn't matter where we say it originates, so long as it is "among us" and moves us toward action.

As I see it, this kingdom that Jesus proclaimed can be experienced by us as peace in the present and hope in the future. First, there must be a deep sense of self-acceptance and identity that is peace. But since the future is most uncertain—and this was Jesus' greatest emphasis—peace in the present is not possible unless accompanied by and predicated upon hope, expectancy of the good that the future holds.

This is somewhat vague. Let me give examples of what this reality is that is the equivalent of the Kingdom of God, which has a place in our lives and is a prologue to moral decision. One of the best examples I can think of is a spirit that permeates the home just before the family goes on a vacation, or the spirit among children the night before Christmas. Here we are filled with a sense of expectancy and joy. We all come more fully alive and find ourselves doing things for each other, loving each other in ways we would not ordinarily do. When children are "good" before Christmas it is not just because they're going to get presents and must be well behaved. It is because they are filled with a spirit of expectancy that makes them feel good and they want to do well. The purpose of religion is to encourage such a sense of expectancy and hope all the time.

Another example is a very specific sensation that comes to us just before we are able to make a moral decision, just before making a decision to love. It is a feeling of well-being, of peace and of hope, that wells up within us, and suddenly it is as if we were released from unseen bonds and are able to love. Next time you're in a position of making such a decision and you decide to do what you know is right, even though it may mean difficulty and even sacrifice, see if you don't feel a sense of fulfillment and peace that accompanies or proceeds the moment of moral decision.

The trouble is that we accept such random moments of beauty and meaning as incidental rather than realize that if we emphasized them all the time, our capacity for moral decision would be enhanced. This is the primary task of religion, to give priority and attention to the deepest realities of being that lead to moral decision. Is the absolute ethic of Jesus, is the commandment of love difficult and elusive? Then seek the kingdom of peace and of hope. Under conditions of peace and hope the absolute ethic is practical, even inevitable.

The kingdom Jesus offered was not the one that the Jews expected, either. They looked for a kingdom and Messiah in the tradition of David, who would liberate their country. So, misunderstood and rejected, Jesus gave his life trying to express the nature of his kingdom and out of a faith that it would prevail, even over death itself.

And the wonder of time is that it has. For the deepest message of Jesus for our time is more than the ethic of love; it is the presence of the kingdom of peace and hope that undergirds the ethical and makes it possible. Yet, it may not be the kingdom we expect either; it is also in our power to misunderstand and reject it. We stand as those who, by the lakeside, heard the Son of Man for the first time: "The kingdom of God is not coming with signs to be observed; nor will they say, 'Lo, here it is' Or 'There!' For behold the kingdom of God is in the midst of you" (Luke 17:20–21 RSV).

— 11 —

Life Has Loveliness to Sell[1]

"Life has loveliness to sell" (Teasdale 2019). An unusual expression. Life truly has loveliness and beauty, but why would Sara Teasdale in her exquisite poem "Barter" say that loveliness is something life has to sell, suggesting there might be a price paid for it? Whoever heard of paying for the beautiful things of life—the wonders of the natural world, the blessings of human community? What I would like to do today is talk with you about the wonderful and lovely things of life that we often take for granted, and through our discussion perhaps resolve the mystery of what Sara Teasdale meant when she said that life has these things "to sell."

Life has loveliness and goodness and beauty. This cannot be disputed. We need only lift our eyes and open our ears to the lovely world about us. We need only to look upon the trees in their many-colored graciousness, to feel the full weight of a golden pumpkin in our hands, to run our fingertips over the even, smooth grains of corn still secure on the cob. We need think not only of the precious autumn season, but the many seasons of the year, of the whiteness and purity in cleansing and life-giving snow with which we are so abundantly blessed in Upstate New York, the reawakening of Spring with its promise of new life and loveliness, and the soothing and nourishing warmth of summer. We need only open our eyes and look at the trees, see the miracle of small life underfoot, and lift them and look upon the array of stars which are so awesome that since time immemorial men thought they must have been placed by the gods.

In the words of the poem by Kenneth Patton:

---

1. Sermon delivered by the author at the Church of the Reconciliation Unitarian Universalist, Utica, New York, on October 18, 1964.

> Smell the air; it's good.
> It's your air.
> Your lungs grew in the breathing of it.
> Take a drink of cool water.
> It's yours to bubble through every cell of your being.
> Stand in the wind and sun. . . .
> It's all yours, the fields, the clouds, the sky.
> The same life that is in me runs through all the earth.
> Pull up the slender blade of grass.
> Nibble the white tip.
> Take life into your living body.
> Run down the hill.
> Jolt your bones a little.
> Stretch your muscles.
> Heave the air in and out of your lungs. . . . (Hudson 1962)

How long has it been since we've done these things? Perhaps not all of us are still able to. But there is an undeniable loveliness and beauty in this world of ours. It is ours, it is our home. We may travel to other planets, but this will always be our home, just as our hometown is always special. It is our paradise, our Garden of Eden from the first rays of the morning light and the stirring of the birds, through the new day, to the quiet and peace of night.

Life has other loveliness, the loveliness we find in human beings. People are lovely to look upon, and there is a deeper loveliness yet that is within them. We delight in children, we cherish our babies, but armfuls of tomorrow. We find in our husbands, wives, and partners the deepest loveliness of all, the loveliness of loyalty and trust and acceptance. We take each other as we are, with our imperfections and failures as well as good qualities, but if our hearts are at all open to each other, we see unmistakably inscribed on the other soul an image of loveliness beyond compare. In our parents, we can or should find a loveliness that springs from their devotion and care for us, from their giving us the greatest gift of all, life itself. In our many friends is the loveliness of trusted companionship with whom we can be ourselves, to whom we can reveal our deepest secrets. In old age, there is an honored loveliness of wisdom and patient acceptance, the sanctity of serenity and peace.

It is as Patton said: "We feed our eyes upon the mystery and revelation in the faces of our brothers and sisters, we seek to know the wistfulness of the very young and the very old, the wistfulness of men in all times of life" (Patton 2015). So, there is a beauty in people, life has loveliness here also.

Finally, we can turn to what might appear the least obvious place to look for loveliness, and that is within ourselves. Each of us may possess an image of loveliness within. As someone once said, "I pray that I may be lovely . . . within!" There may be within us reserves of compassion and strength, honor and courage. We may meet life without fear, and live life with joy and exuberance that wells up from deep within. We sometimes do things that are not very lovely, and we may not feel lovely within all the time, but what we are within may shine forth with glory and radiance. I like the way Rabbi Tagore put it in a prayer we sometimes use:

> Our true life lies in a great depth within us. Our restlessness and weakness are in reality merely the stirrings of the surface. That is why each day we may retire in silence far into the quiet depths of our spirit and experience the real strength within us. If we do this our words and actions will come to be real also. (Tagore 1943)

There is the loveliness that may be within our souls, if we can only nurture it, and learn to look for it there.

So, life has loveliness, beauty and abundance to harvest. A splendor that we can only begin to garner. But there is one hard, cold fact that we come up against, and as religious liberals it is important that we learn to cope with it as do other religions and that is that although life has loveliness, life is not necessarily always lovely! And perhaps here is the key to Sara Teasdale's words "to sell." The truth of the matter is life's loveliness is not always free and the price we might have to pay is the possibility of losing it. Some of these things that are freely given may be repossessed at any time; we do not pay for them in advance and therefore are assured of them; we buy them, so to speak, on a time plan. The mistake we must not make as other churches do is thinking that the good things are taken away and we are visited by misfortune because of personal delinquency in meeting payments, because of guilt or sin, and therefore God repossesses them. This is the story of Job. It doesn't happen because of cosmic control and correction. It just happens. It is a fact that life has loveliness, and also a fact that life is not always lovely. In losing some of the lovely things we pay a price, and in that sense, we can say with Sara Teasdale "life has loveliness to sell."

How do we pay this price, how do we lose some of these lovely things in the course of life? I think you know as well as I. As we grow older, we are able to appreciate fewer of our physical and natural interests; our eyesight dims and our hearing fails. We meet other disappointments. People sometimes fail and disappoint us or do unlovely things to one another: man's inhumanity to man. We go through such prolonged suffering and difficulty that something happens to us, and we are not as lovely as we once were before. Yes, life has loveliness, but we must not forget that it is loveliness to sell, and this may mean eventually paying a price.

One of the best contemporary examples of the fineness and loveliness of life, and the price that we must sometimes pay in losing it, is the story of John Glenn. He was a national, world hero, of superb physical, mental, and psychological condition, a man of brilliance, a man of humility, a man whose personality warmed all who met him. The first man from the free world to step upon the threshold of space and return. A man who at the height of fame resigned his post in the space program to run for the Senate in Ohio. Thousands of John Glenn buttons and bumper stickers were in warehouses; the campaign had begun; people were giving him promising support. What happened? A man who had literally traveled into space, went through two world wars, flew 149 combat missions having his plane hit 12 times by ack-ack fire, who never suffered an injury through all of this—slipped on a rug in his bathroom and struck his head on the bathtub causing severe brain damage.

So, life has loveliness, but is not always free; there may be a price exacted from each of us and we should know this in advance and be prepared for it, so that when that day comes we will be ready. And of course, each of us must eventually pay the dearest price for life's loveliness when we face our final hour. This is the way of life, the Tao of the Chinese, and that is something we must find a way of facing with a measure of serenity and acceptance.

Do we then end on a note of pessimism? No, we would not. We would be reminded of the glories of life that we have mentioned. I would ask only that as religious liberals we also learn how to cope with the lack of loveliness we sometimes experience. One thing that can be said is that life has a kind of justice to it: it can take no more away from us than has been given us in the first place. It is for us to cherish and be sustained by what is lovely, and not to be diminished or defeated by what is unlovely.

— 12 —

No Greater Love Hath Any Man[1]

> Greater love hath no man than this,
> that a man lay down his life for his friends.
>
> —John 15:13 KJV

This morning I want to talk about what it means for people to have such great love and devotion for friends, country, or principles—that they are willing to lay down their lives for them. This is the greatest sacrifice a person can make. Yet throughout the centuries, there are those who have made it without hesitation. This morning it is appropriate to honor some of these individuals.

The first example that occurs in our culture is that of Jesus. Jesus is revered by the Christian church for being the Christ, a God, a supernatural being. He can be revered by us as Unitarian Universalists for his human conviction that was so strong that it led him to deliberately forfeit his life for what he believed was right.

If what we know about Jesus was right, he had ample opportunity to remove himself from danger. It was an entirely voluntary act for him to go to Jerusalem, the center of Roman power and authority. He knew he would face arrest there, but he knew it was the place where his presence was most needed, where he had to preach his message, and knew that if he did not go he would in effect be running away. For some men there

---

1. Sermon delivered by the author at the Church of the Reconciliation Unitarian Universalist, Utica, New York, on December 1, 1963.

are places of destiny. For Jack Kennedy it was Dallas. For Martin Luther King, Jr., Memphis. For Robert Kennedy, Los Angeles. For Jesus, the man, it was Jerusalem.

So, Jesus and his disciples marched to Jerusalem. They set up headquarters at a friend's house, and Jesus showed himself publicly and began to preach. He entered debates and came into conflict with orthodox Jewish leaders. He threw the money changers out of the temple. Even then he had the chance to leave, but he stayed. In the garden, he prayed for the cup to pass from his lips, but it was not to be.

It was only a matter of time and the soldiers found him. As the story goes, he did not resist arrest. Nor did he try to defend himself at the trial. And so, he was killed, knowing that by dying he accomplished what he could not do by living.

A second example of self-sacrifice in our culture is that of Socrates. Socrates was an outspoken critic of much that went on in Athens. This was almost 400 years before the time of Jesus and only four years before a great war that devastated Greece. The politicians of Athens were determined to keep the peace, and Socrates was only stirring things up. So, it should not have been a surprise when one day the news came that he had been arrested. He had the chance to remain quiet, of not being so radical in his teaching, but he spoke and taught as he saw fit. His "subversive" activities included teaching philosophy—the skill of independent thought. His ultimate recourse was to reason which denied the traditional place of the Greek gods and he was branded "atheistic."

Even now, though, it would have been easy for Socrates to get off. All he had to do was to remain quiet and pacify his accusers at the trial, but he was not cut out to do this. He spoke truthfully, bluntly to the court. He did not beg to be let go. He did not bring his wife and children to gain the sympathy of the court, as was the custom. Instead, he judged the court, reproving them for their lack of principle in the political life of Athens. "Men of Athens," he said earnestly, "I am your friend, I love you. . . . But so long as the breath and the power are in me, I will not cease the practice of philosophy. I will exhort anyone I meet. . . ." (Gross 2002).

The trial was over. Socrates was found guilty. Now he rose to speak at the sentencing. It had been a close vote; he could easily get exile instead of death. But even now, it was no time for Socrates to hold back his words. "And I cannot keep quiet, because the God has ordered me to speak, though I know that you do not believe this. And I say that it happens to be the greatest good that a human being can have, to talk everyday about goodness, and the other things which you have heard me discussing, examining myself and others—if I say for a human being the unexamined life is not worth living—you will believe this still less. But it is true as I say, men of Athens" (Stewardson and Weiss 1998, 16–17).

The rest of the story we know. The vote was for death. Even now, there was ample opportunity for escape, for banishment. All that was necessary was a bribe to the guard by his powerful friends, but Socrates would have none of it. The end came. It is not just what a man lives for, but what he dies for that is worthy.

One of the greatest martyrs in our tradition of Unitarian Universalism was the impetuous Spaniard, Michael Servetus, who lived and died in the early sixteenth century. Turning to scriptural proofs and the power of his own reason, Servetus came to the position of opposing the dominant Trinitarian theology of his time. Thus, he was one of the first Unitarians to believe in one God, rather than a God of three persons. During his early life Servetus traveled and studied with the great teachers of his day: Erasmus, Capito, and Bucer.

But it was not enough for him simply to converse about his ideas or spread his heresies by mouth. In these early days of the printing press, Servetus found a publisher and issued his book on *The Errors of the Trinity*. Servetus said, "I should prefer not to use a word foreign to the Scriptures, lest perchance in future the philosophers have occasion to go astray. . . . May this blasphemous and philosophical distinction of three beings in one God be rooted out from the minds of men" (Parke 1957, 6).

The Catholic Church branded the book heretical. Even early Protestant reformers felt the book went too far and refused Servetus support and sanctuary. It was not long before the Inquisition in France and Spain put Servetus on their list. Servetus was forced into exile to Lyon, where he changed his name and dropped out of sight for twenty years. During this time, he turned his great mind to the topics of geography and medicine and wrote remarkable books on these subjects.

Finally, however, knowing the great danger that awaited him and unable to refrain from his original ideas, Servetus returned to the arena of religious controversy. He entered into a correspondence with the great Protestant leader, John Calvin. The correspondence led to debate, and the debate to bitter exchange. Calvin vowed that if Servetus ever came to Geneva, he would be sorry.

Not long after when Servetus was passing through Geneva on his way to Naples, he was recognized and arrested. Calvin directed the prosecution and the result was perhaps inevitable. On October 26, 1553, Michael Servetus was found guilty and sentenced; the next day he died in the flames. In more recent years in America, religious martyrs have been blessed, probably because we have found more civilized ways of dealing with dissent. We no longer require that men literally lay down their lives for their faith; heresy is no longer punished so violently. Yet, from time to time, there have been those in the tradition of Unitarian Universalism who have showed the same devotion and courage and who, in a sense, have given their lives for what they believed in.

Perhaps the most controversial Unitarian because of his views was Theodore Parker. Parker spent his life fighting for his religious convictions, struggling against the orthodox Unitarianism of his day which was based upon the Bible, and asserting the new ideas of Emerson, that religion is based upon man's experience, reason, and encounter with the natural world. Parker was ostracized from polite society and refused membership in the Unitarian Ministers Association. Fellow ministers refused to let him preach from their pulpits. As he said, "I see men stare at me in the street, and point, and say, 'that is Theodore Parker,' and look at me as if I were a murderer" (Frothingham 1874, 345).

Parker could have backed off from the fight, but he was never one to do that. He waded into the controversy, writing thousands of letters a year, preaching twice each Sunday, and lecturing to 100,000 people a year on the Lyceum circuit. It was the combined strain of controversy, and the added effort that he undertook to meet its demands that finally broke Parker's health and took his life, as surely as if he had been executed for his heresy. He suffered pleurisy and an effusion of water on the lungs that lasted eight months. He wrote to his beloved congregation, "I shall not speak to you today, for this morning, a little after 4 o'clock, I had a slight attack of bleeding in the lungs or throat" (Frothingham 1874, 504). The "slight attack of bleeding" proved to be a serious hemorrhage of the lungs.

His doctors ordered him to the West Indies and Europe to recover lost health, but even here his voluminous correspondence continued. On May 10, 1860, he died in Florence, Italy—close to the spot where Michael Servetus was burned at the stake, and not far from the place where Socrates was condemned.

We have time to mention just one more person who, in our tradition of liberal religion, could be said to have given his life for our cause. The last person I have chosen to talk about is someone who was connected to our own Utica church. Such a man was the thirtieth minister of our church, T. Conley Adams, who died on Thanksgiving Day just seven years ago. In the joy of what he had found in the liberal church, Adams gave his all for the cause of a free faith. He became ill and was confined to the hospital for six weeks. Just when it was thought that he was recovered and had returned home, he was struck down by a heart attack.

I would like to read part of one of his sermons which I think is as fitting a tribute as can be paid to anyone: "There is another factor to keep in mind as we struggle for the mastery over our worries. We do not stand alone in our efforts. Whenever we surrender our lives to the pursuit of a worthy cause, we are joined in the search by what William James called a 'something more.' That 'something more,' call it by whatever name you will—if you must name it—multiplies our strength, speaks words of courage to our hearts, and upholds our hands along the way...."

Adams concluded, "One of the greatest stabilizing things a person can ever learn is not to be afraid of life. The greatest teachers of spiritual truth in the past have had one thing in common—they have called upon common people to renew their faith in themselves, in their fellowmen, and in life itself. Life may look hopeless today, brute force is in the ascendency. But truth and integrity are on the throne. In the end, truth and beauty and justice and love will prevail" (Adams 1963).

Few of us are called upon to give our lives in the dramatic way that Socrates, Jesus, and Servetus did. But we may still give of ourselves, of our lives, for that which we believe in. How many of us have the conviction and the devotion to live our lives, to give our all for our beliefs? No greater love hath any man. As T. Conley Adams says, "Wherever we surrender our lives to the pursuit of a worthy cause," we find that something "multiplies our strength, speaks words of courage to our hearts, and upholds our hands along the way" (Adams 1963).

— 13 —

Out of the Stars[1]

OUT OF THE STARS we have come. Stardust and sunlight, spinning through time and space. Time out of time in the vastness of space, earth spun into orbit around the sun. Kindled by sunlight, on earth arose life. Out of the sea to the land, rising to walk and to fly, trembled life. This is the wonder of time, the marvel of space: out of the stars swung the earth, and upon the earth there arose life.

We lift our eyes in wonder at it all. We ask, "What does it all mean? Why are we here? What is the meaning of it all?" With Robert Browning we would say, "Life has meaning; to find its meaning is my meat and drink" (Durant 1926). It doesn't matter much what age we are, whether in the flower of youth, at the height of maturity, or the pinnacle of age. We wonder, and we search. Sometimes the more we search, the less we find. "How strange is a lot of us mortals," said Albert Einstein, "Each of us is here for a brief sojourn; for what purpose he knows not, though he sometimes thinks he feels it" (Einstein 2014, 13). In the words of a poet, "What is the great compelling reason of the flowing through time and space of the liquid, musical river of life?" Of all the great and noble purposes of life, of living in love, seeking right and doing what is just, there is one reason for living more basic than any other. It is that we find peace and joy.

It is so simple that it is the easiest to overlook and brush aside. Perhaps it has been so for you. In our ordered, automated, committee-laden lives; in our frenzied rush to one place and then another, to do one thing

---

1. Sermon delivered by the author at the Church of the Reconciliation Unitarian Universalist, Utica, New York.

and then another—perhaps it is something that you have lost too. Regardless of how busily organized our lives are, or how many things we fill them with, we may lose happiness.

The wonderful thing about this underlying meaning of life is that it's not something reserved for those few who are wise enough to reach it. It is equally accessible to us all. It lies at our doorstep. It lies within the framework of what lives we have, families, jobs, and circumstances that belong to each of us. If we are unhappy about our jobs, or families or lives, the fault is apt to lie as much with us as with these external things. It depends on our attitude, on which way we look at things.

A young man sat by a commuter train window. Beside him was an elderly workman. Suddenly, on the opposite track, an express train thundered by, shaking the window glass, obliterating the countryside. Snapping his fingers, the boy turned and glared at the old workman as he grumbled: "There it is. It's always there. Every time I begin to enjoy something, like the scenery, something gets in the way and spoils it."

The other nodded thoughtfully, "That often happens," he conceded. "But did you ever stop to think that there are windows on both sides of the train? Look over there now." As the boy looked across the aisle and out through the window on the other side of the train, he saw the open waters of the sound, blue under the summer sky, and a young ship with an orange mast and a bellying sail, all quite lovely to behold. "You'll often find," the old workman murmured, "That a lot depends on which way we look at things." Happiness is at our doorstep. Look not afar for happiness, for it is a flower blooming at your door.

Sydney R. Montague of the Royal Canadian Mounted Police was stationed at Edmonton, Alberta. One day he was handed a warrant to arrest an Indian by the name of Little Joe Calf-Child. The date was midwinter. When Montague rode into the small settlement of Letrowitch, there was not a soul on the street except an Indian sitting by an empty store front.

"Here's the man I need," he thought. He beckoned the Indian and clapped his hands twice which means, "What's your name?" The Indian answered in a long string of grunts. "Okay," the policeman answered, "I'll call you Joe." Through an interpreter he said, "I need a guide to go into the bush with me—seven weeks—ten weeks maybe. I pay money." The Indian got his bundle and horse and they rode off. For ten weeks they traveled north and westward to track down the ever-moving tribe that Little Joe Calf-Child belonged to.

At last, when they came upon his tribe, the mounted policeman greeted their chief, who spoke English. "I search for one of your people—do you know little Joe Calf-Child?" The chief smiled as he replied, "Yes, I do." "Well, where is he—how do we travel to find him?" There was a long silence. At last the chief responded, "Maybe the white man has been looking too far from himself." He raised his hand and pointed—pointed directly to the guide, who stood lazily leaning against a tree not three feet from Montague.

We can look for happiness in everything near and precious, in our wives and husbands, our friends, our children, our work. We can look in the world of beauty about us. We can look for it in the mornings and the evenings. We can look in others, or when we are by ourselves. But we must not overlook that which is closest, that which is within ourselves.

We can and must find happiness and satisfaction in our work. Three stone cutters were driving their chisels into a massive block of Vermont granite. A stranger who passed by asked the first cutter what he was doing. "I'm cutting stone," growled the laborer. "And you?" He asked the second. "I'm working for $7.50 a day," he replied. When the question was put to the third, his face lit up and he answered, "I'm building a cathedral."

We can find happiness in the world of nature and with Byron say:

> There is a pleasure in the pathless woods,
> There is rapture on the lonely shore,
> There is society were none intrudes,
> By the deep sea, and music in its roar;
> I love not man the less, but nature more, for these our interviews.
> (Byron n.d.)

We can look to the mornings and the evenings, to Longfellow's evening when, "The night shall be filled with music, and the cares that infest the day, shall fold their tents, like the Arabs, and as silently steal away" (Longfellow n.d.). There it is, happiness on every hand, every place we look for it.

But there is one last, most important place to find happiness, and that is within ourselves. "Why dost thou wonder, O man," proclaimed Francis Quarles, "at the height of the stars or the depth of the sea? Enter into thine own soul and wonder there" (Quarles 1881, 188). We need to know ourselves, the hardest of all tasks, to know our limitations and our strengths, and be able to say, "I am enough." We need to be at peace with ourselves, to feel that we are worthy, to feel a sense of inner adequacy. This is the root of all happiness.

We need to explore the real depths of ourselves. We need to realize that as much as we think we know ourselves, we have only touched the surface of our fathomless spirits. As Tagore said, "Our true life lies at a great depth within us. Our restlessness and weakness are merely the stirrings of the surface. That is why we may each day retire in silence far into the quiet depths of our spirit, and experience the real strength within us" (Tagore n.d.).

One of the best ways of being able to do this, of finding the key to inner-reflection and searching, is through the use of solitude. We need to learn how to be alone without being lonely. We need to realize we don't always have to surround ourselves with people, immerse ourselves in activity, constantly watch TV, but there should be times when we find solitude. We need a quiet place where we can pause to look within ourselves. "It is very seldom that a man is truly alone," said Emerson, "There is one means of procuring solitude which to me, and I apprehend to all men is effectual, and that is to . . . look at the stars" (Emerson 1910, 263–64). And so, we return to the stars to know our true nature.

Easy as it is for us to say that finding happiness should be our foremost task, we must recognize that there are those for whom happiness is particularly hard. There are those for whom life has not been kind, those who have known pain and sorrow we cannot imagine. It may be that as the years pass, we will be likewise tested. It is hard for such people to take another chance, to risk living fully again. They must, as the Buddha said, "draw out the arrow of lamentation, and complaint, and grief. He who has drawn out the arrow and has become composed will obtain the peace of mind" (Carus 1894, 188–89). When we get down to it, what we need to be able to do is to believe in life. "Nothing else matters much," said Harry Emerson Fosdick, but that man "should be able to believe in life" (Fosdick, n.d.). We must be able to say as two astronomers, husband and wife, had inscribed on their tombstone: "We have loved the stars too fondly to be fearful of the night" (Williams 1936, 613–14).

— 14 —

Palm Sunday[1]

Long ago and far away
There was a land
Near the dawn of day.

There lived a man
Who was the son of man,
And he lived his life
On the roads of clay.

He had no home,
No resting place;
There was always the horizon
On his face:

No place to stop,
No place to rest
His head,
Until he was dead.

---

1. Service presented by the author at Harvard Divinity School, Cambridge, Massachusetts in 1959, and at the Church of the Reconciliation Unitarian Universalist, Utica, New York, on April 15, 1962.

MARK 10:32-34—PROLOGUE

"And they were on the road" (Mark 10:32 RSV). There was something of destiny about that road to Jerusalem. None of the disciples understood it, Jesus barely did himself. But all knew that the dusty clay road to Jerusalem lay at their feet and follow it they must. It was as inevitable as the on-moving tide reaching slowly across the sand. Jesus knew the tragedy that awaited him in Jerusalem: he knew he would die. Yet to Jerusalem he must go.

There was something irresistible, magnetic about the city. When one of the disciples would mention in conversation the word, "Jerusalem," Jesus would involuntarily turn and his eyes would look straight ahead as if they could see into the future. At night when some of the band huddled about the campfire and talked and lowered tones, the word "Jerusalem" sometimes escaped their lips. Then, Jesus lying asleep on his side would hear it and wake with a start. The city drew them onward, irresistibly. There was choice for the man of Nazareth. Yes, but there was only one choice for him to make. The city beckoned and would claim him as the sky claims a bird of flight.

"And Jesus was walking ahead of them" (Mark 10:32 RSV), this strange little band of men. They walked steadily and patiently. All their lives they had been walking. They were too poor most of them to know any other way. Many of them wore ragged robes, and the perspiration ran from under their matted hair down their cheeks. The dust rose from the road and caked their faces an even deeper brown than the bronze from the hot Palestine sun.

Yet there was something unusual, compelling about them, as they strode along together. The tramp of their feet could be heard well ahead of them. Farmers working their fields, shepherds tending their herds, travelers meeting them on the road—all stopped what they were doing to watch silently as the determined band of men swiftly swung past.

There was something striking about them. In a land where many men wandered aimlessly over the dusty roads, and where all men traveled at a respectful slowness beneath the burning sun, these men were striding along—yes, almost marching—as if they had some place to go, as if they had something important to do.

And they did. They were going to Jerusalem. Some of those who saw the group march past were so compelled that they turned in their footsteps, left their flocks, or put aside their hoes and fell into the ranks, thus unknowingly enrolling themselves in the greatest drama ever to be played beneath the sun.

MARK 11:1-10—TRIUMPH

Yet it was not only a trail of tragedy that this band travelled. They knew full well, at least Jesus and the disciples knew, that this road to Jerusalem was the goal of their lives. All their lives they had looked for courage to go into their Jerusalem, to stand for what they believed in, to face their fears. There had been enough of being afraid, abused, scorned. Now they would announce to the world who they were. Even Pilate would know it. After a lifetime of waiting they finally decided to walk into the stronghold of the enemy and take the consequences. Oh, what fearful consequences, my brave little band, brave Jesus. But they walked proudly, their heads held high. Their feet rose and fell together. They held their shoulders back.

They marched triumphantly. The happiness and victory of their whole lives poured into this one moment. Then someone took up the shout, "Hosanna. Hosanna in the highest!" Fragments of palm and robes showered down before their feet. The shepherds with their horns and lutes played for joy. Oxen, donkeys, and other beasts of burden added their startled voices. People gathered along the road, shouting and stamping their feet and cheering. They bordered the road on either side for miles.

We strain our eyes. We jump up and down hoping to see Jesus. We lean forward. And here he comes! "Hosanna!" But what is this? He isn't marching boldly. He isn't even being carried on a litter. Nor is he being carried on the shoulders of his men. Where are his men? Where is his army? I don't see a single weapon among them. How can he be a leader, how can he set us free, how can he bring in a new kingdom, without an army and weapons?

What a farce! What a waste of time to come down here! I'm leaving. But, hold on a minute, here he comes. He's coming abreast of me here. I might as well stay and see him. That's what I came for.

He looks just like the others—the robe, the beard—but what's that about his face? Let them come closer. Why, he's not shouting and cheering like the rest. He is sitting there quietly, almost humbly. His shoulders are even stooped over a little. But his face. Such quietness, such peace. I've not seen such beauty in the setting of the sun, or the calmness of the after-storm air; but there's the striving of an ocean there too, there's pain and such great sadness. I've never seen such a face before. Why, everyone I've ever seen is in that face. Everything I've ever felt is there. I've seen that face every time I've looked into the sky or gazed into the sea.

But wait, he's turning his head, he is searching the crowd around me, as if he felt me tugging at him with my eyes. He's—he's looking at me! Me, among all these hundreds, he's looking straight at me. He's holding me with his eyes. And I can hear him speaking. But his lips aren't moving, and if they did, I couldn't hear in this crowd. But I do hear his voice, speaking to me. There, can you hear? He's saying—I can hear him saying, "Follow me!"

And he's gone. The crowd breaks from the sides of the road, closing in behind this man, and I am half running, half swept along by them, and the crowd is shouting and cheering, "Hosanna!"

MARK 11:15-19—CONFLICT

It is now the day after Jesus entered Jerusalem. The road into Jerusalem is abandoned, littered by palm branches and the rags of cloaks from the day before. An old, bent man sweeps them up and puts them into a big basket.

The crowd has gone home. The disciples wish they could. But Jesus knows that it is all or nothing now. He knows that this is the most difficult part. Those in power consider him a dangerous man: they would hush, ignore, and brush him aside. He knows that this is the very thing that must not happen. He must plant himself firmly before them; his presence must be felt; he must do something impossible to ignore.

So, squaring his shoulders and swallowing a lump in his throat, Jesus walks up to the doors of the temple and with the mighty lunge bursts them open. He glances to right and left. His jaw is set and his eyes flash. He charges down upon the astonished moneychangers and the knuckles of his hands are white and the carpenter muscles of his back are taut as he grasps the heavy wooden tables and hurls them across the chamber. The coins go spilling and jangling on the stone floor as the sprawling moneychangers awkwardly scratch after them.

This is not the way of Jesus, to fight and brawl. His disciples are startled at him. But Jesus knows what he must do. It is time to act. It is time to draw a line and take a stand. All his life a man can talk about it, he can tell parables, he can preach. But there comes a time when if he's going to be believed, or believe himself, he must do more than speak, he must act.

But it is not enough for Jesus to call attention to himself and force those in power to deal with him. They would misrepresent him; they would trick him into a false confession and condemn him unjustly. Jesus knows that he must make his position clear so that if action is taken against him, he cannot be misrepresented, so that the entire world would know the injustice of his fate.

So, Jesus seeks out the priests and scribes and elders, the Pharisees and Sadducees. He goes again to the temple, and the moneychangers cringe as he enters. The scribes and priests clamor around him and try to trick him with their questions. But Jesus is too shrewd for them. He stands face-to-face with them and matches them question for question. His eyes twinkle as he recognizes the obvious traps laid for him. His big hands gesture as he speaks and his brow knits as he summons the wisdom of his teaching. His voice is rich and vibrant as he pronounces his truth. And after that no one dared asking him any questions.

LUKE 22:31–34—BETRAYAL

I don't know how long it's been since that moment Jesus looked into my eyes when he entered Jerusalem. Everything's been so unreal, as though I were in another world, or as if I were dreaming. Everything's been so confused.

Jerusalem is a changed city since the day Jesus came. There is no more joy, there is no more celebration. It is a quiet city—there is death in the air. It is a restless city. It is like the stillness in the hills before a thunderstorm. There is much uneasiness in the city. There are rumors of great protest among the scribes, Pharisees, and priests. All over there are mutterings against this man.

He talks about a day of judgment, about the Kingdom of God coming. I didn't know that's what he stood for. I'm not ready for things to change and end; I like things as they are. He's in trouble with the authorities too. And he's not willing to back himself up with arms; he won't let his disciples carry swords. I don't want to get involved with a man like that. Why, the way he broke into the sacred temple and threw things around like a lunatic and insulted the scribes and priests! And didn't he threaten to tear the temple down? Those are words and actions of a troublemaker. Such a man is better silenced.

Do you hear me, you there? Let's go find him. Come on, all of you! The man's clearly a heretic; he's a rebel; he preaches treason. Away with him! Stone him! Crucify him! Here, everybody, they are going to crucify Jesus. Come on, let's help, pick up a stone. Here he comes! Down with Jesus! Hit him! Spit on him! Kick him! Crucify him!

MATTHEW 23:37-38—LAMENT

Now there is no more walking, there is no more walking. There is no more dust, no more unmerciful sun. There have been the accusers, there was Pilate. Then, there was poor Simon, and poor, poor Judas. And there was the man in the crowd.

But they are no more. At least not until they are born again, elsewhere. Now there is only the stillness, the waiting. For a little while. Just a little while.

But there is time to think, time to remember. It was expected—all of it; it was necessary—every bit of it. There is calm and fulfillment now.

Yet, there is a trembling upon the wind. In the early morning darkness, the clouds gather black and hover above the hill. As one life leaves, another comes. There is peace in the going and restlessness in the coming.

> Darkened skies in angry cloud hands keeping
> Rumbling thunder from another world sleeping
> Twisted lightening dream-like leaping.
>
> Hillside looms in early morning weeping:
> From corners of the universe the sad wind
> By a rough-hewn tree slowly creeping,
> Through twin branches of suffering
> Barren except for the spirit of man reaping.

— 15 —

The Last Teachings of Jesus[1]

THERE WAS A YOUNG minister, and he got killed. He was a quiet man: he had a sense of humor, he liked life. He liked ordinary people. He liked to help people who were in trouble, and he was loved by those who knew him. There was a part of the country that was the center of persecution and injustice for many of the people. The police and those in authority were brutal, and the way they punished those in minority groups shocked the whole nation.

One day this man who liked people so much and who was so troubled by the injustice that existed in his country made a decision. He decided that he would go to the city where the atrocities were being committed, and through nonviolent methods and his very presence register his protest and try to change what was happening. As soon as his plans became known to his friends, however, they tried to talk him out of his idea. "What can you do by yourself?" They asked, "As an outsider, why stir things up? Pressure tactics, even if nonviolent, will never do any good; social change is a gradual thing. You're too much of an idealist to think that all people can really be treated equally, with dignity and love!"

The young minister—he was still in his 30's—listened patiently to the objections, but still knew he had to go. His arrival in the city of bitterness and conflict was not unnoticed. The townsmen who stood in clusters on the street corners singled him out. The police undoubtably spotted him and marked him as a troublemaker who had to be watched. He was welcomed by some of the people, those who were

---

1. Sermon delivered by the author at the Church of the Reconciliation Unitarian Universalist, Utica, New York.

The Last Teachings of Jesus

being persecuted. He stayed with them in their poorer section of town; he shared their simple food.

He did what he came to do. Through nonviolent and orderly demonstrations, he helped protest the injustice of this place. There were meetings, some of them after dark and behind closed doors. His friends knew the pressure was mounting; they begged him to get out of town while he could. But he stayed. And one night with a man on each side of him, he was killed. The man's name was Jesus.

I wrote this parable, with its obvious parallel to the Unitarian minister who died in Selma, James Reeb, to illustrate that the situation and problems of Jesus are not so far removed from our own time. Who was Jesus? Not a supernatural individual, magically resurrected. But the Jesus we know was a brave prophet, a Jewish rabbi, a liberal minister; a religious leader of the best sort whose teachings and life were an inspiration to those who knew him. What were the teachings of Jesus? I think that the basic teachings of Jesus are nowhere better stated that at one point in the New Testament.

The point that I want to direct your attention to is the last time that Jesus is known to state his ideas to his disciples. It is the time after the Last Supper before Jesus was arrested when he was in the garden with his disciples. It was here, as the Book of John records, that Jesus spoke to them simply, directly, and led them in prayer before ascending the Mount of Olives for meditation and returning to be arrested. After that, he spoke no more of his beliefs, but simply answered questions. The New Testament lapses into narrative from this point forward—there are no more words of wisdom. So, I submit that these final words of Jesus to his disciples before his arrest are of utmost significance. Knowing he was going to die, there can be little doubt that what he said to them then was what he wanted to remain in their minds after he was gone.

We read at length from the book of John:

> As the Father hath loved me, so have I loved you: continue ye in my love. If ye keep my commandments, ye shall abide in my love; even as I have kept my Father's commandments, and abide in his love. These things have I spoken unto you, that my joy might remain in you, and that your joy might be full. This is my commandment, That ye love one another, as I have loved you. Greater love hath no man than this, that a man lay down his life for his friends. . . . for all things that I have heard of my Father I have made known unto you. Ye have not chosen me, but I

have chosen you, and ordained you, that ye should go and bring forth fruit, and that your fruit should remain. . . . These things I command you, that ye love one another. If the world hate you, ye know that it hated me before it hated you. If ye were of the world, the world would love his own: but because ye are not of the world, but I have chosen you out of the world, therefore the world hateth you. (John 15:9–19 KJV)

His disciples said unto him, Lo, now speakest thou plainly, and speaketh no proverb. Now we are sure that thou knowest all things, and needest not that any man should ask thee: by this we believe that thou camest forth from God. Jesus answered them, Do ye now believe? Behold, the hour cometh, yea, is now come, that ye shall be scattered, every man to his own, and shall leave me alone: and yet I am not alone, because the Father is with me. These things I have spoken unto you, that in me ye may have peace. In the world ye shall have tribulation: but be of good cheer; I have overcome the world. (John 16:29–33 KJV)

Let us take these simple parting words of Jesus, and see if we can we capture their essence, see if we can get some understanding of his life. We have no disciples here, but if we were in Jerusalem 2,000 years ago shortly after Jesus died, what do you imagine we would believe about the religious life after we heard these words? First, as I have already acknowledged, we would be reminded of Jesus' theism. We would be aware of a deeply personal, fatherly God, who Jesus turned to, and with whom he felt a close relationship. This was doubtless an elemental reality for Jesus, the source of all. For some of us it is so also. Others of us are content without the leap-of-faith involved to accept the qualities formally attributed to God as simply a part of life.

The second quality which we find mentioned in Jesus' last words to his disciples is that of finding joy in life. Jesus wished for them, "That my joy might remain in you, and that your joy might be full" (John 15:11 KJV). Jesus must have loved life deeply for one of his greatest desires to be that his friends' joy would be full. We often forget the basicness of enjoying life. Regardless of who we are what we do, if we are not happy, if we do not have joy in our work and our lives we have little. Jesus knew this and wanted and sought, amidst his tragedy, joy.

Third, we find Jesus' basic tenant, "This is my commandment, that ye love one another, as I have loved you. Greater love hath no man than this, that a man lay down his life for his friends" (John 15:12–13 KJV).

It is strange for us to imagine someone going about giving commands, making pronouncements, but Jesus did this with apparent acceptance. He asked not for some theoretical kind of love, not something he preached about; his only qualification for the kind of love he hoped for in his disciples was the kind that he showed for them. And finally, perhaps somewhat anticipating his end and realizing he would die, Jesus gives the supreme example of love, that of laying down one's life for his friends.

One of the most important points in this passage is Jesus expecting love of others only to the extent to which he was able to give it to them. We often expect people, our husbands or wives, for example, to do things for us, to give us love, without giving thought as to whether we have first shown consideration to them. This is perhaps the only kind of love we have a right to expect, the kind we give in which we go over halfway.

Fourth, Jesus says something else that's important about love, and that is what he says about hate. He says not to worry if you find hate in the world or if people dislike you. Jesus says if you were just like everybody else, if you conformed, if your standards were no higher—you would have no trouble getting along: "If ye were of the world, the world would love his own: but, because you are not of the world . . . therefore, the world hated you" (John 15:19 KJV). I think this means simply that if you bring something to life, if your standards are higher, you will be a threat to others. You will be misunderstood, and you may be rejected. Hostility from others can be a paralyzing and disturbing thing but is not something that should worry us so much.

The final part of Jesus' message is that of peace and hope. Jesus must have known how deeply disturbed his disciples were at their last meeting with him, and so it is consistent with his sensitivity that a concern of his should be to comfort his friends. "Peace I leave with you, my peace I give unto you: not as the world giveth, give I unto you," and "These things I have spoken unto you, that in me you may have peace. In the world ye shall have tribulation: but be of good cheer; I have overcome the world" (John 14:27, 16:33 KJV). With these words, Jesus imparts what is perhaps the universal message of religion, that there is that which is important and that which is unimportant in life; there is that which is basic and that which is superficial. What should trouble us is not those things of the material world which can be given or taken away, the things of cause and effect which are external to us—but that spirit with which we meet the world and which the world can never touch. It was this peace Jesus pointed to, not whatever peace the world could give. It was not the outer world of tribulation that Jesus wanted men concerned with, but the inner world which each soul can shape to its own heaven of hope and happiness.

But of course, there is one other thing that must have been impressive about this occasion when Jesus last talked to his disciples. In addition to the ideas in his message, it is the deed he was committing. It is not just the words and beliefs and inner life which were important to Jesus. It was his conduct and acts. And this is the final quality of Jesus' religion we must recognize, the courage to encounter and transform society.

Jesus said, "you have not chosen me, but I've chosen you . . . that ye should go and bring forth fruit, and that your fruit should remain" (John 15:16 KJV). Did Jesus' disciples bring forth fruit? We will never know how fully. Will the fruit of his religion—not the religions created about him—remain? Will the fruit which was so painstakingly garnered on the barren soil of Palestine survive to the present day, or somewhere along the centuries has it been lost and misplaced forever? That is up to us to decide.

— 16 —

The Prophets[1]

It is interesting to note the number of times this year that we have had occasion to refer to the similarities between Unitarian Universalism and Judaism. When we spoke of the nature of the liberal church, we acknowledged that our emphasis upon the goodness of life is shared with the Judaic tradition. When we spoke of the Supreme Court's prayer decision, we recognized how much we have in common with Judaism in matters of social concern. And of course, the belief in one God at least historically underlies both. The name Unitarian literally means belief in one God and arises from the sixteenth century when our forefathers rejected the idea of the divinity of Jesus and the doctrine of the Trinity. The Jews, on the other hand, have always been Unitarian since they never accepted Jesus as the Christ or the Messiah.

There is very little in one religion that is contradictory to the other. That is why liberal Jews frequent our churches when there is no synagogue in the area, or in the event of interfaith marriages. About the only thing we do not have in common with Judaism, and it makes all the difference, is their cultural heritage and history. For this reason, a Unitarian Universalist has been defined, perhaps with tongue-in-cheek, as "a Jew without a history!"

This morning, however, we turn our attention to one of the most important periods of Judaism, in the history of religion for that matter, for the results underlie the rise of Christianity and the emergence of Western civilization. It is the eighth through sixth centuries B.C., the age of the

---

1. Sermon delivered by the author at the Church of the Reconciliation Unitarian Universalist, Utica, New York, on October 7, 1962.

prophets. It was during this time that the Jewish concept of God evolved from a petty, tribal deity to a universal God of righteousness and holiness. It was during this period that the Western world was first touched by a burning concern for social justice and high moral standards. And it was then that the importance of the individual and of inner religious experience first emerged. As H. Wheeler Robinson says in his book on the Old Testament, from the eighth to the sixth centuries "we find the golden age of Israel's creative powers in religion" (Robinson 1937, 17).

Before proceeding with a consideration of the individual prophets, a word about the general historical setting might not be amiss. Prior to the settlement in Canaan, Judaism was a primitive religion of a wandering tribe of Arameans, of whom Abraham, Isaac, Jacob, and Joseph are best remembered. Next is the period of captivity in Egypt and finally the Exodus led by Moses. So, it was not until the Hebrews settled in Canaan, now known as Israel, giving up their nomadic life and removed from the threat of Egyptian enslavement, that their religion had the opportunity to come into its own.

Even here, however, there were obstacles. The dominant religion of the Canaanites was Baalism, and in these surroundings the Jews were quick to forget their God, Yahweh, and to become corrupted. And even in this land they were not free from the threat of aggression: To the north and east Syria and Babylon massed their armed might. During these years that the Jewish nation was on the verge of assimilation and destruction, the prophets appeared who called the Jews to their faith and, perhaps not fully realizing it at the time, to even greater heights than Judaism had known before.

The earliest of the prophets whose writings are extant and of undisputed date is Amos, who prophesied during the prosperous reign of Jeroboam II, from 760–746 B.C. Amos was a shepherd and a pruner of sycamore trees. Yet he was so troubled by the degenerate and immoral lives led by his countrymen that he left his simple life for one of prophecy. His unforgettable phrase, "Let justice roll down like waters, and righteousness like an everflowing stream" (Amos 5:24 RSV), is typical of his regular, sweeping style. In denouncing the corrupt ways of his time, Amos was the first prophet we know of who stressed the universality of God and the moral relationship of man to God. Thus, Amos declares, "'Are you not as children of the Ethiopians to me, O children of Israel?' saith the Lord. 'Have not I brought up Israel out of the land of Egypt? and the Philistines from Caphtor, and the Syrians from Kir'" (Amos 9:7 KJV).

Amos, then, may be considered the first Universalist. This was a significant step in the history of religion. It not only signifies a widening social consciousness as Israel took her place in the community of nations, but is a recognition that the principles of good and righteousness then considered as the God, Yahweh, were not reserved for just one people but were found everywhere, a recognition basic to liberal religion today.

Following closely on the heels of Amos was Hosea whose prophecy saw the end of Jeroboam II's reign and the decline and fall of the Northern Kingdom. As S.R. Driver comments in his *Introduction to the Literature of the Old Testament,* "what Amos perceived in the distance, Hosea saw approaching with rapid steps, accelerated by the internal decay" and disintegration of the Jewish nation (Driver 1957, 304).

Hosea's prophecy is marked by a personal life of tragedy. His wife proved faithless to him—she may even have been a harlot—and although this faithlessness tortured him, he could never cease loving her. His life became a series of futile attempts to win her back. Thus, the main theme of Hosea's prophecy, and this is most interesting to read, is that Israel had proven faithless to God, but God loves her so much that he cries out, "How shall I give thee up. . . . how shall I deliver thee, Israel? . . . .mine heart is turned within me. . . ." (Hosea 11:8 KJV).

Hosea's prophecy is also characterized by a deep concern for right conduct. Man's failure to relate to God is considered primarily a moral one—also an emphasis of liberal religion. Hosea says in the sixth chapter, "What shall I do with you, O E'phriam? Your love is like a morning cloud, like the dew that goes away early. Therefore, I hewn them by the prophets. . . . For I desire steadfast love and not sacrifice. . . ." (Hosea 6:4-6 RSV). Driver observes, "particularly noticeable is Hosea's conception of *love* as the bond uniting Jehovah and Israel . . . as well as individual Israelites one with another" (Driver 1957, 305).

Perhaps because Hosea's experience tends to be so introspective, in him we find emphasis placed upon the individual and the value of inner religious experience. Hoenig and Rosenberg state in their volume titled, *A Guide to the Prophets*: "Hosea looks to the individual, and preaches the importance of an intimate, personal relationship between God and Israel, between man and man, based on a feeling of mutual love" (Hoenig and Rosenberg 1942, 110).

The third prophet that we would turn our attention to is perhaps the best known of all, certainly the most widely quoted, Isaiah. To Isaiah is credited the words which have become the inspiration of our Unitarian

Community Church in New York City—not to mention the United Nations—"they shall beat their swords into plowshares, and their spears into pruning hooks; nation shall not lift up sword against nation, neither shall they learn war anymore" (Isa 2:4 RSV). Isaiah is the author of the sayings, "Comfort, comfort my people" (Isa 40:1 RSV) and "The wolf shall dwell with the lamb, and the leopard shall lie down with the kid" (Isa 11:6 RSV). Isaiah was responsible for the prophetic passages foretelling Jesus: "Behold, a young woman shall conceive and bear a son, and shall call his name Immanuel" (Isa 7:14 RSV), and "For to us a child is born, to us a son is given. . . . And his name will be called 'Wonderful Counselor, Mighty God, Everlasting Father, Prince of Peace'" (Isa 9:6–7 RSV).

Of the life of Isaiah, little is known. He lived and prophesied during the distressing years, 740–700 B. C. when the Northern kingdom fell to Syria and Judah itself was threatened. Probably of royal descent, Isaiah was not only a prophet but a statesman who took part in the events of Judea, and he was eventually martyred by his execution.

One of the most important contributions of Isaiah was his emphasis upon the ultimacy and holiness of God, thus taking a step beyond Amos and elevating God above the petty deity of tribal Judaism, and creating an image of the divine that made Christianity and historical Unitarianism and Universalism possible. One of the best examples of this quality Isaiah ascribed to God is in Chapter 57:

> For thus says the high and lofty One
> Who inhabits eternity, whose name is Holy:
> "I dwell in the high and holy place,
> Also with him who is of a contrite and humble spirit,
> To revive the spirit of the humble,
> And to revive the heart of the contrite.
> For I will not contend for ever,
> Nor will I always be angry;
> For from me proceeds the spirit,
> And I have made the breath of life." (Isa 57:15–16 RSV)

After Isaiah, prophecy is silent during the long reign of Manasseh, which is marked by pagan reactions to Yahwism. Then, in the remaining third of the seventh century, we come to the fourth and final prophet that we will consider this morning, Jeremiah. It was Jeremiah who first coined the expression, "Can the Ethiopian change his skin or the leopard his spots?" (Jer 13:23 RSV).

Jeremiah, who was of priestly dissent, led a life of sorrow, contention, and suffering, as our reading this morning only too well illustrated. When Nebuchadnezzar won his great victory over Egypt, Jeremiah could see that Judah also would soon fall to Babylon. To yield to the inevitable and to avoid the destruction of his people, Jeremiah counseled surrender, even desertion to the enemy. Needless to say, his advice did not meet with favor among many. He was ostracized as a traitor, beaten, arrested, and thrown into a dungeon, practically starved to death, witnessed the destruction of the Temple of Jerusalem, and carried against his will to Egypt where he died.

Of a gentle, susceptible, deeply emotional nature, this adverse course of events impacted Jeremiah profoundly. The conflict left a scar on his soul. Isaiah's voice does not falter with emotion, but Jeremiah's does. His writings are highly self-disclosing, for example when he says, "My grief is beyond healing, my heart is sick within me" (Jer 8:18 RSV).

Yet Jeremiah never lost heart. Despite despair, bitterness, and loneliness, in the face of death and pain, he was compelled to speak out. As he said:

> If I say, "I will not mention [the Lord] . . .
> or speak anymore in his name,"
> there is in my heart as it were a burning fire
> shut up in my bones,
> and I weary with holding it in,
> and I cannot. (Jer 20:9 RSV)

So, by example as much as by precept, Jeremiah represents the importance of the individual and of inner experience in religion, portraying suffering and courage that are as relevant in our day as in his own. There is no better tribute to Jeremiah than that given by Robinson:

> [In Jeremiah] the lesson of all history is exhibited with peculiar emphasis—the dominance of the spiritual factors over the physical, the power of the attitude of human personality over the events which seem to crush it, yet are forced at last to yield to its own interpretation of them. This is seen most of all in Jeremiah, in whom the religion of the older Israel reaches its highest point, and the foundation of a new and more individualizing religion is laid. (Robinson 1937, 70–71).

These, then, are the prophets: Amos, Hosea, Isaiah, and Jeremiah. They were men of sensitivity and integrity the likes of whom the world had never seen before and has seen too few of since. They comprise one of the greatest eras in the history of Judaism.

Yet, as I'm sure you have sensed by now, it is not just Jewish history of which we've been speaking. It is our history too. It is not true that we don't have a history. This is our history, not just because our culture stems from Judaic roots, but because we find in exploring all the world's religions, that everything great that man has ever done belongs to us. Nothing that is human is alien to us.

— 17 —

The Story of a Diabetic[1]

"I HAVE BEEN A diabetic for 41 years." The man talking to a group at our church was Arthur H. Jones, one of the oldest living users of insulin. As a sickly child recently arrived from North Wales, none of the local doctors expected him to live out the year. "Well," one of them advised more as an afterthought, "you might take him to the Presbyterian Hospital in New York City. They are trying some new things there in treating diabetes." Nor was the reception very much more encouraging at the hospital. The admitting officer insisted upon a deposit of $55 to ensure funeral expenses. Yet the emaciated boy lived (as a 12-year-old he weighed only 50 pounds), and today is the father of two children and the principal of a public school. His life is a testimony that with an illness such as diabetes, one can look forward to a long, vigorous, and relatively normal life.

The story begins with that day in 1922 when his cousin led this boy, who was told he would not live out the year, up the steps of the Presbyterian Hospital. For many days there was only the diet of sterile vegetables. Then, gradually began the new drug insulin, and finally the return to a more balanced diet. With strength returned hope, and this young boy began to take an interest in the hospital routine. He helped plan the diets and train the younger children in the use of insulin. The rabbits that were used in experiments were entrusted into his care.

When young Jones first started the use of insulin, the drug cost $10.75 for a 5-cc vile which would last about two weeks. At this time his father was earning only $12.50 a week working in the mills of Upstate

---

1. Sermon delivered by the author at the Church of the Reconciliation Unitarian Universalist, Utica, New York.

New York. To pay for the needed insulin his brother took a job and his father started to work overtime.

When the boy returned home to Utica after a year in the hospital, he had gained 15 precious pounds. After his father died within a few years, Arthur quit school and went to work in a bakery. "At least," his employer wryly surmised, "the cookies were always safe around Arthur." Working over the bakery ovens, however, the slim boy dropped back to 62 pounds. One advantage of the Depression was that as jobs closed, working boys like Arthur went back to school. He walked the eight miles to school along with other students.

Diabetes was a strange disease and this boy who gave himself insulin injections must have seemed very different. Further education was out of the question for most diabetics; there was a kind of taboo on such young men going to college. But not for Arthur. He worked one summer picking crab apples for 25¢ a bushel and hitchhiked to Oneonta State Teachers College with $28.25 in his pocket. "Well, if you really want to come," Dr. Charles Hunt said after listening to his story, "Let's try it for ten weeks."

One day when returning home from the *Oneonta Star* office where he tried to get work delivering newspapers, young Jones overheard two men discussing some pigs that they had to slaughter. "I'll do them for 50¢ apiece," Jones eagerly interposed. Perhaps somewhat taken back by the prospect of this scrawny young man proposing to do what they themselves were reluctant to undertake, the two men agreed. Not only did he walk the 7 ½ miles to slaughter the three pigs, but the enterprising student bought farm eggs with the money and returned to Oneonta and sold them for a profit.

Arthur Jones finished the three-year course in two and a half years. By this time the hard work, careful dieting, and discipline had molded his body into a wiry, solid frame. Although he was slight of build, he now took pride in his vigorous strength and refused to let his illness put him second to anyone.

He passed the Senior Red Cross lifesaving test when he weighed only 70-pounds. Later in life when he was at his top weight of 120-pounds, he hiked 26 miles carrying a 55-pound backpack. The day before he left college a 180-pound fellow student made the mistake of patting him patronizingly on the head and saying, "Now, now, little man!" The "little man" hit him so hard he buckled up and fell through a window.

After graduating from Oneonta State Teachers College, he went to work as a teacher in a small country school. It was a tough school and on the first day three boys, all over 6 feet, stood up menacingly and blocked his way. Without hesitation his fist shot out like a cannonball and the biggest of the lads toppled over unconscious. The other two sheepishly took their seats.

Arthur Jones looked up at the clock on the wall and quietly excused himself. It was 2:30 p.m., and time for his cup of tea.

— 18 —

Where Rivers Begin
*A Theological Assumption
of Unitarian Universalism*[1]

SOMEWHERE HIGH IN THE mountains is a secret spring or an unknown glacier—where rivers begin. It is only the most intrepid explorers and adventurers who seek this place, only those who search for the mystery of origins.

So, too, in our religion there are sources, predispositions, assumptions from which our attitudes and actions spring. From time to time it is good to press beyond our outward behavior to the basic presuppositions that lie beneath them, to that place where rivers begin. This morning I propose to explore with you what I consider is or should be such a fundamental theological presupposition in the Unitarian Universalist church that I venture to suggest it without knowing you intimately as a congregation.

The theological presupposition I have in mind is nothing particularly obscure, although I intend to take up some of its not so obvious implications. It is almost an inevitable presupposition in a culture whose forerunners were the Greeks and Hebrews where people were created in the very image of God, and yet a presupposition which we Unitarians and Universalists were particularly identified with at a time when Calvinist Christianity was undermining people's faith in themselves. I'm speaking, of course, of our belief in the worth and the value of human beings.

---

1. Sermon delivered by the author at the Church of the Reconciliation Unitarian Universalist, Utica, New York.

Our heritage from the Greeks and Hebrews is one which glorifies humanity's moral and intellectual character. To my way of thinking, one of the chief contributions Jesus brought was that of hope in our estate and enterprise. It was not until a disenchanted Augustine and later in the same vein a disgruntled Calvin wrote of human inadequacy and inherent sinfulness, that the belief in our essential goodness became a characteristic of a minority of Christians, a minority then called Socinians, but soon to be known as Unitarians. At a time when Calvinism was insisting the salvation was for only a predestined few, the basic tenet of Universalism came to be that all were destined to be saved. Unitarianism, on the other hand, met Puritanism's emphasis upon the depravity of humanity with Channing's optimistic pronouncement of our perfectibility. Today our denomination has come to be distinguished as much, if not more, by our view of people as by that of God.

Where rivers begin. Rivers sometimes lose their way, however, and dissipate upon the sand. Despite our ideals, we are sometimes content to let people come second to the things we do. This is true with our friends and families, and all others we know. Another area where the principle of the worth of persons is consistently denied is with people whom we have difficulty getting along with and dislike. We are often apt to respond to those who are unappealing or threaten us in a way that, in effect, denies their value.

This principle of the worth of persons has many applications for us in the liberal church. It underlies our approach to religion, in which the individual is trusted to find what is ultimately true. It forms the basis of our position on social issues such as civil rights and nuclear disarmament. It underlies our conception of democratic relationships, of family living, of child-rearing and development. In short, it permeates every area of our lives and comes to bear upon our associations with all those we encounter, however casually.

Where rivers begin. As we have said, rivers sometimes lose their way. Much as this principle of the worth of persons means to us, there are instances where we neglect it; there are cases where we fall short in the performance of our professed belief. There is one instance that has occurred to me which puts our beliefs sorely to the test. Almost all of us repudiate the principle of the worth of people in our attitude towards people we have trouble getting along with, people we dislike. It has occurred to me that we consistently act toward such people in a way that suggests that they are not worthwhile as persons.

I think for almost all of us there is someone, or some kind of person that we just can't seem to get along with. "Well, you can't get along with everybody," we say. Will Rogers' claim, "I never met a man I didn't like," is to most of us incomprehensible.

If a person is uninteresting or unimportant by some standard we're influenced by, we often don't even make the attempt to get to know them. Or if a person is strange and disturbs us there are several ways we can respond. We may resort to verbal or even physical attacks. However, these are not socially acceptable and may hurt our prestige. So, we often turn to more subtle ways of dealing with those who bother us, and that is akin to our reaction to those who simply don't interest us—we turn our backs upon them. This is a form of reprisal more vicious than outright assault: a retreat, a withdrawal of relations, leaving the person isolated; not free to take the initiative as perhaps the metaphor would imply, but denied further interaction at all. By interaction I'm not referring only to physical proximity. We may continue seeing the person, or even being overtly cordial as in the case of business associates where it serves our best interests, but we have turned away inwardly, we have withheld our real selves, we have denied any closeness of spirit.

We have all experienced this, in varying degree of seriousness; it can happen in the best of relationships, in marriages for example. We are all aware of the tragic toll that such repeated experiences can take about someone's sense of identity and self-acceptance for its meaning is clear, "I don't think you're worth even being around!"

Although we may formulate our uneasiness in such general terms, there are certain groups of people that I've observed even in our churches are slighted. Our standards for people's acceptability begin on such subtle grounds as vocational and economic status, involve such distinctions as cultural background and national origin, include such harmless categories as the divorced or single person, and run to such extremes as the African-American, the mentally unstable, or the LGBTQ individual.

Of course, such a reaction on our part says something about the other person—usually the same people are the ones affected—but it also says something about us. You may wonder what it is that determines the type of people we dislike; it's what we dislike and fear in ourselves. It is as if written by a finger on the ground. Will Rogers' statement is remarkable not only for its social tolerance but for the inner security it reflects. So, we wall ourselves off from that which we fear, locking ourselves away from others and not realizing that what we fear is in ourselves and can never be left behind. We can numb ourselves to it by intoxicating work or drink. We can exhilarate ourselves by feverish speed or vicarious violence; we can project it and hate it, but we can never rid ourselves of its burden until we too, with our imperfections, are accepted by a knowing love.

In our personal relations, then, we can no longer afford the luxury of selective associations. Obviously, I'm not suggesting that we spend the same amount of time and energy with everyone we know. That would be impossible and absurd for it would mean forfeiting special friendships that are so important. What I'm suggesting is that we be open and available to all, truly receptive and acceptive as the needs of others as well as our own fluctuate on the tides of life. It is said that this is a creedless church. This is to me, however, one of the chief doctrines of life, the responsibility of circumstance. We are not responsible just for that which appeals to us. We are responsible for all that we know, for all we encounter. For, in truth, if not us, then who?

We need, then, to find our way once more to the place where rivers begin. We need to reaffirm that principle which has long marked our liberal religious tradition and of which we have need in our lives. We need to say more than all of us are of value, more even than all people are worthy of acceptance, we must say and believe that even those who have characteristics that are unattractive or offensive to us are worthwhile, that there is something in us more important than transitory defaults and deficiencies. The Christian church traditionally called it "soul." Call it what you will, but believe that there is something in us worthy of acceptance and care regardless of who or what we are. This is true of a political opponent, the segregationist, the person who runs the liquor store, or the local mortician.

This is the attitude of our religious heritage. This is Martin Buber's attitude, that only aspects of a person can be hated, that when you see people in totality, including the part that binds particular qualities which is called "Thou"—you cannot help accepting them. This is Schweitzer's attitude of reverence for life, regardless of scale or apparent merit. This is the attitude underlying the practice of medicine that sustains the lives of even the hopelessly ill, of our legal and political system that guarantees the rights of all. It's about time it became our attitude in our everyday relationships with other people. We need a church that unconditionally guarantees people.

This is precisely the task of religion, the acceptance of the unacceptable, the redemption of the unwanted. Jesus knew this. The record of his ministry is impressive for its association with and care for the lowly working man, the twisted cripple, the feared Roman, the blind man, the outcast adulteress, the despised tax collector, the distained prostitute, and the feared leper.

From the days of my childhood I recall a story, at once touching and thrilling. It was a wonderful story about a Canadian Indian boy whose father showed him that place in the mountains where rivers begin. The boy had an idea. He worked all summer carving a small wooden canoe with an Indian paddler crouched in its stern. The night before the first Spring thaw the Indian boy worked late putting the final, loving touches of paint on his canoe. The first rays of the morning sun found him clambering to that high place in the mountains where his father had said rivers begin. There he reverently placed the canoe on a snowbank. Morning became afternoon, and the drops of water rung from the icy bank trickled into a flowing rivulet; the stream undercut the snow and the canoe slowly slid forward. At first hesitatingly, then gathering speed, it bobbed along, with the boy first walking, then running alongside in breathless excitement, until the rivulet joined a speeding torrent and the small canoe sped out of sight. There were tears in the boy's eyes as he watched its bright colors disappear in the distance.

The story follows the long journey of the wooden canoe as it travels down the stream and tributaries that eventually become the St. Lawrence River, and finally into the ocean. From time to time, strangers help the canoe on its way: some rescue it from snags; one repaints it; another saves it from a lumbermill's saw.

With the basic belief of the worth of all men and the acceptance of the unwanted, as with the small canoe, we find ourselves placed by an unseen hand at the source of what is good, where rivers begin. From there, if we will, to be carried down the stream of life, and even though ourselves unworthy, to be tended and helped by caring hands until we too find our way to the great sea.

PART II

A Soul in Transition
Sermons in Central Square, New York

— 19 —

75th Birthday of Church[1]

TEN YEARS AGO, I completed my ministry here. It hardly seems possible that it was that long ago. The years seem like yesterday, full and golden on the mind. The faces, the friends, come rushing back to fill the mind's eye.

The Hudson family had just moved from Utica to Cortland where I had accepted a teaching position at the college in 1966. I love the ministry and wanted to keep my roots firmly planted in it as I began teaching at Cortland College. Central Square understood and needed a part-time pastor. I came for an interview, and I gave you a sample sermon one Sunday morning in 1966. The deal was closed with a handshake. Only a few of us shook our heads at how I would make the forty-mile trip Sunday after Sunday, as well as Tuesdays and some Thursdays. Route 81 hadn't been completed through Syracuse, and the trip took a full hour or more with the bypass down Salina street.

We were all young—or so it seemed. We had a wonderful seven-year association that was to last until 1973. I still have the silver charm bracelet presented to me by the Sunday School with the date subscribed as 1966–1973.

The Universalist Church was a warm and friendly place. The services were seldom longer than an hour—unless I got long-winded. The music was superb. Peggy Burrell surpassed herself Sunday after Sunday, reaching down into her love of music and uplifting us spiritually. Yes, "Music was her life!" The choir was large for a church our size, bolstered by Bob McPherson, who had just finished a successful period as your

---

1. Sermon delivered by the author at the First Universalist Church, Central Square, New York, on October 2, 1983.

part-time minister before I came, and helped by Marcia, with her lovely alto voice. I recall our beloved Arnold Goettel and his fine strong voice. I remember Arnold every time I hear the memorial chimes on our organ. There were others whose voices joined Sunday after Sunday. If I close my eyes, the music comes flooding back in my heart.

Our children, Deborah and Wendy, loved the church too. They looked forward to Sunday school—or so I thought—especially their classes with "Mr. Hank" (Henry Ladd). When Sean was born, he was christened in this church by Ellsworth Reamon of the Syracuse Universalist Society. Today, Debbie is out of university. Wendy is a freshman at Wells College. Sean is in high school. You used to warn me that the years would go fast. You used to tell me to enjoy my family while they were still young. I'm glad I took your advice because the years have cascaded by.

I remember the special occasions of Christmas and Easter. I remember the lovely, uplifting Palm Sunday services and the experience of serving communion which meant as much to me as it could have to you. I remember the beautiful silver service and chalice that Charles and Lena Cleveland provided so painstakingly. I can see the ushers standing before us straight and proud to pass the plate.

I close my eyes, and it is Christmas Eve week and we are having our children's service, "The King of Hearts." All the children have a part, so carefully rehearsed at home. All goes well, even with last minute lapses of memory. We join in a medley of Christmas carols, with the strains of "Silent Night Holy Night" ever so softly creeping back into my heart from yesteryear. Waiting for Santa and for the Christ child.

Today what is left is a rich legacy of memory. The joy of being with you and sharing in the lives of you and your children. Of joining in their Sunday school classes, of leading their Sunday school worship services, which we always had to finish on time so our choir could practice. Of leading the Liberal Religious Youth group. The bending down to lift your children high for a hug or a kiss—if I was lucky—in those days when my back was good.

I remember the spaghetti suppers, the roast beef dinners, the pancake breakfasts. I remember the clay pancakes put on my plate one morning as a joke, but I didn't bite. Just as the spaghetti sauce got better and better due to Mel Nessmiller's skill and love, our fellowship got closer and closer. People came for miles for both the spaghetti sauce and the fellowship. "A friendly place to worship"—that's what our church came to be known as.

I remember the long days, the snowy blustery winter days when I wondered how I would get back to Cortland. I remember the Tuesday nights with the committee or board meetings and the many gracious invitations for your homes for "something to eat." I ate too well and before I knew it there was 40 pounds more of your parson in the pulpit. The diet, and the short haircut came later. I remember especially the hospitality of Bob and Vi Kimberly, and Steve's first steps at his graduation.

You took me into your homes and into your hearts, and I will always be grateful to you. Central Square is a special place and came to be a little bit of heaven on earth for the Hudson family. When Jesus was asked when the Kingdom of God was coming, he told his disciples not to look afar, for Lo, they were in the midst of it.

We found many friends at Central Square. We left many here as well. Some of you are still here carrying on the good work of this church. Today is a special tribute to you.

And on this wonderful 75th birthday celebration, I would recognize those who gave so much to this church who are no longer with us. The friends I said goodbye to on the hill. They are still with us in memory and deed, smiling their approval on this beautiful day and giving us their benediction. As Tennyson said:

> Come, my friends
> Tis not too late to seek a newer world.
> Push off, and sitting well in order smite
> The sounding furrows; for my purpose holds
> To sail beyond the sunset, and the paths
> Of all the western stars, until I die.
> It may be that the gulfs will wash us down:
> It may be we shall touch the Happy Isles,
> And see the great Achilles, whom we knew.
> Tho' much is taken, much abides; and tho'
> We are not now that strength which in old days
> Moved earth and heaven; that which we are, we are:
> One equal temper of heroic hearts,
> Made weak by time and fate, but strong in will
> To strive, to seek, to find and not to yield. (Tennyson 2019)

— 20 —

Christmas 1988[1]

DEAR FRIENDS, IT IS the holiest night of the year. All over the world, people are coming home. They're coming in quietness and peace. Their bags are packed with gifts, for it is Christmas Eve.

We, too, come home. We return again to this beloved church. We bring our families back to our spiritual home. Some of you grew up in this church as children and return tonight bringing your families with you.

Marcia and I feel special joy this Christmas Eve and having our entire family return here with us: Sean, Wendy and her friend Russell Beck, and Debbie and her husband Mitchell Hartquist. And we come bearing gifts. What gift can I give you this starlit night? What message can I bring you on our Christmas Eve together?

It has to be this—we come here to celebrate that night almost 2,000 years ago, when God gave us a gift. He gave us his greatest gift. A gift of life and love. According to legend and faith, he gave us his only son. His son's name was Jesus.

Jesus was born to Mary and Joseph. They raised him and taught him in the ways of the world. But he was not their child. He was God's child. God gave him as a sign. The sign was that God loves us. Despite all the things we do wrong, all the mistakes that we make, all the sins that we commit, God has not given up on us.

God sent us a beautiful baby. Clear of skin, and strong of limb. Angels foretold his coming. Wise men came from afar to look in wonder.

---

1. Sermon delivered by the author at the First Universalist Church, Central Square, New York, on December 24, 1988.

Shepherds abandoned their flocks on the hillside to worship at his cradle. And Mary pondered these things in her heart.

The baby grew into a healthy boy, and the boy grew into a strong and wise man. The man became a rabbi, who taught and showed us how to live. During the past week I saw a movie called "The Seventh Sign." It was a story about the end of the world. The most frightening thing about the story was that God's grace ended.

Christmas Eve is the time we rejoice in God's gift of love and hope. God gave us his son, Jesus. Great as this was, however, this gift was but a sign of a greater gift: God's love for us. Before Jesus was born, God loved mankind. But on that holy night in Bethlehem, God showed us how much he cared. He loved us enough to send his only child. Now, God's grace could not be doubted.

The magic of Christmas is that it re-creates each year the miracle of God's gift. If our hearts are open to this night, if we lift our eyes in awe of the bright star overhead, if we join our voices with the sound of angels, if we bring our gifts to the manger—then God's miracle happens all over again, and God's grace is renewed once more.

In closing, I would like to share with you what Marcia wrote on our Christmas card to the church this year:

> May the peace of the season,
> The glory of God,
> And the serenity of snowcapped hills
> Be with you today
> And always. Amen.

— 21 —

Christmas 1990[1]

CHRISTMAS IS A TIME of gifts, of giving and receiving. The presents are wrapped carefully and arranged under the tree. All is ready, almost.

Are you sure you thought of everything? Do you have a gnawing feeling you forgot something? Did you ever go through a Christmas and say, "Is that all there is to it?" Has it ever seemed to you after it's all over and done, that something was missing?

If we want to be sure we thought of everything, we have to remember one gift, a gift that can't be wrapped and placed under the tree like the rest. We must recall the present that in itself is the essence of Christmas. The most precious thing that we have to give and rejoice in this Christmas is our relationships and friendships with one another. Our relationships as husbands and wives, as parents and children, as brothers and sisters, and as friends.

The greatest gift that we have as human beings is our bonding and support for each other. We care about each other. We nurture each other. We support and uphold each other. It is our connection with each other that matters the most. Take away all the other gifts but leave us rich in our relationships, and we have a full and happy Christmas. This is why we remember so fondly the Christmases that we shared when we had little in the way of material things. This is why families who seem poor still enjoy Christmas so much.

---

1. Sermon delivered by the author at the First Universalist Church, Central Square, New York, on December 23, 1990.

Of course, we enjoy our presents, but they mean the most to us when we remember that they are symbols of our relationships with each other. That is why simple gifts, or handmade ones, mean so much.

This is also why it is so futile to buy gifts for ourselves, hoping it will make us feel happy. More than anyone else, we know what we want, but when we gift to ourselves something is missing. A gift without a giver is empty.

Therefore, someone who lacks relationships with others can never get enough. We've all experienced times in our lives when regardless of all the stuff and toys we got, we had the pervasive feeling that "it was never enough." We were looking for our satisfaction in the wrong places, in things, not in people.

Two thousand years ago Jesus of Nazareth lived and died as a testament to the truth that fulfillment in this life is in people, not things. He preached and taught and practiced the value of relationships, of connection and bonding between human beings. People in his time were much like people today, like you and me. They thought many of the same thoughts, struggled with many of the same problems of war and peace, of government and the governed, of illness and death, of work and play. And they had much the same feelings—of happiness and sorrow, of joy and rage, of ecstasy and pain.

But Jesus told these people, people like you and me, that the most precious gift is to care for each other and to establish relationships. And so, he reached out to people, to his disciples who were his closest friends, to lepers and sick people, to Romans and the politically outcast, to prostitutes and tax collectors. And he loved them. He cared enough to enter into relationships with them and risk everything.

He risked rejection, misunderstanding, death itself. But his cosmic gamble paid off. The adoration and praise and glory of Christmas is our response to him. Christmas, then, is our celebration of giving—it is a celebration of the birth of Jesus. It is a curious mingling of both in this season. Christmas is a celebration of the giving of ourselves through deep and lasting relationships with each other. In all the world, and all of heaven, there is nothing more sacred and holy.

— 22 —

Christmas 1991[1]

MY DEAR FRIENDS, AS is my custom every Christmas, I want to bring you a special message, to share with you my deepest truth this year, the greatest reason for hope that I have found this season. This Christmas is no different. Circumstances change. Circumstances have been difficult for many of us this past year, and I am no exception. We are all still grieving the loss of our dear friend, Eva Willenbrock.

Difficulties and pain are opportunities for growth. Growth can be painful. Show me a person in spiritual torment, and I will show you a person in the process of growth. How have you and I grown, what have we learned this past year?

I have received a gift, a spiritual experience if you will, that I'd like to share with you. A gift I'd like to pass on to you. It is the age-old truth that life and relationships are based on giving, not taking. This is to me the message of Christmas this year, the fundamental rule of giving.

As long as we are obsessed with what we receive, it will never be enough. Once we have decided we have enough and are enough, that we already have everything we need and that we are everything we should be, then we are free, truly free to give to others without reserve. Our lives and relationships need to be based not on demand of what we want, but on the giving of what we are.

Do you want serenity and happiness? Then take away your expectations, your conditions, your demands, and surrender your "rights." Give without measure, and in a miraculous way you will find that you

---

1. Sermon delivered by the author at the First Universalist Church, Central Square, New York, on December 22, 1991.

get much more in return. Instead of preoccupation with what "I need and feel and want," let our lives be ruled by concern for what others feel and need and want. Our lives and relationships become not a series of demands for ourselves but of gifts to others.

This Christmas and always, do this and you will be reborn. Christmas is about birth, about beginnings. There is no reason why we can't experience rebirth. Let the child come forth. I pray, let us give up our selfish and controlling ways, and let the new being within us come to life. Remember always that love is like five loaves and two fishes. There's never enough until you give it away. This is what the psalmist meant when he said, "he restoreth my soul" and "my cup runneth over" (Psa 23:3–5 KJV). We are so preoccupied with our cup being half empty or half full, that we have lost sight of the fact that our cup has long since run over.

A minister friend in Cortland told the story of his wife who died after a long illness. He said that all her life she had given to her family, to her children, to him. Then they learned she had a fatal illness. That allowed him to get in touch with what he could do to give to her. She liked to sew. Every week he would drive her to the fabric store, and as she went in, she'd say, "I'll only be a minute." He'd say, "take all the time you want. I have errands to run at the hardware store." He never did. He sat in his car and waited. It became his privilege to give to her, to live for her. The blessings he received were incredible. We do not have to wait until someone is ill or dying. Seize the moment. Do it now.

The truth of this Christmas message is contained in the wonderful prayer of St. Francis of Assisi:

> Grant that we may not so much
> Seek to be consoled, as to console;
> To be loved, as to love.
> For it is in giving that we receive,
> It is in pardoning that we are pardoned;
> It is in dying that we are born to eternal life. Amen. (St. Francis n.d.)

— 23 —

Crossing the River[1]

AFTER BEING RELEASED FROM captivity in Egypt the people of Israel were alone wandering in the desert—what the Old Testament calls the wilderness—trying to come to terms with who they were. You have probably wondered where I've been during the past year since I left here just after last Easter. I've also been wandering in the wilderness, spending time in my spiritual desert learning who I am. I'm here this morning to give you a report of this spiritual odyssey, a kind of a state of the soul message.

I want to begin by acknowledging, however, that a year is too long for friends not to get together, and I trust it will not be so long the next time. In my sermon last year, I talked about the losses in life. I reported that Ruby had been hit by a truck and was paralyzed. I talked about not remaining a ship in harbor, but of having the courage to take to sea in life.

Today I want to share with you what I have learned during my sojourn in the wilderness, especially where I am today in my relationship with God and myself. In doing this I owe a debt of gratitude to Henri Nouwen's book *Life of the Beloved* which I recommend to you (Nouwen 1992). The Universalist in me always believed in God. The Unitarian in me always believed in myself. The Unitarian figured if you tried hard enough you can work everything out. The Universalist believed that God was good enough to provide whatever tools are needed to work things out.

Today I have come to a different conclusion. I do not think I need to or can fix everything about myself and life, nor do I think God will give me all the tools. Today I do not think I need to have all the answers. I do

---

1. Sermon delivered by the author at the First Universalist Church, Central Square, New York, on February 27, 1994.

not think I need to fix myself. I do not think I need to be perfect or in control. I have come to believe that I am OK the way I am created—that is the way God wants me to be. Peace in life comes from accepting myself and giving myself to God and others the way I am.

In Mark 1:11, we find an account of how Jesus was baptized by John the Baptist. As Jesus came up out of the water, the heavens opened and the voice of God said, "Thou art my beloved Son, in whom I am well pleased" (RSV). Nouwen's remarkably simple thesis is that we are all God's sons and daughters with whom he is well pleased. Stop and think about it and you'll realize that this is the basic tenet of Universalism, that God's love is universal and certain.

Yet we live in an age when we do not like ourselves very much the way we are. We think we are too old, too young; too fat, too skinny; too tall, too short; too rich, too poor; too uneducated or too intellectual. We do not like our body image and so we become anorectic or bulimic. We exercise at gyms; we diet. We do not like our moods and our emotions, so we see counselors who help us change them—or we cover them with alcohol or drugs. We do not like our lives, so we overwork to escape the pain. To fill our sadness or emptiness, we keep busy or spend money. We live in an age of self-recrimination and self-rejection.

We have lost sight of the fact that we are the beloved. We are first, now, and always God's beloved children. We are intimately, purposefully, and unconditionally accepted by an everlasting love.

In the sacrament of communion, there are four steps. The bread is taken (or chosen), blessed, broken, and given. Nouwen suggests the same steps occur in our spiritual lives. First, we are chosen. Long before we were born and became a part of history, we existed in God's heart. We are irreplaceable, unrepeatable, precious children of God. Yet, the world is controlling, guilt and shame-based, and power-hungry. The forces of darkness are strong. They tell us lies about who we are. In an existence marked by so many broken relationships, the world tells us that we are nothing special. We don't matter.

Second, we are blessed. God has blessed us. We need to affirm that blessing with each other. As human beings we are continually in need of blessing. To give a blessing creates the reality of which it speaks. We need an ongoing blessing that will allow us to hear in an ever-new way that we belong to a loving God who will never leave us alone.

Third, we are broken. We have all had to live through difficult and painful experiences. We have all been broken, whether it has been growing old, loss of health, the death of someone close, divorce, losing jobs, or financial losses. We are unique in how we have been broken: probably no two people have experienced the same traumas or hurts. Frequently our brokenness is experienced in regard to our sexuality. The great task becomes accepting that we are chosen and blessed precisely because we are broken. Our brokenness is not something to fix, but to understand and embrace.

Fourth, we are given. We live for others and we give ourselves to them, not in perfection but in our reality, our humanity, our brokenness. We give, not expecting something in return, but as God gives to us, out of joy. This is the meaning of what is called covenant love or relationship. Thus, God's love becomes a model for our love of each other. Nouwen says there is a "mysterious link between our brokenness and our ability to give to each other . . . just as bread needs to be broken in order to be given, so do our lives" (Nouwen 1992, 87–88).

So, today I remember I am blessed, I am beloved of God. I give myself to God and to those I love just as I am—in my incompleteness and imperfection, in my brokenness if you will. In doing this I take God and those I love at their word, that their love is unconditional, that they accept and value me just the way I am. And so, I learn to give myself unconditionally, not in a withholding or measured way, but completely.

To do this means trusting. I am learning to trust God, to trust others, and to trust myself. I am learning that this is what life is about, trusting and giving. So, we teach old dogs new tricks. We are not too soon old and too late smart. We are given the grace to enter the future differently than we exited the past. We break the cycle.

The people of Israel wandered in the wilderness for many years. Then they came to the banks of the river where they could cross over into the promised land. Some were destined to cross; some were not.

Will we cross over into the promised land on our spiritual journey? We may choose not to. We may choose to stay in the wilderness which is familiar and feels comfortable. Or we may cross into the promised land. But it is not an easy place; it is a land of giants and fortresses. One thing God tells us, however. If we dare to cross over, we will not be alone. He will be with us. He will be our strength. And we will endure and prosper.

– 24 –

Easter 1987[1]

MY FRIENDS, HAPPY EASTER. On this day the Christian world celebrates the triumph of the Nazarene over death. It is said he was resurrected from the grave. As Christian Universalists, we celebrate his triumph over death. To us, he lives. Not physically resurrected, but spiritually arisen in our hearts and minds. Not magically restored to life, but emotionally alive in word and deed. He is forever an example and inspiration for our lives. For us he never died. He never will. So, we join our hearts in celebration. Christ is risen! Alleluia!

As we look to Jesus to understand the essence of life and his teaching on this day of days, we are humbled by our own limitations and shortcomings. It seems we spend so much of our life growing up. We struggle to grow up from being children to become teenagers. From being teenagers, to becoming young adults. From being young adults to becoming middle-aged. And still we haven't caught on to everything there is to know about life. We strive to attain the wisdom and grace of old age. And still we are awed by how much growing up is left to do.

From time to time we see ourselves as still being children within. We are plagued by insecurities and fears of the very young. There are so many ways we haven't grown up. We spend so much of our time feeling sorry for ourselves and want others to feel sorry for us too. We indulge ourselves in self-pity.

So many people think the world owes them a living. We think society should accommodate us personally and make things easy for us. We

---

1. Sermon delivered by the author at the First Universalist Church, Central Square, New York, on April 19, 1987.

think the whole world should revolve around us. Everything should exist for our convenience. Everything should be done for our benefit. Rules and regulations were made for others, and for us they were meant to be bent or broken. We are not made for the world. The world was made for us. If the world is inconvenient, it should change. So often we try to avoid taking consequences for our actions. We see ourselves as exceptions to the rule. We fudge on our tax returns, we litter, we take things that don't belong to us. It doesn't matter what we do, as long as we're not caught—or others don't do it too.

The spirit of the age tells us not to take responsibility for ourselves. Nor do we want to be responsible for others, either. We do not want to accept the authority of others, nor do we care to exercise authority over them.

In short, we do not want to accept life as it is. We pout and hold our breath waiting for it to change! In so many ways we are still children within. We do not see ourselves as grown-ups or adults. We avoid growing up emotionally. We do not want to be big people. We balk at being spiritually mature.

Just as we are overcome by our limitations, we are overwhelmed by the example of Jesus' mastery of things human on this Easter. We know that Jesus took responsibility for himself and others. He did not expect the world to be an exception for him—he became an exception for the world.

Jesus was an adult. He left childish things behind. "When I was a child . . . I thought as a child: but when I became a man, I put away childish things" (1 Cor 13:11 KJV). He did not harbor insecurities and petty fears. He put his fears behind him: "Get thee behind me, Satan" (Luke 4:8 KJV). Nor did he indulge in self-pity. He set a manly example of courage and strength.

We want attention and recognition from others. The mistake we make is thinking the only way to get it is by asking for pity from others for our weakness. Jesus showed us that there is an alternative. It's receiving the admiration of others for our strength. He became for others a spirit that was remembered with gladness. I get tired of being around people who continually feel sorry for themselves and want pity. I feel happy being around people who are cheerful and accepting of life. Do you really want other people's pity, or their true appreciation?

Jesus did not expect the world to revolve around him, or to make an exception for him. He knew he would have to abide by the regulations of Rome. "Render to Caesar the things that are Caesar's" (Mark 12:17 RSV), he said. And entering Jerusalem where he knew he would die, Jesus signaled he was willing to accept the consequences of his actions.

Jesus accepted the authority of others. Just as he accepted the authority of Rome in the physical world, he accepted the authority of God in the spiritual world. Perhaps no one in all history has accepted God's will as well as Jesus did. Thus, Jesus becomes singularly well-suited to exercise authority over us and be a rallying point for our faith. And so, "the last will be first" (Matt 20:16 RSV). As Jesus accepted God's authority, we accept his authority and will. When he says, "Follow thou me" (John 21:22 KJV), men and women do not hesitate. Of those who have gone before, Jesus embodies the qualities of a mature person, a grown-up, a spiritual adult.

He did not sit around feeling sorry for himself and moaning and groaning about how unfair life was to him. "Ahh, I am sunburned, poor me!" "I am so hungry." "I don't have a thing to wear." "I don't have a home." "It's cold here." "I have to walk every place I go." "The Romans are picking on me." "Why does everything happen to me?" "Poor me. . . ."

If Jesus had been this way, no one would have followed him. Instead he rejoiced in life and the good that he had. He was a pleasure and an inspiration to be around. He was giving towards others. He listened to them. He didn't ask for pity, he gave pity! He didn't ask for understanding, he gave understanding! He didn't ask for help, he was helpful! Others sought him out, rejoiced in his company and followed him, even to the gates of death.

He believed in God's will. He believed that things are the way they are for a purpose. He accepted life and death with a trusting spirit. He lived his life with a sense of spiritual peace and serenity that he referred to as the Kingdom of Heaven. Not a mystical kingdom outside the world, not a magical kingdom you had to die to reach, but kingdom that exists here and now! A kingdom that was not greater than life.

God had told Jesus the Kingdom of Heaven was within. Jesus did not doubt God. He did not quibble. He saw no reason to try to improve upon the teaching. He accepted it. He accepted God's love without question, without reservation.

This is perhaps our greatest challenge also. To believe that God is good. To believe that life is good. To believe that God is in life. To believe that God wants us to be happy and grown-up spiritually. The greatest challenge we must meet is accepting the fact that we are loved by God, that He wants us to be happy. Our greatest purpose is to make others who depend on us happy also. That is how God works.

And so, on this Easter morning, Jesus passes on to us his legacy of a caring, loving, and believing spirit. He calls this spiritual reality the "Kingdom of Heaven." Jesus promises us that we can grow up spiritually. And once having done so, it is the way we can help others grow.

He warns us that this is addictive. Once having started along this path it will become an obsession, a "magnificent obsession" as Lloyd C. Douglas titled it (Douglas 1929). Jesus said once the plow was put down, or the fishing net set aside, there would be no turning back. The way will take over our lives.

And He whispers a final benediction in our ear. The Kingdom of Heaven isn't far off. It is close at hand. It is within the reach of each of us. It is here. It is now. It is Easter.

— 25 —

Francis[1]

JOHN DONNE ONCE WROTE:

> No man is an island
> Entire in itself:
> Every man is a piece of the continent,
> A part of the main
> And if a clod be washed away by the sea,
> The continent of which he and we are a part remains.
> This man's life increases me,
> Because we are involved in mankind.
> Therefore, never send to learn for whom the bell tolls,
> It tolls for thee. (Donne n.d.)

We are here because we love Francis. We love him because he loved us. He gave us his time, his patience, and his wisdom. He took the cotton out of his ears and listened to our problems. We're not quite sure why, but he did.

Somehow, he always seemed to be there. You could set the clock by his phone calls. He remembered things. His encyclopedic mind held the details of our lives. He never forgot a birthday—except his own.

We would go back in time and remember him as he sat on his porch on Elm Street looking out at the hills, or near his apartment window on Court Street. We sat with him and passed the time of life. Sometimes we would say nothing at all. These were serene moments when he taught us how to be quiet inside. He had learned the secret of life, of how things

---

1. Eulogy for Francis Garvey delivered by the author at a Memorial Service in Cortland, New York, on February 20, 1988.

come to those who are patient and wait. Of how we get what we need, not necessarily what we want.

The ripples of his life have reached from Cortland to the West Coast, to Utah, to Missouri, to Oklahoma, to Texas, to Florida, and many other places. His life touched countless others and they have been permanently affected. We are fortunate, indeed, that he "came downstairs for coffee and doughnuts" and stayed.

He gave new meaning to the word "friend." He gave unselfishly of himself. His deep reservoir of caring never seemed to run dry. His gift was that he made each of us feel special and cherished. He helped us learn to love and value ourselves, because inexplicably he treasured us.

With profound respect, we commit this spirit who dwelt lovingly among us. He added to the sum of human joy. Were everyone to whom he did some loving service to bring a blossom to his grave, he would sleep tonight beneath a wilderness of flowers.

Goodbye, my good friend.

— 26 —

Road to Emmaus[1]

MY DEAR FRIENDS, THIS is in all probability the last sermon I will preach to you. As you may have heard, I've taken a "final" retirement from Cortland College, am closing on a house in Key Largo, Florida, over Thanksgiving week, and come mid-December Ruby and I are heading down to stay. You and I have had a wonderful friendship as pastor and congregation since 1966. I was your pastor from 1966 to 1972, and then again from 1986 to 1992. That is a total of 12 years of a mutually rewarding relationship. If I have not been faithful in returning and keeping in touch, it is not because I love you the less but the more.

Now, it is time to say goodbye. And I'm here to preach my final and last message to you. I remember a sermon I gave a number of years ago titled, "The Last Teachings of Jesus." I said that his last teachings to his disciples must have been especially significant for them, because they knew he was leaving. So, too, I have pondered my last words to you, knowing how special they would be for me and perhaps for you also.

As a Unitarian, I've always believed in the goodness of man. As a Universalist, I have always believed in the goodness of God. But I must make a confession. Deep down inside I believed that other people were worthy, but I didn't think I was. I believed other people were worth God's salvation and love, but I doubted that I was. The experience of loving myself and being loved by God was always reserved for others more deserving; it was not something I felt I was entitled to.

---

1. Sermon delivered by the author at the First Universalist Church, Central Square, New York.

And so, I lived my life, and finally when I separated and divorced, I came to a spiritual crisis. I was alone with myself and found myself in the company of someone who didn't know who he was, and certainly didn't like or love who he was. I didn't trust or feel close to God. I was certain that after what had happened, God must not like or love me either. I was as alone as any man could be. I felt this, even though I had three wonderful children and friends like you. I cannot express to you the fear and loneliness, the anger and sadness I felt.

And so, as you know, I left the ministry and started participating in my daughter's church in Cortland, the First United Methodist Church. There, for the first time in my adult life, I did something radically different. Instead of trying to get my spiritual needs met through helping others meet their needs, I turned directly to getting my needs met.

It was a slow and unfamiliar process, but in time it began to work. Gradually the ice around my heart began to melt, the pain subsided, the fear and rage diminished, and hope tiptoed in. Through a trip to Arizona and a month at the Sierra Tucson Rehab Center, I learned about who I was. I was not in imminent danger of alcohol or chemical dependency, but clearly, I had hit a bottom emotionally and needed to recover. For the first time in my life, I became fully honest with myself, accepted myself for who I was, and started to get to know who I am. I didn't like everything I learned, but I met myself on the road.

Another period of time passed, and with the support of a new church community, my friends including members of this congregation, my vocation as a professor, and one or two special relationships in my life, I began to accept and love myself. But I stayed broken, burdened by the failure of my marriage, desperately in need of healing, needing deep-seated acceptance and forgiveness.

Ruby's accident two years ago, her paralysis and eminent loss underscored my loneliness and pain. Yet something remarkable happened. I turned to prayer and belief in God in a way I never had before. When Ruby recovered, I was deeply convinced and am to this day that it was a miracle of God, a gift from Him, a demonstration of His love and grace. I was convinced of how powerless I was and of how completely in control He was.

Cracks had begun to appear in my tough exterior, but still I kept up the walls, the barriers so carefully constructed over many years. And so, I remained burdened, hurting, in deep need of acceptance, freedom of spirit, and peace of heart. Then, two months ago, something wonderful happened in my life. I went to a retreat organized by Methodist laity called the "Walk to Emmaus."

It was held in Syracuse at the West Genesee Street Methodist Church. Thirty-five men and the team of fifteen to twenty laity went through a full three days of fellowship, singing, eating, story and joke telling, fun and laughter, speeches (fifteen in three days), workshops, worship including Communion every day, and services of reconciliation and healing. We were completely engulfed in prayer support from our churches, from team members, and from others who had done the retreat previously. There were gifts and many tangible tokens of love and support through the weekend.

I had never experienced the presence of God and His love this fully in my life. The evidence was overwhelming and completely convincing. As I prayed during my first day on the Walk, I felt the walls start to crumble; the barriers fell away between me and God. Tentatively, I cracked the door open between me and Him, and then flung it wide open. I came to a point of trust and love of Him that I had never experienced before, and I found Him as promised waiting just on the other side of the door. I was to learn that He loved me without qualification. I told Him I was open and ready to accept His grace in His time. And you want to know what the greatest miracle was? His time began almost immediately.

No, I didn't hear voices in my ear, nor was there a clap of thunder or a flash of lightning. But over the next few days as I listened to speakers at the retreat, I heard God speaking through them, telling me what I needed to hear. Telling me that I needed to let go of hurt and anger, and forgive. I had to let go of the past, and I found a measure of acceptance and peace I had not known before.

Ever since, the hand of God has continued to mold my life, and He has continued to be in control, shaping and leading me. The house I wanted in Florida, previously unavailable to me, was offered to me in October. Financing has been approved, and the closing is set. I am finishing my college job this semester, packing up my house, saying goodbye to friends, and will be moving down to Key Largo in a few weeks. Just this past week I received a phone call and was offered a job teaching part-time at the Florida Keys Community College!

Today, I know who I am. I know who God is. And I know I am His. My life and my will belong to Him. He is my friend, not my boss. He is always with me. Although I step out into the unknown by myself, I am not alone. He is at my side, holding my hand, loving and keeping me safe.

The feeling of freedom and peace is greater that I have known before. I am blessed.

I am also blessed by all of you, my many friends here at the First Universalist Church of Central Square. You will always be in my heart and in my prayers. Goodbye and God bless you always.

— 27 —

The Sunday After Easter[1]

COMING TO SPEAK TO you, as I do several times a year, is like writing a letter to an old friend, telling you how I have been and affirming my affection and love for you. Last Sunday, Easter, brought many messages to mind, but the one that stands out most clearly for me is what the angels reportedly told Mary and others when they came to the empty tomb, "Do not be afraid" (Matt 28:5 NIV). All the things that happened to us in life, the losses we all must bear, have the effect of making us cautious, vulnerable, and afraid. If we have lived at all, had close relationships, and lost some of them for whatever reason, the net result can be to make us hurt and angry and afraid.

We all have had parents die. This leaves hurt and anger. The pain is so overwhelming, we resolve that never again will we put ourselves in a position where we can be vulnerable and hurt. Our fear is so great, fear of being hurt, of being alone, of abandonment and rejection. Some of us have lost our relationship or spouse through death or divorce. This leaves us with incredible hurt and anger and guilt and fear. The pain is overwhelming, and we resolve that we will never again put ourselves in a position where we can be so vulnerable or hurt. Our fear is too great, fear of being hurt, of being alone, of abandonment.

Very recently I suffered another loss in my life. My beloved German Shepherd dog, Ruby, was hit by a truck a week ago and may not walk again. There is a real danger of losing her. During a very difficult period of my life, she has been my family, my best friend, my companion,

---

1. Sermon delivered by the author at First Universalist Church, Central Square, New York.

even my spiritual connection. Her faithfulness and constancy have been unbelievable. I love her very much. And yet within a matter of days she could be gone forever.

Why, we ask, must life be so fragile? Why must life be so delicate and uncertain and vulnerable? The unsatisfactory answer, "Because that's the way life is," brings us little comfort or reassurance. I may lose Ruby, and if I do my pain will be great.

One thing we learn from life is that our acceptance of loss takes place through grieving, through what is called grief work. It is called grief work because it is very painful and hard, because it takes a lot of energy and effort and commitment. Commitment to hurt and hurt, until there is no more to the hurting and it passes of its own accord, and we move on to another level of being. We must move through the stages of denial, anger, guilt, remorse, forgiveness, love, until we finally reach acceptance.

It takes time and is painful, but this process of emotional and spiritual disengagement and realignment is necessary for deep and lasting healing. It is only thus we can "fear not," and dare to love again. If we do not heal, if we do not do the needed grief and separation work, if we do not resolve underlying emotional conflicts, we will be stuck and unable to move on for the rest of our lives. We will live in fear forever. It will be as if the angels never speak to us again.

And living in fear is no way to live. It would be, as Thoreau said, "to live what was not life" (Thoreau 2012). It is being held captive, being emotionally chained. It is being in a prison of our own making. There is no jail, no dungeon anywhere that is as dark and isolated as that within our own soul. To be sure, we might be safe there. We will protect ourselves from being hurt again. We limit our vulnerability, but at what cost?

There is a saying that I painted on a rock and gave to a special friend in Arizona, "A ship in harbor is safe, but that is not what ships are built for" (Hopper 2013). Can you imagine having a great boat, outfitting it, getting it seaworthy and ready to sail, and then being so afraid of having it damaged that you leave it tied to the dock or moored in the harbor? How pointless and futile. But that is precisely what we do with ourselves when we have spent our lives getting prepared and ready to live, and then because we are afraid of being hurt, we hide and stay in an emotional space that is protected and safe, where we are not exposed to risk but also where we receive none of the satisfactions of living.

Ships are not meant to be permanently moored, but meant to sail the ocean. We are not created to be carefully kept in a safe place. We should be out in the sea of life where we can we bounced and banged around, scuffed-up a little, even scraped and bruised. Only thus will we become beautiful. It is not by being without scars that we are beautiful. The vessel that has weathered the storm is beautiful. As in the story *The Velveteen Rabbit* we will be real. Remember, being real isn't something that happens all at once, it takes a long time, and it "doesn't often happen to people who break easily, or have sharp edges, or have to be carefully kept" (Williams 1997, 13).

So, on this Sunday after Easter, I affirm that those of us in the midnight hour of our souls, need to be "born again." We need to step forth into the sunshine and dare to live again. And we do this by healing from the past and believing the angel's admonition, "Do not be afraid!"

The world awaits. A world of nature and springtime beauty. Of cascading streams and rivers, of flowers pushing through the soil, of starlit nights and silver moons, and warm balmy days.

A world of people. Of all those friends and family that are left in the lives of each of us. "Although much is taken away, much remains" (Tennyson 2019). Those who care, who depend upon us, and who need us and our example, and our presence in their lives. Hard to believe, isn't it, that you and I are actually needed by someone, that we really do count in the course of things?

A world of special relationships. Of love that awaits us, of the fulfillment and happiness and joy that only comes from the most special, committed relationships. These relationships are at our fingertips, awaiting our decision to venture out of harbor. Can we stretch our souls and reach them? Will we take the chance? The chance of living and loving again? The rewards of loving are so great. Can we afford to jeopardize them? Yet, it takes special courage to go on living, to dare to care again. Courage to take a chance. "The courage to be," as Paul Tillich said (Tillich 1952).

Lao-Tse put it succinctly when he said, "the invincible shield of caring is a weapon from the sky against being dead" (Lao-Tse 2018). It is as simple as that. Caring is living. Not caring is dying. Will you then be vulnerable, and can you be hurt? Well, certainly. But, my friends, that is living, but with vulnerability and risk comes greatness. Through it all we become beautiful, not polished and perfect on the outside, but appealing and real on the inside.

Through such freedom from fear comes true peace, of knowing we have become all that we were meant to be, of being a ship at sea not in harbor. So, entertain the presence of angels in your life. And the next time one of them whispers in your ear, "Do not be afraid," take them to heart.

– 28 –

Thy Will, Not Mine[1]

IT IS INTERESTING TO view life from the vantage point of a few years. It is remarkable how different some things look. What once seemed important is relatively insignificant now. What once looked insignificant, now seems very important. It is true that how you perceive something depends much upon your vantage point, and how you experience life depends upon your point of view.

Life has a disconcerting way of reversing perspectives and values. In gentler moments, we refer to it as a "mellowing" process. In cynical moments, we refer to it as fickleness of mind or the beginnings of senility. Some of my earliest memories are what I thought I wanted out of life, and how I could get it. First and foremost, I wanted success and prestige. I wanted to be accomplished and respected. They say you better be careful about what you wish for—you might get it!

As life progressed, there were people and things I wanted to prove myself to. I felt driven to compensate, even at times to get even. Revenge is a harsh taskmaster. Resentment is a terrible companion. Think twice before you consciously entertain them.

I don't think that early in life I considered happiness, serenity, and peace of spirit to be goals. I guess I figured they would be obvious by-products of success and prestige. Early in life, I concluded that I could not rely upon other people to help me get very far; if I was going to accomplish very much in this life it had to be by my own will power. Early I became obsessed with worship of self-will. I was convinced that if I

---

1. Sermon delivered by the author at the First Universalist Church, Central Square, New York, on October 13, 1991.

wanted something, all I had to do was to will it, and it would come about. If that did not work, I was simply not trying hard enough and all I had to do was to will it harder.

Actually, this philosophy worked well enough for a number of years. It saw me through school and marriage and early family life. But the day of reckoning came. The day came when self-will was not enough. I found that well-practiced even well-motivated as I was, there was more to life than I could handle on my own will power.

Needless to say, I fought this realization tooth and nail. I did not want to admit that I had been wrong for so long. I did not want to give up, admit defeat and surrender, but as time went by, this was precisely what I had to do on one after another of the major struggles in my life. I gradually came to the realization that as an individual I did not have enough strength to solve the problems of the universe and cope with the mysteries of life. Lack of power was my dilemma.

Gradually I came to the conclusion that a power greater than myself was necessary for life. I had always given lip service to the idea of God, but that was a different thing than desperately needing and coming to believe in Him. In retrospect it was fairly simple. If I did not possess the power sufficient for living within myself, and if it was indeed necessary for life, that power had to come from a source outside of myself. Bit by bit, I came to believe in a Higher Power. Mind you, I do not say I came to understand him. I still do not understand fully. I don't understand electricity or atomic power either, but I know they are real.

I realized that I lie in the lap of immense intelligence and care. If I would only relax my fragile hold on life and let go of some of my greatest problems, I would be caught securely by hands larger and stronger than my own that would uphold me on my way. I came to believe in a God of love who I can trust, who cares for me. He doesn't want me to be unhappy or hurt, but wants me to have serenity of spirit and peace of soul. He finds it totally unnecessary for me to hold resentments or seek revenge on others, and doesn't seem to care very much about the quantity of success or prestige in my life but only about the quality of my days.

Now, every day I say a simple prayer to my Higher Power. I thank him for another day, and I ask him to be with me today. I pray for the strength to turn my will and my life over to his care. I ask that his will, not mine be done. I have come to realize that there are so many things in life I cannot control, that are beyond the power of my will. At the most I can change myself. I cannot change others. I cannot change nature. I cannot change life itself. I am happiest when I recognize this and let the uneven struggle end, and let go and turn things over to God. When I take myself out of the driver's seat, and let God do the driving, I have a better trip.

There are many implications to such a change in life. One of the most significant has been how it impacts my attitude toward being right and wrong. When I relied on self-will, I felt that somehow, I could indeed be perfect. I could not stand the idea of being wrong. I hated most having someone else see I could be wrong about anything. I had swallowed the myth that I was perfect, or I could be if I only tried hard enough. I didn't like myself when I was wrong, and being human I was wrong enough of the time that I didn't like myself very much of the time.

When I started to turn my life over to the care of my Higher Power, an interesting change occurred. I came to accept the fact that being human, sometimes I'm wrong, sometimes I'm right. I learned that being human, it is OK to be wrong. And it's OK to take credit when right. I learned that no one's keeping score. It's not necessary to be perfect.

As a matter of fact, being perfect is pretty intolerable. It sets unrealistic standards for us. It makes life hell for those around you. How can they love you? We love people for both their strengths and their shortcomings, because part of loving is forgiving. If there's nothing to forgive, there would be less to love. If those we press and strain within our arms were perfect, "perhaps that love would wither from the earth" (Ingersoll, n.d.).

Today, I'm just human. I'm not perfect; there is another who is. He takes care of the perfect department just fine. Today I try not to confuse myself with Him. Today I have the right to be wrong. Today I've learned that being right or wrong has little to do with being happy. I used to think that if I was right, I would be happy. Now I have learned that happiness derives not from being right but from being a caring, loving person.

— 29 —

Wings Like Eagles[1]

> They who wait upon the Lord
> shall renew their strength,
> they shall mount up with wings like eagles,
> they shall run, and not be weary; they shall walk and not faint.
>
> —Isaiah 40:31 KJV

I WANT TO SPEAK to you today about life, of how I see life, and why I believe in it. The first thing I would say is that life is profoundly spiritual. God fills every moment, and lives at every turn for me. His spirit and force animate me. He is my breath. With every breath, with every sigh, his spirit moves in me. He is the blood pulsing through my body. His energy moves my heart. His intelligence fills my mind with wonder. His emotion, his pain and suffering are in my soul. His love and compassion, his gentleness and goodness and kindness animate my spirit.

He has made me a profoundly passionate man. I care. My caring is His caring. "The invincible shield of caring is a weapon from the sky against being dead" (Lao-Tse 2018). Passion means suffering. To be passionate means to have suffered. As all men I have suffered, but it was never meant by God to break my spirit. It was his gift to me. It was meant to bring me a blessing. Today, my cup runneth over.

---

1. Sermon delivered by the author at the First United Methodist Church, Cortland, New York, on October 24, 1993.

The suffering of Job completed his love of God. Christ's suffering and death was inseparable from his relationship to God. As Martin Luther King, Jr. said, unearned suffering is redemptive. It purifies and cleans the spirit; it burns away arrogance and selfishness. Suffering in my life has prepared me for glory crowned by humility and peace and closeness to God's presence. I love God for the pain he has given me. It has fulfilled me and proven to be a source of strength. It has not taken away, but given me faith.

God also moves in my reality and masculinity as a man, as he has given you femininity if you are a woman. My sexuality is God-given and good. It is a divine gift and is not a cause of shame but of grace for me. As any of his gifts, it is not meant to be taken lightly or abused. It is to be used lovingly and caringly.

I see God in every moment, most especially in the present. He fills the present. I would be alive and open to this moment, for this is where He stands. This is holy ground. I would be present to life and God. I see God in every part of this natural world, and the sky, the stars, my friend the moon, the bright and pure sun, the mountains, the desert, the trees, the grass, the sunset and particularly the sunrise, the ocean, the prairies of Illinois, the hills of New York. The air, the wind, the sun that blends in me reenacts the miracle of creation.

But most of all, perhaps I see God's hand in my relationships with other people. God is a God of relationship. His relationship to me is a model for my love. I see God's presence in my relationship to my children, truly not "my" children, but his. Now they are no longer children but friends, and I praise God for the miracle of that transformation. They were a gift to me for a while but as so much of life, they have moved on, and become transmuted into something more beautiful than I could have created or controlled. Now they are their own people, and God's gift to others, their spouses and their children. So, the power of God is passed on, from generation to generation, the miracle of life without end.

God is present nowhere more convincingly than in the relationship I am privileged to have with the one I love. A lifetime ago I prayed to God, for his miracle for my beloved dog, Ruby. He revealed his miracle to us all, and today she walks and runs unassisted. Great as that miracle was, for me it was but a foreshadowing of a greater miracle. For you see, I dared to pray a second time and thank God for yet another miracle, for someone I could love. God is good. Everything that has happened to me for so many years has prepared me for the discovery and recognition of this miracle.

Are prayers answered? Most certainly. Not right away perhaps, not when we expect, sometimes not in the way that we expect, but God gives us the eyes to see, ears to hear, arms to hold, hearts to trust. So, my life today is different. To say that it is different is an understatement, it is a new life. I have been born anew. Today I live in God's presence each moment, perpetually humbled and uplifted on "Wings like Eagles."

My humanity brings me imperfection, chaos, terror. God's intervention brings me love, joy, and peace. I live life today, feeling every emotion, frequently being overwhelmed, but I have courage. There is no more hiding. Life is to be met face-to-face. "Now we see through a glass darkly, but then face-to-face. Now I know in part, but then shall I know even as also I am known" (1 Cor 13:12 KJV).

I am never alone, never abandoned. He is with me to the end. That is his promise, his covenant of unconditional love, a haunting model for my love. So, I take my fear in one hand, and my love in the other hand, and putting my love ahead of my fear, I walk into the future. And the future is mine. At the present I stand with God, and in my freedom I make choices and commitments. I commit to God, I commit to myself, and I commit to those I love.

Michael Johnson said, "Your fear will tell you that you are lost in the forest. Your love will tell you that you are the forest" (Johnson, personal communication, 1992). "Those who wait upon the Lord," who pray and hope and expect a miracle, who seek only to know and trust his will, "shall renew their strength. They shall mount up with wings like eagles" and will soar to heights of joy and fulfillment unknown to our earthbound and finite ways.

"They shall run, and not be weary." Our strength and vigor shall be sufficient for this venture. "They shall walk and not faint." We shall prevail and be equal to the adventure of life and love.

PART III

A Seasoned Spirit
Sermons in Key Largo, Florida

— 30 —

A Better Love[1]

THERE ARE PROBABLY AS many sermons given in churches on love, as there are on God or Christ or Heaven. But somehow, I prefer the ones on love. Maybe it's the Unitarian Universalist in me. At any rate, I think it's as good a topic as any to begin the New Year, and before I forget it, Happy New Year to all of you!

In the New Testament Jesus says much about love. In John 13, he says, "A new commandment I give to you, that you love one another; even as I have loved you, that you also love one another" (John 13:34 RSV). In John 15, he says, "My command is this: Love each other as I have loved you. Greater love hath no one than this; to lay down one's life for one's friends" (John 15:12–13 NIV).

Strong words indeed, to lay down one's life or to die for a friend. Even stronger, however, would be to live one's life for a friend. Certainly, Jesus spoke of a better love than the world had known before. Jesus set a new standard that has prevailed to this day, and that is one of the reasons I am proud to consider myself a Christian.

All my life, I have sought a better love. I sought it in my family of origin. I have sought it as a minister of churches, as a teacher, as a husband, as a father and now as a grandfather. Sometimes, I even looked for love in "all the wrong places." You never did that, did you? When none of that worked out, I looked for a love—at least for escape—in addiction. There is a saying that sometimes the more you look for something, the

---

1. Sermon delivered by the author at the Coral Isles Church, Tavernier, Florida, on January 1, 2012. A video of this sermon as originally presented is available online: https://youtu.be/fnXT8gG7yc4

harder it is to find. Love eluded me. I always thought it was something I had a right to and was entitled to, something that others should give me. Then I discovered it was something I had to give away.

Kahlil Gibran wrote in his book, *The Prophet*:

> Love one another, but make not a bond of love; let it rather be a moving sea between the shores of your souls. Fill each other's cup but drink not from one cup. Give one another of your bread but eat not from the same loaf. . . . Give your hearts, but not into each other's keeping. For only the hand of Life can contain your hearts. And stand together yet not too near together, for the pillars of the temple stand apart, and the oak tree and the cypress grow not in each other's shadow. (Gibran 1942, 19–20)

I learned that love was something I had to give to others. I had to grow up a little and become responsible. I had to learn that it is not all about me. I am responsible for my happiness. I don't need anyone else to do that; no one else can do that. And I need to be responsible toward others, although I am not responsible for their happiness. Responsibility means the ability to respond, to respond appropriately.

Love is being first and foremost a friend to others. I enjoy the way Antoine de Saint-Exupery talked about love in his story when the Little Prince asked the fox how to tame him: "You must be very patient," replied the fox. "First you will sit down a little distance from me—like that—in the grass. I shall look at you out of the corner of my eye, and you will say nothing. Words are the source of misunderstandings but you will sit a little closer to me every day" (De Saint-Exupery 1943, 67). Friendship and love involve a level of comfort, but more than that, they involve trust. We must learn how to trust others, and we must become trustworthy ourselves.

Twelve Step programs offer insight into not drinking and not using, but also in having functional relationships. The book *Twelve Steps and Twelve Traditions* states, "it is from our twisted relationships with family, friends, and society at large that many of us have suffered the most . . . we fail to recognize . . . our total inability to form a true partnership with another human being. . . . Either we insisted upon dominating the people we know, or we depended on them far too much." The book concludes, "if ever we are to feel emotionally secure . . . we would have to put our lives on a give-and-take basis, we would have to develop a sense of being in partnership or brotherhood with all those around us" (*Alcoholics Anonymous* 2011, 53, 116).

Why is this sometimes so hard? Many of us have been adversely affected, if not badly mangled, by past relationships in our family of origin or in adult relationships. Under these circumstances, it is normal to carry "some baggage." We carry expectations, emotions, and stereotypes from previous relationships into our present ones. If there was negativity, anxiety, control, and punishment in former relationships, we tend to continue reacting to that, even in present and different circumstances. This is what psychologists called "transference." We need to learn to check our baggage at the door.

A better love needs to learn the art of friendship-making, of trusting, of being direct and forgiving when others hurt us, and of being honest and accountable when we hurt them. Good relationships take time and they take work, but they are a joy to behold.

Most of all, a better love is a pathway to God. Human relationships, community, or fellowship are the way to that which is holy. This is referred to by the Greek word, *koinonia*. Sam Shoemaker referred to the church as being a quiet place of "unhurried people with time enough for souls" (Shoemaker 2008, 107). To be in loving relationships is to be in *imago dei*, the image of God. To live in the image of God is to live in relationship. To live alone is but a fracture of His image. When asked when the Kingdom of God was coming, Jesus answered, "The Kingdom of God is in the midst of you" (Luke 17:21 RSV). God is in relationship; in a mystical sense He is relationship itself. Entering into a better love is not only to have a gift from God, it is to be in that which is holy. It is to glimpse the face of God.

— 31 —

Celebration of Life for H. E. Hudson, Jr.[1]

FOR YEARS, THE HUDSON family has played a part in making America great. The Hudson legacy can be traced directly to Henry Hudson, according to a genealogy compiled by my great aunt, Ruth Hudson Wexler. A descendent, William Hudson, lived in Boston in the mid-1600s. His cow path became Beacon Street, and he was one of sixteen public spirited men who gave Boston Commons to the city of Boston. Eli Hudson was a Revolutionary soldier. William Perkins Hudson fought in the war of 1812. Thomas Jefferson Hudson was killed in the Civil War at the Battle of Chickamauga. Asa Sherman Hudson was a lifelong friend of President James A. Garfield. Asa's second son, named Herbert Edson Hudson I, was a dentist. His first son, my grandfather, Herbert Edson Hudson II, was a veteran of World War I and a founder of the Tennessee Valley Authority. Dad, then, was actually Herbert Edson Hudson III, although he preferred Herbert E. Hudson, Jr. out of respect for Grandpa Hudson. He was called "Boone," by family and older friends since the day he played the part of Daniel Boone so convincingly in a school play.

Dad was born in Chicago in 1910, and married Annabelle Woods in 1932. Into this heritage my brother, Ken, and I were born. Dad's grandchildren, Laurie and Christopher on Ken's side; and Deborah, Wendy, and Sean on my side, proudly carry on the Hudson tradition.

---

1. Speech by the author at Memorial Service, Gainesville, Florida, on October 26, 1983.

Celebration of Life for H. E. Hudson, Jr.

Some of my earliest recollections were visiting Dad's office in the Water Treatment Plant of the City of Chicago where he worked. I remember the huge filtration basins. I remember visiting his office at the Illinois Water Survey in Urbana, and I vividly recall the many bottles of strange smelling chemicals in the lab. Dad's work and his professional life were more important to him than I can express. I was always warmly greeted by his colleagues who consistently thought so highly of him. There was always a clean smell and taste and air to his work. To him water was something sacred, to be protected and respected. In an age before environmental protection became popular, he believed and lived conservation of what he considered our greatest natural resource.

World War II caught Dad squarely in mid-career. He volunteered for the Engineer Corps and was stationed at Fort Belvoir, Virginia, where our family moved to join him. He then served in Europe. I remember living in Virginia where I was branded a "Damn Yankee." I remember Dad's homecoming from Europe late one night, and Mom waking Ken and me early in the morning to tell us he was home. We celebrated with a bottle of French champagne he brought home in his duffel bag. I mixed mine with orange soda pop.

Dad was a product of the Depression and working for governmental agencies was his first preference. As our country settled into the post-war, however, Dad moved into private practice as a consulting engineer, first with Hazen and Sawyer in Detroit and New York City. Then, as you know, he moved to Gainesville to become president of Water and Air Research in 1972.

If I had to characterize Dad, it would be as one of the best-informed men I have known. He was a Renaissance man living in the twentieth century. He could carry on a perceptive conversation on almost any topic, and just when you found the subject where you thought you had the edge, you were in for a surprise. Whether it was history, agriculture, religion, geography, art, stock market, music, or mechanics, Dad knew what he was talking about.

He was a thoroughly practical man, well-versed as a designer and builder. Concurrently, he was a brilliant theoretician and teacher. He was destined to become one of the most distinguished figures in the field of water treatment and supply in the middle half of the century.

He was a humorist. He was a prolific and gifted writer. His mind was unclouded by prejudice or unwarranted bias. His attitude was inquisitive, his method investigative. "He climbed the heights, and left all superstitions far below, while on his forehead fell the golden dawning of a grander day" (Ingersoll 1900, XII: 390). He was an international man and belonged to the world. Others have observed how he contributed so much in a single life. His work was his life. My brother and I are proud of him, and we are pleased to join in the celebration of the life of an extraordinary man.

I want to express the appreciation of the Hudson family to those responsible for this celebration. First, to the partners and staff of Water and Air Research for arranging this gathering. Second, to the University of Illinois Alumni Association, in particular Lewis D. Liay, chief administrative officer and past president of the Alumni Association, who has come some distance to be with us this evening. We thank the Alumni Association for the honor they bestow on Dad this evening. Finally, I want to express the appreciation of our family to all of you who have come to share in this lovely occasion.

Herbert Edson III . . . Herbert Edson II . . . Herbert Edson I . . . Asa . . . Thomas . . . William Perkins . . . Eli . . . William . . . Henry. Dad is in good company and leaves a legacy in the example of his life. We salute and celebrate the life of a man who dwelt faithfully among us.

— 32 —

Dark Night of the Soul (*Kenosis*)[1]

LIFE IS EASY—WHEN EVERYTHING goes alright. But what about those times when things don't go OK, when life is difficult? What about those times when nothing seems to work, when things stop clicking, when we fall into a hole? You have heard about the pessimist who not only slips into a rut but furnishes it!

We all have those moments when the bottom seems to fall out. We despair of ever being whole or happy again. There are times when we are tempted to give up, to quit on life. There are times when some people call it quits. These are the moments when some of us contemplate the ultimate surrender, suicide. It is said that suicide is the permanent solution to a temporary problem. There are moments when we are overcome by depression and hopelessness and despair.

In fact, however, these are sacred moments, full of possibility. These moments when we don't feel we can go down any further are the times when the only direction we can go is up. There are times when we experience what John of the Cross in sixteenth century Spain referred to as "The Dark Night of the Soul" (John of the Cross 2003). Who here has had a "dark night of the soul?"

Alcoholics Anonymous teaches that "lack of power was our dilemma" (*Alcoholics Anonymous* 1955, 45). Addiction recovery tells us that it is necessary—indeed, essential—that we hit bottom before we can begin

---

1. Sermon delivered by the author at Coral Isles Church, Tavernier, Florida, on January 6, 2019. A video of this sermon as originally presented is available online: https://youtu.be/sAwsQI_wzFo

to climb, to recover. It is difficult to start our upward ascent until we are at our lowest point. We become willing as only the dying can be.

It is one of the ironies of life that there is a gift in desperation, a victory in surrender, a sunrise that follows the night. Let us not make the mistake of trying to shun all loss and tragedy in life—these things are inevitable. Let us learn to find the potential inherent in them. There is something special and sacred about the low moments, the times of despair. Traditional Christian theology talks about how Christ voluntarily divested himself of divine powers to become human and live as a man. It is said that he "*emptied himself*, taking the form of a servant" (Phil 2:7 RSV).

This teaching of being emptied out is known as *kenosis*, taken from the Greek word *kenoo*. Emptying out is essential to make room to be filled with something else, something more. As one theologian puts it, "For Paul, to have the mind of Christ is specifically to be *kenotic* in accommodating the needs of others, especially those who are poor or weak in the community" (Lee 2018). We then realize what scholars mean, "genuine love has a kenotic quality" (Lee 2018). So, too, let us not begrudge the moments we feel defeated and depressed. It is only by the emptying of self that we can identify and empathize with others who likewise suffer. In a sense, we create space for them, we validate them and give them permission and encouragement.

Unmerited suffering is the theme that we find in ancient times, going back at least as far as the Book of Job. Job, as we know, was a wealthy, upright and blameless man who lived in a land called Uz—many have reflected on the similarity to L. Frank Baum's *Wizard of Oz* (Baum 2019). According to the Old Testament, God allows Satan to torment Job, but forbids him to take Job's life. Job's livestock, servants, and children die. Job himself is afflicted with severe skin sores. Friends visit and tell Job that although he comforted other people, he never really understood their pain. Job's losses thus become a means to understand and empathize with others. The meaning of Job's hitting bottom and being emptied out is expressed in his affirmations: "Shall we receive good from God and shall we not receive evil?" and "The Lord gave, and the Lord hath taken away; blessed be the name of the Lord" (Job 1:21 KJV).

In sixteenth century Spain, Teresa of Avila wrote a poem: "Nada te turbe; nada te espante; todo se pasa." Translated it means, "Let nothing disturb you; Let nothing make you afraid; All things pass" (Thomas 2016). Teresa was mentor to another Carmelite, a short man less than five feet tall. This cleric became known as John of the Cross who wrote the book *La Noche Oscura,* or *The Dark Night of the Soul* (John of the Cross 2003).

In the 1980s, Harold S. Kushner wrote his popular book, *When Bad Things Happen to Good People* (Kushner 1981). Our friend Richard Agler, rabbi of the Keys Jewish Community Center recently published his book, *The Tragedy Test,* provoked by the untimely death of his twenty-year-old daughter. He concludes that the "God of Law and Spirit is one with, and does not overturn, the laws of the universe. This God . . . may not be all the God we want. But it is a God we can have" (Agler 2018, 122).

Before I moved to the Keys, I lived in Upstate New York. I knew a man there named Julius. Julius was an alcoholic who had newly found recovery, but he had trouble accepting the fact that he couldn't drink any more. Day after day, he would moan, "Why me? Why me? Why me?" One day he began to say something different. He started to say, "Why not me?"

Teresa and I enjoy children's stories like *The Little Prince* and *The Runaway Bunny.* I think her favorite is *The Velveteen Rabbit* by Margery Williams. If you haven't read it, or if you haven't read it in a long time, it bears rereading. In the story, the Velveteen Rabbit meets another toy in the boy's nursery, an old Skin Horse. The rabbit asks the Skin Horse:

> "What is Real. . . . Does it mean having things that buzz inside you and a stick-out handle?" "Real isn't how you are made," said the Skin Horse, "It's a thing that happens to you. When a child loves you for a long, long time . . . you become Real." "Does it hurt?" asked the Rabbit. "Sometimes," said the Skin Horse for he was always truthful. "When you are Real you don't mind being hurt."
> "Does it happen all at once, like being wound up," he asked, "or bit by bit?" "It doesn't happen all at once," said the Skin Horse. "You become. It takes a long time. That's why it doesn't often happen to people who break easily, or have sharp edges, or have to be carefully kept. Generally, by the time you are Real, most of your hair has been loved off, and your eyes drop out and you get loose in the joints and very shabby. But these things don't matter at all, because once you are Real you can't be ugly, except to people who don't understand." (Williams 1997, 12–13)

So, my friends, try not to despair if you are going through a "Dark Night of the Soul." Try not to despair if you feel you have hit a bottom in life, if you feel an inner emptiness, or if you feel you have fallen into a hole and can't seem to get out. Don't despair even if your hair gets thin, if you have trouble seeing, or if you get loose in the joints. If we are to believe the Skin Horse, let us be assured that we are not becoming ugly, but are finally becoming lovable, complete, and real.

— 33 —

Earth's the Right Place for Love[1]

EARLIER THIS MONTH, I led a discussion group at our church on Henri Nouwen's book *Life of the Beloved* (Nouwen 1992). Nouwen's premise is that life parallels bread from the sacrament of Communion in that we also are chosen, blessed, broken, and given. According to Nouwen, our brokenness as human beings can be physical and is experienced in death, but is often an "inner brokenness—a brokenness of the heart" (Nouwen 1992, 72). He reflects, "I see the immense pain of broken relationships between husbands and wives, parents and children, lovers, friends, and colleagues... feeling rejected, ignored, despised and left alone" (Nouwen 1992, 72). Clearly, the human condition includes being vulnerable, being hurtable, being broken, but is that the end of the story?

You all know from my prayer request several weeks ago that Maxwell, my German Shepherd dog, has only a few weeks or at best a few months left to live. At twelve years of age, he has disabling arthritis and now has a breathing problem called laryngeal paralysis, which means his larynx is paralyzed and he has trouble getting enough air to breathe. Just walking for short distances makes him gasp for breath. All Teresa and I can do is to keep him as comfortable as possible, make sure he doesn't suffer, and continue to love him while we can.

All our grief could have been avoided. My first German Shepherd was Ruby who came with me when I moved to the Keys twenty years ago. She was with me for over twelve years, and then I lost her. My heart was

---

1. Sermon delivered by the author at Coral Isles Church, Tavernier, Florida, on March 23, 2014. A video of this sermon as originally presented is available online: https://youtu.be/WA_RiEzP4Bs

so broken, I resolved I would never get another dog—I would never go through that again. But as the years went by after Ruby died, I realized something else. By living alone and protecting myself from the pain of loss, I was hurting myself in a different way: I was depriving myself of love and companionship. I was safe from the hurt of loss, but I was also forfeiting the rewards of love and closeness. So, after five years of living alone, I decided to take another chance, I decided to risk loving again, and I adopted Maxwell who was already full grown. Together we have had eight years of joy and happiness.

I tell you this story because it is what life is all about. Life is about love: about becoming close, forming attachments, and making commitments—and it is also about taking risks and accepting loss. Yes, it is also about being broken and being hurt. These are two sides of the same coin: one side is love and closeness; the other side is vulnerability and becoming hurtable. You can't have the first without the other. It's a package deal. Just as part of our call as human beings is to love, part of our call is to become vulnerable.

We think of God as all-powerful, but God knows about vulnerability, too. Even God became vulnerable when he gave us free will, when he gave us freedom of choice. For me, Jesus is God become vulnerable. God became man, and experienced the pain of loneliness, misunderstanding and criticism, rejection, betrayal, torture, and death. He did this because he loves us and wants to know us better.

But of course, we still don't like the idea of being vulnerable and being hurt. As in my stories about Ruby and Maxwell, our human tendency is to try to avoid pain, to rise above God and life—a self-centered attempt to be in control, to exempt ourselves from being hurt. Sometimes we try to compensate for pain and suffering. We say, "I'm never going through that feeling of loss and grief again. I know what I'll do: I just won't get involved any more, I won't let myself care so much, I won't risk loving again. Then I can't be hurt. That's my way of beating the system."

A very important concept of mental health and psychotherapy that I have studied in conjunction with my post-graduate courses is what psychologists refer to as "transference." In addition to my study, Teresa and I have attended seminars at Baptist Hospital in Miami on this topic. Negative experiences, often in early childhood, predispose us to not trusting others (men, women, parental figures, authority figures, etc.). So, in life when we meet those types of situations or people, we are predisposed to not trusting them; we avoid them; we will not let ourselves get close; we will not risk love and involvement. As M. Scott Peck says in his book *The Road Less Travelled*, "Transference is that set of ways of perceiving and responding to the world which is [sometimes] developed in childhood ... which is *inappropriately* transferred into the adult environment" (Peck 1978, 46). He concludes, "The problem of transference is not simply a problem between psychotherapists and their patients. It is a problem between parents and children, husbands and wives, employers and employees, between friends. . . ." (Peck 1978, 50).

In the case of Ruby, I carried and transferred the pain of grief and loss and my fear of being hurt again, so that I would not consider committing and loving another pet for over five years until I finally adopted Maxwell. For those five years I was protected and exempted from being hurt, but at the expense of depriving myself of love. I became impoverished, and my emotional life was diminished. I am strongly convinced that fear, and the transference of negative experience from the past onto the present, is one of the greatest enemies to our living happy and loving lives.

Is hurt or grief really so terrible? Is it not what every great and courageous soul who ever lived has experienced? Sometimes I think we underestimate human resilience and our capacity for growth. In the musical version of *The Man of La Mancha*, called "The Fantasticks," El Gallo sings, "Without a hurt the heart is hollow" (Donson 2004). Kahlil Gibran, the Lebanese poet, writes, "The deeper sorrow carves into your being, the more joy you can contain" (Gibran 1942, 35). We need to have the strength to take yet another chance on life.

We need to practice discernment, and we need to have courage if we are to live and love. Karle Wilson Baker originally stated that, "Courage is fear that has said its prayers" (Popik 2014). We need to say our prayers, and we need to pray for the daring to live, to live fully and without fear, to give ourselves to the uncertainty and vulnerability of life, to enter into relationships and caring for each other, and not when we come to die, as Thoreau observed, "discover that I had not lived, I did not wish to live what was not life" (Thoreau 2012). Just for today, we need to commit ourselves to live fully and to love with reckless abandon.

Robert Frost testifies in his poem "Birches":

> It's when I'm weary of considerations,
> And life is too much like a pathless wood
> Where your face burns and tickles with the cobwebs
> Broken across it, and one eye is weeping
> From a twig's having lashed across it open

I'd like to get away from earth awhile
And then come back to it and begin over
May no fate willfully misunderstand me
And half grant what I wish and snatch me away
Not to return. Earth's the right place for love:
I don't know where it's likely to go better. (Frost 1969, 122)

— 34 —

Endings and Beginnings[1]

GOOD MORNING, MY FRIENDS. As you may realize, one of the challenges of being a retired minister and at the same time a member of this congregation is not to meddle in things and to mind my own business. Today is one of the first opportunities I have had since Bonnie and Richard left to fill the pulpit and express my views. First, I want to go on record as saying how very blessed I feel we are to have Kerby as our interim minister. She has been a breath of fresh air and we are so fortunate to have a pastor of her maturity and stability during the interim period.

Last Fall at her request, I undertook the job of coordinating Focus Group discussions, which took place the end of February and during March as part of the interim process. These discussion groups were unprecedented in the numbers of members involved: 40–50 of our membership participated! Every week I gathered reports from the groups and typed a summary, which I passed on to Kerby. It is not appropriate for me to go into detail on what was said, but I would like to share with you an observation.

The strongest impression I have from the Focus Groups was how much love and unity there is in our congregation. Clearly, we are a group who cares very much for each other, as well as our God. And what better way can we manifest our love of God than by our love for each other? As Jesus said in the Great Commandment: "Love the Lord your God with all your heart and with all your soul, and with all your strength, and with

---

1. Sermon delivered by the author at Coral Isles Church, Tavernier, Florida, on April 26, 2015. A video of this sermon as originally presented is available online: https://youtu.be/Rt9CzHd89no

all your mind, and your neighbor as yourself" (Luke 10:27 RSV). Our congregation is conspicuous in its lack of dissension or division of any kind. There are virtually no factions. We are united in our resolution to move forward. We are all bozos on the same bus.

The second impression I have from working with the Focus Groups is how gifted many of our members are. We are blessed by so many capable and talented people. Those who are in need are intuitively drawn to this fellowship, and the support they receive does not diminish but only increases us.

My subject this morning is "Endings and Beginnings." When Bonnie and Richard left, we were faced with an Ending, but at the same time, we were given the opportunity for a New Beginning. I perceive that we are now well on the way to that New Beginning.

And is this not what life is all about? Endings and Beginnings. I think back on my life and the tragic divorce from my ex-wife. For such a long time I was overwhelmed by the Ending of that marriage, but time passed, and I have found someone else to love in a special way. And I am free to give my heart again. A New Beginning.

I lived most of my adult life in Upstate New York before I moved to the Florida Keys. An Ending and a New Beginning. When I moved here, I had lovely German Shepherd dog named Ruby. I lost her in the first years I lived in Key Largo, an Ending. I will remember the comforting words of my friend, the Vet, who explained to me, "she has left on her journey." Five years later, I adopted Maxwell, a New Beginning. Eight years later Teresa and I lost him, an Ending. This last month we adopted Libi, a New Beginning.

The lesson I learned is that we cannot allow ourselves to be so overwhelmed or distracted by the inevitable Endings in life, that we forfeit the opportunities for New Beginnings! "Ah, but I shall be wounded. I shall be hurt." That may be so, but is it so terrible then to be hurt? Has not every great and noble soul who ever lived experienced that? We must never forget the words of Tennyson, "'tis better to have loved and lost than never to have loved at all" (Tennyson "In Memoriam" 2019).

The world of nature offers many lessons in Endings and New Beginnings. The sunset is an Ending of day, but also the Beginning of night; the sunset here is an Ending, but it is a sunrise somewhere else, a New Beginning. The summer changes to winter, an Ending; but it gives way to spring and summer, a New Beginning. The caterpillar dies, an Ending; it gives birth to the butterfly, a New Beginning. The seed dies, an Ending; but it grows into a plant, a New Beginning.

As we grow older, we forfeit the gifts of youth. We get wrinkles, we gain weight. We get out of breath easier; we don't move as fast; we have two new friends, Arthur and Itis. It is harder to see; we have more trouble hearing. Every morning we have to gulp a handful of obscenely big pills. We have so many doctors listed in our cell phone contact list that sometimes we have trouble finding anybody else. Every time we go to the doctor's office, they find something else wrong with us.

But along with the Endings come New Beginnings. Grandchildren, whom we can spoil and then send back to their parents. Quiet, peace, serenity, calm, stability, happiness, and contentment. True friends, companionship. We lose old friends, Endings. But we grow and become capable of new, deeper friendships, New Beginnings. Gibran said, "the deeper sorrow carves into your being, the more joy you can contain" (Gibran 1942, 35). Appreciation for the sunset, the ocean, the sky. Walks, if not runs. Most of all for me going back to school, for learning and hopefully for wisdom. I am 80, and this is a most wonderful, if not the best time of my life. And what about the end of life—when we all leave on our final journey? Thoreau wrote, "our human life but dies down to its root, and still puts forth its green blade to eternity" (Thoreau n.d.). Will it then really be so terrible? Tagore said, "life as a whole never takes death seriously" (Tagore 1996, 65).

I realize it is not as easy as it sounds. How do we let go of the especially jarring and hurtful Endings we all experience? There is one way that I know, and that is acceptance and forgiveness of others, of the past. Forgiveness is not only for the benefit of the other person, but it is a benefit for ourselves. For, you see, it frees us for New Beginnings. Teresa and I recently attended the discussion group about the Holocaust book *The Sunflower* at the Keys Jewish Community Center led by one of our local rabbis. In the history of the world, there are few things that come close to the evil of the Holocaust and the injury done to humanity. The Holocaust continues to be a burden borne by the Jewish people and by the world.

The Bible is a book of New Beginnings. Moses murdered a man, but he was chosen to lead his people. David committed adultery with Bathsheba and had her husband killed, but was later called "a man after . . . [God's] own heart" (1 Sam 13:14 NIV). Peter denied Christ and ran away, but became the leader of the church. Paul persecuted early Christians, but became an apostle and author of much of the New Testament. Jesus knew that the Samaritan woman at the well had several husbands, but he befriended her. The parable of the Prodigal Son is about a man lost in the world who was welcomed home. New Beginnings.

Years ago, Jesus died on a cross. By all contemporary standards, his life ended as a failure. He never went to school. He never wrote a book. He never traveled more than 200 miles from the place where he was born. He wasn't married, he didn't have any children. At the end, his friends deserted him. He was executed between two thieves. His executioners gambled for the only possession he had, his cloak. He was buried in a borrowed tomb. A pitiful Ending? Or was it a New Beginning for humankind, perhaps the greatest beginning since creation itself?

— 35 —

Feeding of the 5,000[1]

WE HAVE A SAYING here at the Coral Isles Church, "If you feed them, they will come!" Food is a common theme in Scripture. Adam ate the apple. The Jewish Passover centers on the Seder meal. In Christianity we are told that Jesus is the bread of life. In the Lord's Prayer we ask God, "Give us this day our daily bread." We learn of the spiritual value of fasting, giving up certain food for specified periods. Communion is one of our sacraments, partaking in bread and wine (or juice) that symbolizes Christ's life and spirit.

Two other stories in the New Testament that center on food are the feeding of the 5,000 in Matthew 14:13–21, which Marsha has just read for us; and the feeding of 4,000 described in Matthew 15:32–39. These are considered two of the miracles of Christ.

These stories parallel each other in a number of ways. The feeding of the 4,000, also known as the "miracle of seven loaves and fish," is reported in Mark and Matthew, but not in Luke or John. The feeding of the 5,000, known as "the miracle of five loaves and two fish," however, is reported in Matthew, Mark, Luke, and John, and thus is the only miracle reported in all four Gospels. It is this second story, the feeding of the 5,000, which we will consider this morning.

Recently, Bonnie has been preaching on stories of the ministry and miracles of Jesus. This morning we continue in the same vein. This, then, is the "rest of the story." When Jesus had heard that John the Baptist was

---

1. Sermon delivered by the author at the Coral Isles Church, Tavernier, Florida, on June 21, 2013. A video of this sermon as originally presented is available online: https://youtu.be/-oeuPMkEPrg

killed, "he departed thence by ship into a desert place apart and when the people had heard thereof, they followed him on foot out of the cities" (Matt 14:13 KJV). When Jesus saw the multitude, he was "moved with compassion toward them, and he healed their sick" (Matt 14:14 KJV). This had gone on all day, and they were tired—and hungry. It was evening and the disciples urged Jesus to send the people away, so they could find food.

But these were poor people. They had no place to go. They did not have any money; they had no way to get anything to eat. They had been sent away, put off, marginalized all their lives. So, Jesus replied, "They need not depart; give ye them to eat." And the disciples said, "We have here but five loaves, and two fishes," barely enough to feed themselves. He said to them, "Bring them hither to me." He had everyone sit down, and "took the five loaves, and the two fishes, and looking up to heaven, he blessed and brake" the loaves and fishes and gave them to his disciples who passed out the food to the multitude. And the Book of Matthew reports, "They did all eat, and were filled. . . ." (Matt 14:16–20 KJV).

A miracle indeed! I remember a church in Upstate New York that had a banner on the wall of the dining room that a Sunday School class had made. It showed a basket with bread and fish. Below the picture of the basket appeared these words: "Love is like a basket with five loaves and two fish. There's never enough until you give it away."

But wait, there's more to the story of the feeding of the 5,000. After "they did all eat and were filled," Matthew goes on to tell us that the miracle was not over. There was one more thing to be done. Jesus directed the disciples to gather up the leftovers, "and they took up of the fragments that remained twelve baskets full" (Matt 14:20 KJV).

Now, there's a miracle for you! The story is not about the five loaves and two fish. It's not about the miracle of multiplying. It's not about feeding 5,000, and that did not include women and children. The story, my friends, is about all the food that remained. There was twelve times as much remaining as they started with—after feeding everyone.

The hungry people were important to Jesus. The five loaves and two fish were important to Jesus. Feeding the people was important to Jesus. But ultimately, what was important was that Jesus told his disciples to gather up and bring to him the broken pieces. Nothing was to go to waste. Nothing was useless. Nothing was to be thrown away. Nothing was expendable. The pieces were as important, if not more so, than the whole loaves or fish. Everything had a place and a use. Everything was needed. Everything was special and holy. Everything was valuable and was to serve a purpose.

Those of you who have heard me speak before know that I sometimes quote Henri Nouwen. His book *Life of the Beloved* was life-changing for me (Nouwen 1992). There are few books that I can say that about. Nouwen, a Jesuit priest, talks about the sacrament of Communion. He says there are four stages in the Eucharist. First, the bread is chosen. Second, it is blessed. Third, it is broken. And fourth, it is given. Nouwen says that there are also four stages of our lives. In our lives we are chosen by God, and then we are blessed by him. Next Nouwen says something that at first seems a little odd. As with the bread in Communion, he says we must be broken.

He argues that each of us is broken in a slightly different and special way. It is what makes us unique: it is what gives us character; it is what is becoming to others; ultimately it is what makes us useful to them, allowing us to be able to empathize and be truly loving. Our brokenness "reveals something about who we are. . . . [for] each human being suffers in a way no other human being suffers" (Nouwen 1992, 71). He goes on to say, "our brokenness is often most painfully experienced with respect to our sexuality" (Nouwen 1992, 73).

There are all kinds of brokenness, including physical and mental disabilities, but Nouwen concludes:

> . . . the suffering of which I am most aware on a day-to-day basis is the suffering of the broken heart. Again and again, I see the immense pain of broken relationships between husband and wives, parents and children, lovers, friends and colleagues . . . the suffering that seems to be the most painful is that of feeling rejected, ignored, despised and left alone. (Nouwen 1992, 72)

This gives us added insight into why Jesus would not tell the crowd to go away.

Has anyone here ever felt rejected? Has anyone here ever felt left alone? In Communion, only the bread that is broken can be distributed and given to the worshippers. Nouwen insists that so, too, in life it is only after we have been broken that we can be given to others and be useful to them. In another of his books titled *The Wounded Healer* Nouwen argues that the person who has been wounded themselves can be an empathetic and believable counselor and friend (Nouwen 1972).

How do we do this? First, we face our brokenness squarely and befriend it. Second, we put our brokenness under a blessing. We realize that whatever adversity has happened to us, whatever tragedy and suffering we have experienced can become "a source of purification . . . pruning," discipline and growth (Nouwen 1992, 79). In the Old Testament, Joseph said to his brothers, "You meant evil against me; but God meant it for good" (Gen 50:20 RSV). In the New Testament, the apostle Paul puts it this way: "And we know that all things work together for good to them that love God. . . ." (Rom 8:28 KJV).

No, the glass is no longer seen as half empty, but as half full—and in time we will be able to say with the Psalmist, "My cup runneth over" (Psa 23:5 KJV). So, I say to you, my friends, that regardless of the trials and struggles in your lives, regardless of the pain and hurt, the losses and disappointments, the failure and heartache, there can be value and purpose and redemption. Let us not throw away what is broken. Let us carefully and gently gather all the broken pieces together for the true banquet of life. Nothing is for naught. Nothing is useless. Nothing is wasted. Nothing is lost. We need all the broken fragments. The pieces are as important as the loaf, for what is the loaf except a composite of the pieces? Everything that has happened can be used for good. Everything is special and holy, and everything is valuable and can serve a purpose.

And that, my friends, is the miracle of the feeding of the 5,000.

– 36 –

God Is Nigh[1]

ACTS 2:17 SAYS, "I will pour out my Spirit on all people. Your sons and daughters will prophesy, your young men will see visions, your old men will dream dreams" (NIV).

As you know I was ordained a Unitarian Universalist minister, attended Methodist, Baptist churches, and am now active in the United Church of Christ. When I was a young minister my early churches tolerated my visions of what life was like. But I hadn't lived life; it was only guesswork, albeit well-educated guesswork. Today I am no longer young. As the bumper sticker says, "Young at heart. Other parts slightly older." I have lived and loved; I have made my share of mistakes. So, this morning I will not be sharing guesswork with you about what life is like, but my memories and "dreams" of what life has actually been.

Years ago, I would have said I believed in God, but I didn't know who God was. I hadn't lived and had the life experience, the gifts and losses, the grace and suffering that leads to relationship with Him. I knew only that I was tough and smart, and by myself I could handle anything. As for God, Well, He was up there somewhere, sort of like the bush-league pinch hitter who could be called upon when all else failed.

God was my hero. I wanted to be like Him, All-wise and All-loving—and I wanted it right away. But that was not to be. The world has turned over many times. It took years, and much loss and pain, but I have

---

1. Sermon delivered by the author at Coral Isles Church, Tavernier, Florida, on November 4, 2012. A video of this sermon as originally presented is available online: https://youtu.be/tUdb4kNRuSM

learned some patience and a little humility. It's about time, because if truth be known, I am closer to the end of my life than to the beginning.

I hope I have learned not to be afraid so much. I think my life today is less fear-driven and more love-driven. I am human and the two will always be part of me. What we need to do is to place our fear in one hand, and our love in the other. Then with the hand holding the love in front, walk into the future.

Now, having lived more of life, I know that God is with me all the time. He is my constant companion. He is in my mind; He is in my breath. He is as close as my heartbeat. I not only have a relationship with Him, He is my friend. I have learned to love and trust Him, particularly in moments of loss. This is the meaning to me of the statement attributed to Job: "The Lord gave, and the Lord hath taketh away; blessed be the name of the Lord" (Job 1:21 KJV).

God is All-Wise, All-Present, All-Powerful. He created me. I didn't create Him. Twelve Step programs say, "There are only two things you have to know: There is a God, and you're not Him."

I have come to know Him as a God of relationship. He created the world and those of us in it for one reason only, because He wanted to be in relationship with us. He created Adam and Eve to be his friends, and when they ran away and hid from Him, He cried out: "Where art thou?" (Gen 3:9 KJV). The Bible is an extended story about God establishing relationship.

A month or so ago, Bonnie asked us in a sermon, "Who is Jesus for you?" Several of us responded, but I didn't answer at the time. For me, Jesus is the ultimate attempt of God to be in relationship with us. An All-Powerful God took the form of human frailty, so He could understand who we are, and be closer to us. Jesus is God becoming vulnerable—living, hurting, being alone, crying in despair, being abandoned, being beaten, and being killed in the most brutal way known at the time. You might have heard the riddle, "What is the one thing in Heaven that is man-made?" The answer is, "The scars that Jesus bears." God didn't have to surrender being All-Powerful. He did it because He loves us and wants to know us.

God, who truly moves in mysterious ways, has come to me not only in the form of Jesus, but there are many who have given their time, their lives, and their love to me. It is not necessary that I name them here, only that I acknowledge my debt. They were His angels, in poor disguise.

God has also come to me in the form of animals. I love the old Anglican hymn:

> All things bright and beautiful,
> All creatures great and small,
> All things wise and wonderful,
> The Lord God made them all. (Alexander n.d.)

My pets have taught me friendship, unselfishness, spontaneity, honesty, courage, and love. Lord Byron put it most eloquently in a tribute to his dog:

> Who possessed Beauty without Vanity,
> Strength without Insolence,
> Courage without Ferocity,
> And all the Virtues of Man without his Vices. (Byron n.d. Epitaph)

In 1994, I moved to Key Largo and became a PADI Master Instructor. I was searching, but I didn't know what for. The words of the 139th Psalm fitted me very well: "If I take the wings of the morning, and dwell in the uttermost parts of the sea; even there shall thy hand lead me, and thy right hand shall hold me" (Psa 139:9–10 KJV).

I came to the Keys to heal, and it has come to pass, to grow up a little. I became active in a Twelve Step program and have been helped and had the privilege of helping others. Twelve Step programs, perhaps not best understood by outsiders, embody principles of love and service that emulate first century Christianity.

In this avocation, I have come to believe in the power of changing the world one person at a time. Once an unusually strong tide covered a beach with thousands of star fish that were washed up and would soon perish under the hot sun. In the middle of the beach was a man picking up the star fish one at a time and throwing them back into the ocean. A passerby confronted him and said, "What good do you think you are doing? With these thousands and thousands of sea stars stranded here, what does it matter if you throw a few back?" Lofting another into deep water, the man replied, "It matters to this one."

Where can God be found? There is a Country Western song, "Looking for love in all the wrong places." I have finally learned to look for love in the right places. As Scripture tells us: "Neither shall they say, Lo here! or, lo there! for, behold, the kingdom of God is within you" (Luke 17:21 KJV).

When I was a boy at Scout Camp, I would drift off to sleep at night listening to the bugle play "Taps." I am haunted by the words of that song:

Day is done,
Gone the sun,
From the hills,
From the lake,
From the skies.
All is well,
Safely rest,
God is nigh. (Taps n.d.)

May the words of my mouth, and the meditations of my heart, be acceptable in Thy sight, O Lord, my strength, and my redeemer. Amen.

— 37 —

Happiness in an Imperfect World[1]

The wonderful thing about sermons is the opportunity it gives the pastor to contemplate something important about life. If it then has a positive impact on the congregation, so much the better. Today I want to talk about some very broad ideas about what life is like. First, by definition, we as human beings are imperfect. Try as we can to deny and change that, we cannot. We can will being perfect with all our might, but inevitably someone like Angie pops up and asks, "How did that work out for you?" I've told some of you the story about the man who was looking for the perfect woman, and he returned to his friend and said, "I found her—the perfect woman." The friend asked, "Where is she?" He answered despondently, "She's looking for the perfect man."

Why do we try to be perfect? My experience is that we think if we are perfect, we will be more loveable. That is a fallacy that I have bought into for some time. We don't have to be perfect to be loved. If anything, being perfect makes it harder for others to be comfortable around us and to love us. It's easier to love someone who is flawed. The imperfections and faults of others contribute to making them more human and more becoming. Kahlil Gibran said, "The only time a juggler appeals to me is when I see him miss the ball" (Gibran n.d.).

The next broad idea is that as human beings at our best, our role is to be happy. What good are we to anyone if we're miserable? Not to anyone

1. Sermon delivered by the author at Coral Isles Church, Tavernier, Florida, June 12, 2016. A video of this sermon as originally presented is available online: https://youtu.be/KHxsYf-RodE

else—and certainly not to ourselves. There is a saying I'm sure you have heard, "Happiness is an inside job." We attribute all kinds of wise insights to Abraham Lincoln. One saying is that, "Folks are usually about as happy as they make up their minds they're going to be" (Lincoln n.d.). Another is the story about Lincoln traveling by horseback from his home in Salem to his office in Springfield, Illinois. He met a wagon of settlers headed for Salem. They stopped him and asked him, "We're thinking of settling in Salem. What are the people like there?" To which, Lincoln replied, "What were they like where you came from?" They responded, "We didn't like them. They gossiped and argued and were terrible neighbors." Lincoln responded, "Well, you'll find the people in Salem to be about the same."

If we are imperfect, and if our role is to be happy, it follows that we need to learn how to be happy despite our imperfections. I am not saying that it is up to other people to make us happy. That's not their job. For quite a while in life, I assumed it was the job of others to make me happy. First, I imagined my parents should do that. Then I projected that role on teachers and employers. Angie? When that didn't work out for me, I projected the role of making me happy on my former wife. Because she is now my "former" wife, you can tell how well that worked out for me.

Finally, I grew up. I learned it is my job to be happy, warts and all. We are not put here on earth to be perfect or to be right, but to be happy. I had long heard about being responsible. I assumed that meant for others, my children, my parishioners, even my friends. But then I learned, I was responsible for making myself happy. I learned this from other people I admired. It was what they did. I wanted what they had, and they say if you want what someone has, you need to do what they do. Although there is a great deal of sadness and strife in the life of Jesus, I think that essentially he was a happy man. Today I can try to imitate him. That is what being a Christian means to me.

Another thing that being a Christian means is forgiving others. One of the most important ways of growing up and becoming responsible for our own happiness, is by letting go of blame and resentment of others—in short, forgiving them. Forgiveness means giving up our right to get even. Forgiveness is the key to happiness. The crux of the Lord's Prayer is, "Forgive us our trespasses, as we forgive those who have trespassed against us." When we forgive others, we recognize their humanity, and we find true humanity in ourselves. Humanity also involves humility. The path of humility leads to the destination of our humanity. It is our yellow brick road.

Paradoxically, forgiving others includes asking for forgiveness for ourselves. How do you make amends, or ask for forgiveness? First, by being honest and squarely taking responsibility for what we have done. Asking for forgiveness is not, "*If* I hurt you" or "*If* I offended you." Asking for forgiveness sounds like this: "I did this, and I am grieved in my heart. I am convicted by God that I did it, and I apologize. I own it completely, I was wrong" (Van Yperen 2002, 234). A part of making amends or asking for forgiveness is action and restitution. By definition, amends means change. We should demonstrate change in our attitudes and behavior. The change should be immediate and generous. Action speaks louder than words.

So, what is our "take home" on human imperfection? If we're not perfect and in control, how in the world can we learn to be happy? My friends, as human beings we must learn that we will always be incomplete and unfinished. We must learn to live with our longing. We will never rest; we will never be fully complete. This is our most precious gift from God, and not a sign that something is wrong but that something is more right than we can imagine. As Gerald May said: "It is God's song of love in our soul . . . always, leaving us unsatisfied, calling. To claim our rightful place in destiny, we must not only accept and claim the sweetly painful incompleteness within ourselves, but also affirm it with all our hearts. Somehow, we must come to fall in love with it" (May 1991, 181).

> Come, my friends
> 'Tis not too late to seek a newer world.
> Push off, and sitting well in order smite
> The sounding furrows; for my purpose holds to sail beyond the sunset,
> And the paths of all the western stars, until I die.
> It may be that the gulfs will wash us down;
> It may be we shall touch the Happy Isles,
> And see the great Achilles, whom we knew;
> Tho' much is taken, much abides;
> And tho' we not now that strength which in old days moved earth and heaven;
> That which we are, we are;
> One equal temper of heroic hearts,
> Made weak by time and fate, but strong in will
> To strive, to seek, to find and not to yield. (Tennyson 2019)

— 38 —

Hospitality
The Mission of the Church[1]

Two weeks ago, I talked about the "The Keys of the Kingdom," a personal and individual prescription for spiritual living. Today, I want to speak on the purpose of the church in the twenty-first century, as I see it. It is my hope that this may be useful in our church assessing who and what we are as an organization, as we transition from the ministry of the last 20 years through the interim ministry of Kerby to new leadership and direction for the future. This sermon sequel to "The Keys of the Kingdom" I have chosen to call "Hospitality: The Mission of the Church."

In my post-graduate courses, I have spent some time considering the place of hospitality in the church's life. I am convinced that historically and contemporaneously the concept of hospitality describes the church at its best. Unfortunately, many people today see the world as an inhospitable place and come to feel unwelcome in life. People are cautious, skeptical, even mistrustful. The prevailing assumption is one of scarcity, not sufficiency. What is needed in our churches today is a spirit of plenty, of accessibility, and of generosity.

Our Judeo-Christian tradition has long provided this. The book of Genesis portrays God as the perfect host, creating and providing the world as a place for us to prosper and to be comfortable. To this end, he created all that we need: land, water, vegetation, light, fish, and animals—even a wife for Adam. And we find what is referred to as "The

---

1. Sermon delivered by the author at Coral Isles Church, Tavernier, Florida, September 14, 2014. A video of this sermon as originally presented is available online: https://youtu.be/DEkCguCjZWw

Hospitality

Great Mandate": "Be fruitful and multiply" (Gen 1:28 RSV). After the great flood we are told that God will make humankind "as numerous as the stars in the sky" (Deut 10: 22 NIV).

In Matthew comes the "Great Invitation": "Come to me, all who are weary and burdened, and I will give you rest" (Matt 11:28 NIV). The ultimate hospitality is extended by God. When Jesus sent his disciples forth, he prepared them to accept hospitality: "Take nothing for the journey.... If people do not welcome you, leave their town and shake the dust off your feet" (Luke 9:3–5 NIV). In the feeding of the 5,000, Christ played the perfect host when he refused to send people away hungry and instead told his disciples, "you give them something to eat" (Luke 9:13 NIV). On the road to Emmaus, the disciples portrayed hospitality when they told the stranger who traveled with them, "Stay with us, for it is nearly evening; the day is almost over" (Luke 24:29 NIV). You know of Christ's hospitality at the Last Supper as he washed his disciples' feet and gave them bread and wine that became the basis of the sacrament of Communion, and which remains the ultimate symbol of hospitality.

Scripture goes so far as to tell us that when we extend hospitality to the stranger or "the least of these," in effect we do it to Christ: "For I was hungry and you gave me something to eat, I was thirsty and you gave me something to drink, I was a stranger and you invited me in, I needed clothes and you clothed me . . . I was in prison and you came to visit me. . . . whatever you did for one of the least of these brothers and sisters of mine, you did for me" (Matt 25:35–40 NIV). Christine Pohl observes that, "The possibility of welcoming Christ as our guest strengthens our kindness and fortitude in responding to strangers" (Pohl 1999, 106).

Peter and the disciples frequently broke bread together (Acts 2: 42–47). Jesus typically would share meals with tax collectors, prostitutes, and other sinners. And who can forget the Good Samaritan who committed the basic acts of kindness and hospitality to a complete stranger, caring for him and binding up his wounds (Luke 10:30–35)? Finally, we are reminded that in the great commandment of "Double Love" Jesus charges us to "Love the Lord your God with all your heart and with all your soul and with all your mind and with all your strength " and "love your neighbor as yourself" (Mark 12: 30–31 NIV).

In our church, we can express hospitality in the way we greet newcomers and visitors, providing coffee and lunch for them, having potluck dinners together, and sharing through our Barnabas Fund for the needy. Hospitality is that which is humanizing and connecting in a relationship.

It provides respite that leads to engagement. Christian evangelicals consider it the essential first step in evangelism. As a church we also need to cultivate hospitable hearts and provide a refuge for the stranger. We need to move over at the table and make room for those who are on the outside (Pohl 1999).

I perceive these ideas to be a mandate. Hospitality is not a frill, an embellishment, or an "add on." Without hospitality we are not a church. Andi Ashworth declares that, "we cannot separate real demonstrations of care from the gospel itself. When we care for people in imaginative, life-giving ways, we embody the love of Jesus. What could be a grander calling?" (Ashworth n.d.).

The Church should be a place of rest and replenishment. It is a place for "Sabbath," for a "time out" from the world. It should be a place where we can ask for what we need, take responsibility for our feelings, respect and appreciate others, enter into the lives of others without losing our own identity, a place where conflict can be resolved, healing can occur, and people can be forgiven.

The idea of hospitality is expressed in the classic Hispanic statement which I'm sure you are familiar with, "Me Casa es su Casa." A couple of years ago Teresa gave me a greeting card which said, "Me Casa es su Casa. Pero me chocolate es me chocolate!" This concept of openness and welcoming is what the Coral Isles Church does well; it is our strength. It is what our church has done historically with our "open membership policy," and our willingness to provide meeting space for Twelve Step programs. The Christian Church has long withheld hospitality from those embracing alternative sexualities. Those suffering from addiction have likewise been sidelined and treated as modern day lepers by many churches. Coral Isles has been a shining beacon in its offering hospitality to these groups. This is what we must reaffirm in this time of transition. And we must become even better at doing it.

This is summed up in the mission statement written by one of my mentors, Donald Guthrie:

> By God's grace,
> We are not what we once were,
> Nor are we yet what we will be.
> But, having been loved with perfect affection,
> Redeemed at great expense,
> And given new life,
> We live well today because today matters
> And eternity awaits. (Guthrie n.d.)

— 39 —

The Keys of the Kingdom[1]

IN MATTHEW 16:19, WE find the provocative promise made by Jesus, "And I will give unto thee the keys of the kingdom of heaven" (KJV). Some of us hear this as saying Jesus will give us the keys "to" the kingdom, but notice he does not say that. He says he gives us the keys "of" the kingdom. What he is giving us is not the way to the destination of heaven, but a design for living that is heavenly right now, a way of true happiness and fulfillment.

The question, then, is how shall we live in a way that is heavenly here on earth, and right now? To answer this question, I want to tell you about a conversation I had last month when I was in Chicago taking one of my post-graduate courses. You should know that I take a lot of guff about being the oldest student in my classes (I am 79). Sometimes I feel like Rodney Dangerfield, the comedian, who would plaintively declare, "I don't get any respect."

The conversation I had was with a fellow doctoral student, John, who is an associate minister of a mega-church near Gary, Indiana. After a class one day he took me aside and asked me what the secret was of staying young, healthy, and happy at my age. Without hesitation, I answered him it was by giving my time, my energy, and my life to others, by investing in relationships. I was surprised at how quickly and clearly the answer came. Then I knew what I was going to preach about when I got back to the Keys and to the Coral Isles Church.

---

1. Sermon delivered by the author at Coral Isles Church, Tavernier, Florida, August 31, 2014. A video of this sermon as originally presented is available online: https://youtu.be/am9d6zlDEXU

All my life I have searched for who I am, I have sought to be good enough, to be fulfilled, to be happy. For years I searched for meaning and self-esteem. Twenty-five years ago, I went on a Methodist church retreat in Upstate New York called "Walk to Emmaus." I'll never forget one of the things I heard there. What I heard was, if you want to feel self-esteem, do esteemable things!

For over half a century I had my priorities wrong; I had it backward. I was guided by self-will and ego. I thought I was the center of the universe, that it was all about me. If I ran into frustration, well . . . people just didn't know who I was; they didn't know who they were dealing with. I had decided at an early age that if I wanted something, if I wanted to accomplish anything, all I had to do was to will it! If that didn't work, then obviously I had not willed it hard enough, and I had to will it harder. It was like having a toolbox with two tools: a hammer—and a bigger hammer. The box had no tool for cutting me down to size. Just tools for hammering and pounding me into other people's lives. You're supposed to ask me, "How did that work out for you?" My answer would be "Poorly." As someone once put it, it was "self-will run riot." And you know what they say about ego: it stands for "Easing God Out."

After trying to live with this model for half a century, I went to a rehab for a major tune-up. Every morning, those of us who were there gathered for a "house meeting," which we began by sharing a personal slogan. One man's slogan was, "Thorns have roses." My slogan was, "Ride the high road." I'll never forget the slogan of another of the members; it was, "I am enough; I have enough." He was declaring that he was complete and whole in himself, he was fine the way he was. How I envied him. I had never felt I had enough; I certainly never felt I was enough. I wondered how in the world can you ever have enough or be enough.

After returning home, I went to an Episcopal church in Upstate New York, where there was a picture on the wall in the dining room. I mentioned it in another sermon here a year or two ago. It was a picture of a large basket with five loaves and two fish. Underneath was a reference to the story of Jesus feeding of the 5,000 that said, "Love is like a basket with five loaves and two fish. There's never enough until you give it away."

Love has a life that replenishes its power. It was always unfathomable to me how Jesus, Mother Teresa, Albert Schweitzer, Gandhi, St. Francis, and other great saints could give so much without running dry. The secret is that real love is drawn from a well of the soul that has no bottom and has no limit to how much it can give. It is like the "bottomless cup of coffee" that some restaurants advertise; it keeps getting refilled. The more you drink, the more you get refilled.

To return to my conversation with my fellow student in Chicago, I realized that along the way I made the decision to invest my life in relationships with people. My children and my grandchildren are my main investment. Sometimes they are surprised how much time I have for them. But what else could possibly be more important? They are my soul. I also take joy in investing in my students and friends who I mentor and sponsor. They are my immortality. And in the last few years I have been blessed to be able to invest my life in a special friend and partner. She is my heart.

One author I read in my post-graduate studies wrote, "the human enterprise is an experiment in love and connection" and "the deepest wisdom and the most profound expression of your experience are rooted in compassion." Compassion means literally *"to be together with someone's pain"* (Heifetz et al. 2002, italics his). The human heart must open and close every second. If it does not open over and over and over, it cannot perform its life-giving function. The question is how we keep our hearts opening in love—not just closing. Surely, we must do this if we are to live.

There is an allegory about the two seas in Palestine. One is the Dead Sea. The water is stagnant, brackish, and foul. Nothing grows there. There are no fish; there are no trees or vegetation near it. People shun it; travelers go out of their way to avoid it. And, then, there is the Sea of Galilee. Its water is pure and sparkling, full of fish, with trees and flowers bordering it. Children play near its banks and it is a joy to all who visit it. What accounts for the difference between the Dead Sea and the Sea of Galilee? The difference is not in the source of the water that flows into them: Both are fed by the Jordan River. The difference is that the Dead Sea has no outlet; every drop of water that flows into it is kept and hoarded and does not flow on. The Sea of Galilee, in contrast, has an outlet. For every drop of water that flows in, water flows out. One sea is stagnant and dead. The other sea gives freely and is alive.

Which do you want to be? Do you want to have a richer, fuller life that is filled with more and more love? Then freely give what you have, and it will be replenished. The paradox is that the more you give the more you will have.

There was one man in my life, significantly named Francis, who epitomized this principle more than anyone I have ever known. He mentored hundreds of people, kept their birthdays and anniversaries in countless address books, and sent out greeting cards every few days. Like a chief of state, his phone was at his elbow for making and receiving calls. He lived a life of service and love of others. He truly paid it forward. Although poor by material standards, he was rich in heart and soul. He invested his time and life in the lives of people, and it returned to him amazing dividends of serenity and peace.

He contracted and died of cancer of the esophagus. Toward the end of his life I took him aside one day, looked him in the eye, and asked, "Francis, what can I ever do to repay you?" Without hesitation, he replied simply, "Pass it on." At first, I thought he was in fact telling me how to repay him. But I soon recognized that he did not need or want repayment. Instead, he was giving me his final and greatest gift. He was sharing with me the secret of having a full and happy life, the happiness that can only come from caring and investing in others.

He was giving me the Keys. The Keys of the Kingdom. The Keys of the Kingdom of God.

― 40 ―

The Kingdom of God[1]

History tells us there was a man born 2,000 years ago who lived in an inconspicuous village, in a subjugated country, which is one of the poorest and smallest nations of the world. By almost all standards his life ended prematurely and a failure. His ministry, which began at 30, was no more than three years. He was forsaken by his friends and disciples, and his broken body was sealed in a borrowed tomb. Yet this man called Jesus became the most influential person in the course of history, and today commands a response from hundreds of millions of people.

What did Jesus teach and what did he stand for? One of the most obvious things was the commandment of love. "Love one another," he said. When a lawyer asked him what the greatest commandment was, he answered, "Thou shalt love the Lord thy God with all thy heart, with all thy soul, and with all thy mind" and "Thou shalt love thy neighbor as thyself. On these two commandments hang all the law and the prophets" (Matt 22:37–40 KJV). And in the Book of John, "A new commandment I give unto you, That ye love one another; as I have loved you, that ye also love one another" (John 13:34 KJV).

Yet there is something else Jesus taught and stood for besides love, and this something else is mentioned in the Bible at least twice as many times as love. This "something else" is what almost every parable is devoted to. This "something else" is what Jesus called the "Kingdom of God."

---

1. Sermon delivered by the author at Coral Isles Church, Tavernier, Florida, on April 21, 2013. A video of this sermon as originally presented is available online: https://youtu.be/19Bh-9MbNrs

What did Jesus mean by "the Kingdom of God"? Probably no two scholars or pastors agree. Recently our church's Bible study group, based on Marcus Borg's book *Evolution of the Word* considered how the Book of Mark treats the idea of the Kingdom of God as the imminent end of the world. Mark 9:1 is cited: "Truly, I tell you, some who are standing here will not taste death before they see that the kingdom of God has come with power" (NIV). Borg continues, "obviously they were wrong—it didn't happen" (Borg 1989, 155).

There is, however, an alternate view of the Kingdom of God that is expressed in the Book of Luke. The New Revised Standard Version reads:

> Once Jesus was asked by the Pharisees when the kingdom of God was coming, and he answered, "The kingdom of God is not coming with things that can be observed; nor will they say, 'Look here it is!' or 'There it is!' For, in fact, the kingdom of God is among you." (Luke 17:20–21 NRSV)

But I prefer the King James Version:

> And when he was demanded of the Pharisees, when the kingdom of God should come, he answered them and said, the kingdom of God cometh not with observation: Neither shall they say, Lo here! Or lo there! for, behold, the kingdom of God is within you. (Luke 17:20–21 KJV)

This alternative view of the Kingdom of God refers to an inward state or spiritual condition, if you will, that seems to be what Jesus is suggesting in this passage.

What is this Kingdom of God that is "within you"? What is the essence of this inner spiritual experience? For me, it is the giving up of self-will, self-centeredness, selfishness, ego, pride, and grandiosity; and the cultivation of God-consciousness, humility, love, and giving. The Kingdom of God is knowing that this is not our world, but God's world. The Kingdom of God is being content with our lot. It is the sense of being enough and having enough. It is in seeing our glass half-full, not half-empty. It is gratitude and serenity and inner peace. As St. Francis prayed, "make me a channel of Thy peace" (St. Francis n.d.).

The Kingdom of God is not living in fear of life but being in love with it. An unknown author once said, "Fear knocked at the door. Faith answered. And no one was there." Truly, we have nothing to fear but fear itself. Perfect love casts out fear. It is said, people fear two things: losing what they have; or not getting what they want. If we have a sense of well-being with what we have, a sense of abundance, then we have no reason to fear.

The spiritual way of life is knowing that our needs and our wants are not this same thing. Our wants are not our needs—they will always exceed our needs. Our true needs are relatively few, and somehow they are always met.

The spiritual way of life is one of trust: trusting God, trusting significant others in our lives, and ultimately learning to trust and love ourselves. The Kingdom of God is not having to punish or beat up on ourselves, nor being our own worst enemy. It is not in making ourselves into victims, unhappy and miserable. It is avoiding the deliberate manufacture of misery.

It is learning to make healthy choices, set appropriate boundaries, and surround ourselves with positive, loving people. It is eating enough of the right things, and not eating too much of the wrong things. It is getting enough rest and exercise. It is having fun. It is being in love. The Kingdom of God is loving animals and knowing that in doing so we reach out and touch the hem of God's garment.

It is in loving the ocean, and the mountains, and the forests. It is in caring for this planet. It is enjoying the sun and the rain, the moon and the stars, the sunrise and the sunset, the wind and the calm. It is being at home in the universe. It is as described on the tombstone of two astronomers, husband and wife, "We have loved the stars too fondly to be fearful of the night" (Williams 1936).

It is in studying and learning and keeping our minds active, for there is always something more to learn. The Kingdom of God is in choosing the right attitude, no matter what life's circumstances. It is in remembering that what matters is not what happens to us, but how we let it affect us.

It is letting God in and finding out that God is already there. It is in having Christ knock at the door and seeing that the doorknob is not on his side but on our side of the door. It is being grateful to our family of origin for doing the best they could, and trying to be an even better parent and friend for our children. It is remembering that our children and grandchildren are our connection to the future, a future we cannot enter; that they are our immortality.

The Kingdom of God is in being as much as possible a loving person, a friend to those in need. It is not in judging but in accepting and forgiving. It is in caring less about what others think of us and thinking more of how we can care for others.

It is not being anxious for tomorrow, but letting today's trouble be sufficient for today. It is not living and dying and going to heaven, but living is if we are already in heaven. It is not holding onto what we have been so freely given, but in "passing it on." It is in knowing that these are the Keys, the Keys to the Kingdom, the Keys to the Kingdom of God. Amen.

— 41 —

Prayer[1]

IT IS SAID THAT church is a house of prayer. I have heard prayer defined as the "way we talk to God." I once saw a quotation on a sign in the front of a church that said, "Prayer doesn't change things. Prayer changes people, and people change things."

In our church we pray every Sunday morning. There are different kinds of prayer: Praise, Forgiveness, Intercession, and Thanksgiving. In our service, we have a prayer of petition for those who are suffering and ill. We then conclude with The Lord's Prayer. We keep a prayer list and are encouraged to pray for the people on it during the week. When we meet in small groups at the church, such as the Abundance group or Bible Study, we usually pray before we begin our discussion, and often pray again before we go home.

A.A. and Al-Anon meetings in our church always start with a prayer, usually the "Serenity Prayer," and generally end with "The Lord's Prayer." So whatever else churches do, they are about prayer. We do a lot of it around here, and therefore I think it is important that we try to understand it and do the best job we can with it.

What part does prayer play in your religious life? I try to pray every day, usually in the morning when I am walking Maxwell. Theodore Parker, a Unitarian minister and abolitionist from the nineteenth century, put it this way:

---

1. Sermon given by the author at Coral Isles Church, Tavernier, Florida, June 30, 2013. A video of this sermon as originally presented is available online: https://youtu.be/jqG-KfFwfOs

> The natural attitude of my mind has always been prayerful.... A snatch of such feeling passes through me as I walk in the streets, or engage in any work. I sing prayers when I loiter in the woods, or travel the quiet road. (Frothingham 1874, 336)

One form of prayer that has come to me naturally is what is called "aspiratory prayer," that is repeating a short prayer with every breath taken in, and another prayer with every breath out, such as "God in, Anxiety out." Try making up your own. Another I have used is a little longer, "God I love you and trust you. Thank you for loving and forgiving me." That's probably about the maximum length for an "aspiratory prayer."

I used to kneel when I prayed, and that was important to me. I would even kneel in church. Two spinal surgeries later, I pray while sitting with head bowed. I think God understands.

I started praying as a young boy when my father was in Europe during World War II, so it was not unusual for me to think of God as a sort of substitute father, a replacement Dad if you will. Actually, this is quite consistent with New Testament theology, where Jesus uses the term "Abba" when addressing God.

There was a man I knew when I first moved to Key Largo, who used to say that in his prayers he "practiced the presence of God" (Brother Lawrence 1982). This concept came from a medieval monk named Brother Lawrence. A contemporary writer explains it in this way: we need to "make a chapel of our heart where we can retire from time to time to commune with Him, peacefully, humbly, lovingly" (Foster 1992, 124). We need to learn what Kepler meant by "thinking God's thoughts after him" (Kepler 2014).

What does prayer do? As the sign in front of the church said, I don't think prayer changes things. It would be self-centered and egotistical to think that. And it is doubtful if prayer really changes God's mind. We are simply not that important or powerful.

Why pray, then? It expresses our trust in God. It leads to deeper fellowship with God, and it allows us to somehow be involved in activities that are eternally important. Richard Foster said, "We pass from thinking of God as a part of our life . . . to the realization that we are a part of his life" (Foster 1992, 15). "What can you tell God if he knows everything," another writer asks. According to Western logic the answer is, "Nothing." According to Jesus, "Anything" (Hunter 1986, 42). And according to me, "Everything."

A theme which Bonnie touches upon often in her sermons is that we don't always know why things happen, why bad things happen in particular, but one thing that is certain is that God doesn't let us go through it alone, that He is always with us. I think that is an important emphasis of her ministry. Whatever we suffer, as Henri Nouwen promises, "we belong to a loving God who will never leave us alone" (Nouwen 1992, 72). In the Book of Hebrews God says simply, "I will never leave thee, nor forsake thee" (Heb 13:5 KJV).

An aspect of prayer that churches don't seem to pay much attention to these days is Fasting. I think the practice of moderate fasting can increase our focus, our sense of humility and dependence on God. Fasting is a form of discipline and sacrifice; bodily hunger can remind us of our deeper spiritual hunger.

Another form of prayer that churches don't make much use of is the Prayer of Lament or Lamentation, which is very strong and poignant, often a fitting and appropriate response to tragedy in life. The Prayer of Lament cries out, as Job and Jonah did, "Woe is me." It is a cry from deep within our souls, an outpouring of our suffering and pain to God. It can be a Prayer of Tears. Finally, we are so preoccupied with talking and trying to fix things, that we often overlook the power of silence, which can be considered as fasting from words.

In talking about the prayers in our church in Twelve Step meetings, I mentioned the use of the Serenity Prayer. Attributed to Protestant theologian Reinhold Niebuhr, it is an excellent and sometimes neglected prayer that we can all make use of. Here it is in complete or "long form":

> God grant me the serenity
> To accept the things I cannot change;
> Courage to change the things I can;
> And wisdom to know the difference.
> Living one day at a time;
> Enjoying one moment at a time;
> Accepting hardships as the pathway to peace;
> Taking, as He did, this sinful world
> As it is, not as I would have it;
> Trusting that He will make all things right
> If I surrender to His Will;
> That I may be reasonably happy in this life
> And supremely happy with Him
> Forever in the next. Amen. (Niebuhr 2010)

I have learned that it is all-important in our prayers of petition to try not to pray for specific things or outcomes. There is a saying, "You have to be careful about what you pray for. You might get it!" Seriously, we need to avoid being in a position of going to God with a wish list, as if he is some sort of a cosmic Santa Claus. God is not our codependent. Prayer is not our time to manipulate God, but his opportunity to align us. In quiet, we commune with Someone who loves us and is always there for us, willing to go through it with us, to help us find our way.

Instead of asking for specific things, I have learned it is important to pray for God's will, as the Serenity Prayer suggests. The Lord's Prayer also prays, "Thy will be done on earth, as it is in heaven." One writer said we should add to a prayer of petition, "Nevertheless if I am wrong in asking this, and if this is not pleasing to you, then do as seems best in your sight" (Grudem 1994, 383). Another author states that we must not pray to try to "get what you want. . . . People must learn to want what they get. . . . How old must we be before we begin to realize that even prayer can't get us everything we want" (Hunter 1986, 61).

It follows that some prayers will be unanswered and that sometimes the answer will be "No." One theologian said:

> No matter how large a spiritual giant you may become, there will be days when God's answer to your prayers will be no. Despite your seeking, searching and outpouring of your soul, your heavenly Father has decided against your petition . . . "Have thine own way, Lord." (Hunter 1986, 65)

Perhaps we have a bit of growing up to do. If nothing else, it may be that our prayers can help us grow up, get real, or just get over it. It may be that is the best gift that God can give us. It may be that is the best discovery we can make in our prayers, that life is not all about us. There are others who matter, too. And there is a loving God who matters most of all. That it is not our world, but God's world.

I said also that we need to get "real." In the story *The Velveteen Rabbit* there is a conversation one night in the children's nursery between two toys, the rabbit and the "Skin Horse." The rabbit doesn't want to be just a toy anymore; he wants to be "real." The old Skin Horse, who has been around for a long time, has somehow managed to become "real."

The rabbit enviously asks the Skin Horse what it means to be "real." The Skin Horse answers in words that have a universal application:

"Real isn't how you are made," said the Skin Horse. "It's a thing that happens to you. When a child loves you for a long, long time, not just to play with, but really loves you, then you become real." "Does it hurt?" asked the rabbit. "Sometimes," said the Skin Horse, for he was always truthful. "When you are real you don't mind being hurt. . . . It doesn't happen all at once," said the Skin Horse. "You become. It takes a long time. That's why it doesn't often happen to people who break easily, or have sharp edges, or have to be carefully kept. Generally, by the time you are real, most of your hair has been loved off, and your eyes drop out, and you get loose in the joints and very shabby. But these things don't matter at all, because once you are Real, you can't be ugly, except the people who don't understand." (Williams 1997, 12–13)

God loves us with an everlasting love. It doesn't happen all at once. And so, we become. It takes a long time. We change slowly. As with the Skin Horse and the Velveteen Rabbit, we become real—and then can't be ugly anymore.

– 42 –

Spirituality[1]

THEOLOGIAN WALTER BRUEGGEMANN IDENTIFIED three parts of the Old Testament, which correspond to three phases of spirituality. The first part of the Bible is the Torah, in which the people of Israel are given identity and a sense of being chosen through law, tradition, and ritual. This section of the Old Testament corresponds with our childhood, in which we are given containment, security, and a sense of being special. In short, we learn that we are loved. This may be referred to as a secure attachment style that forms the basis of our future relationships as adults, as opposed to an anxious, dismissive, or fearful attachment style.

The second part of the Old Testament is the Prophets, who recognize the dark side of life and pronounce judgment upon it. This part corresponds with our time of spiritual turmoil, when we undergo rebellion and conflict. The third section of Hebrew Scripture is referred to as Wisdom Literature—Psalms, Ecclesiastes, the Song of Songs, and the Book of Job. This part of the Old Testament parallels the period in our lives when our spirituality is strong enough to hold together our contradictions with tolerance, compassion, and forgiveness. We realize that our being chosen is for the purpose of letting others know they are chosen too.

So, the sequence of the Old Testament and of life is order—disorder—reorder. Hopefully, in life we achieve a sense of being chosen and loved. Then comes the inevitable time of being challenged, criticized, perhaps even rejected. Finally, we come to a time of reorder, characterized by forgiveness, love, and acceptance.

---

1. Sermon delivered by the author at Coral Isles Church, Tavernier, Florida, on August 21, 2016.

Spirituality

Spirituality is something many of us seek. Its characteristics are a sense of being free, overwhelming gratitude, and a sense of humility as we rejoin humanity. It is marked by honesty, openness, forgiveness, and the capacity to love and to be of service to others. That, my friends, is why we are told by the Psalmist that we must walk through the valley of the shadow of death. A vital way to fully appreciate and savor the glory of life and love is by experiencing loss. It is only then that we have something to offer others and can be of value to them. And life is about giving and serving others. Life is a symphony, like the waves washing upon the beach. First, the sand is undisturbed; then the wave comes and brings surge and commotion; finally it recedes, and all is smooth and calm until the next wave.

When I moved to the Florida Keys in 1994, I felt like it was the fulfillment of a lifelong dream, a prophecy. As is said in the 139th Psalm that Teresa read this morning:

> If I take the wings of the morning, and dwell in the uttermost parts of the sea;
> Even there shall thy hand lead me, and thy right hand shall hold me.
> If I say, Surely the darkness shall cover me; even the night shall be light about me.
> Yea, the darkness hideth not from thee; but the night shineth as the day: the darkness and the light are both alike to thee.
> For thou hast possessed my reins: thou hast covered me in my mother's womb....
> How precious also are thy thoughts unto me, O God! how great is the sum of them!
> If I should count them, they are more in number than the sand: when I awake, I am still with thee....
> Search me, O God, and know my heart: try me, and know my thoughts.
> (Ps 139:9–23 KJV)

Ernest Kurtz was the leading historian of A.A. Interestingly, Kurtz was not an alcoholic, but when he did his PhD dissertation at Harvard University, he chose the history of A.A. as his subject. His dissertation became a best seller titled, *Not-God*. He also coauthored a book titled, *The Spirituality of Imperfection* (Kurtz and Ketcham 2002).

In addition to his research at the Alcoholics Anonymous archives in New York City, Kurtz had to seek out and attend a lot of A.A. meetings to learn about his subject. One of my favorite stories was when he told of arriving late to a church basement where the A.A. and Al-Anon meetings were held (Al-Anon is a group for spouses and families of alcoholics). The meetings had already started, and the doors were closed. Kurtz didn't know which room was A.A. and which was Al-Anon. Finally, he heard a burst of laughter through the door of one room, and he knew that was the A.A. meeting. He observed that people in the Al-Anon room didn't have much to laugh about!

He once told the difference between therapy and spirituality: "Therapy offers explanations; spirituality offers forgiveness" (Kurtz and Ketcham 2002, 27). Kurtz tells why sinners are closer to God than saints: "God . . . holds each person by a string. When you sin, you cut the string. Then God ties it again, making a knot—bringing you a little closer to him. Again and again, your sins cut the string—and with each further knot God keeps drawing you closer" (Kurtz and Ketcham 2002, 29).

An American tourist visited a famous Polish rabbi. The rabbi's home was just a simple room with books. The only furniture was a table and bench. "Rabbi, where is your furniture?" "Where is yours?" asked the rabbi. "Mine? But I'm only a visitor here." "So am I," said the rabbi (Kurtz and Ketcham 2002, 34). A preacher asked a class of children, "If all the good people in the world were red and all the bad people were green, what color would you be? Little Linda thought for a moment and said, "Reverend, I'd be streaky" (Kurtz and Ketcham 2002, 56).

My best friend told me to change. Then one day he said, "Don't change, I love you just as you are." I relaxed and I came alive. And suddenly I changed. Now I know I couldn't really change until I found someone who would love me whether I changed or not. We find miracles only when we stop looking for magic. As T. S. Eliot said:

> We shall not cease from exploration
> And the end of all our exploring
> Will be to arrive where we started
> And know the place for the first time (Eliot n.d.).

When a man comes to you and tells you your own story, you know that your sins are forgiven (Kurtz and Ketcham 2002, 67), and when you are forgiven, you are healed. The Sufi tell this story:

> Past the seeker, as he prayed, came the crippled and the beggar and the beaten. And seeing them, the holy one went down into deep prayer and cried, "Great God, how is it that a loving creator can see such things and yet do nothing about them?" And out

of the long silence, God said, "I did do something about them. I made you." (Kurtz and Ketcham 2002, 81)

"What do you think of the world to come?" An admirer asked Thoreau. "One world at a time," Thoreau replied (Phillips 2009).

— 43 —

The Least of These[1]

SEVERAL YEARS AGO, WE held a discussion group on Henri Nouwen's book *Life of the Beloved*, first published in 1992 just a few years before Nouwen died (Nouwen 1992). Sometimes people ask me what the source is of my interest and caring for people. This book has influenced me perhaps more than any other single work, so much so that I want to talk about Nouwen's point of view and how it applies to our lives and to the life of our church.

Henri Nouwen was a Dutch-born Roman Catholic Jesuit priest, who wrote dozens of books. He taught at Yale and at Notre Dame University. He was a theologian and a renowned spiritual leader for Protestants as well as Catholics. Yet toward the end of his life, he turned his back on the world of academia and accepted a humble position as chaplain at L'Arche Community in Toronto, a home for mentally retarded young adults. There he lived out his days loving and ministering to those that had been all but forgotten by the world and in some cases even by their families.

It was at this point in his life that he wrote his classic book, *Life of the Beloved*. The text or Scripture for the book is Mark 1:11. It is the well-known story of the baptism of Jesus. You have heard it before: Christ goes to his cousin, John the Baptist, and asks him to baptize him in the Jordan River. John is reluctant at first, but then agrees, and Jesus is submerged in the river. As he comes to the surface of the water and opens his eyes, he has a remarkable experience. As the Book of Mark says:

1. Sermon delivered by the author at Coral Isles Church, Tavernier, Florida, on June 28, 2015.

> And it came to pass in those days, that Jesus came from Nazareth of Galilee, and was baptized of John in Jordan. And straightway coming up out of the water, he saw the heavens opened, and the Spirit like a dove descending upon him: And there came a voice from heaven, saying, Thou art my beloved Son, in whom I am well pleased. (Mark 1:9–11 KJV)

The thesis of Nouwen's book is that being God's beloved child is not a unique status reserved for Jesus: We are all God's beloved children in whom he is well-pleased. Being God's beloved is the most intimate truth about us. Self-rejection is the enemy of the spiritual life. Being God's beloved expresses the core truth about our existence. As Nouwen says, "We are intimately loved long before our parents, teachers, spouses, children, and friends loved or wounded us" (Nouwen 1992, 36).

As a Catholic priest, Nouwen is well familiar with the sacrament of Communion. He says that our lives as God's beloved parallel the stages of Communion. The first step in Communion is that the bread is chosen or taken. So, too, in our lives we have been chosen by God. As he says, "Long before we were born and became a part of history, you existed in God's heart. . . . The world persists in its efforts to pull us into the darkness of self-doubt, low self-esteem, self-rejection and depression" (Nouwen 1992, 54). You "have to keep unmasking the world about you for what it is. . . . These feelings, strong as they may be, are not telling me the truth about myself" (Nouwen 1992, 59). We need to "celebrate our chosenness constantly" (Nouwen 1992, 86).

We all experience difficult things in life. "Why me?" we ask. As the title of a bestseller says, *When Bad Things Happen to Good People* (Kushner 1981). We have a choice: we can decide whether to be grateful or to be bitter. As a friend in a Twelve Step program put it, "It's not what happens to you that matters. It's how you let it affect you."

So, we are chosen. The second step of Communion and of life itself is that we are blessed. The priest or minister holds up the bread and blesses it. So, too, in life we are in need of blessing, an ongoing blessing. As Nouwen says, "I am increasingly aware of how much we fearful, anxious, insecure human beings are in need of a blessing" (Nouwen 1992, 68). Many people suffer from a sense of being cursed. If you had the luck I've had, or if you have had the disadvantages I've had, or if you came from the kind of family I came from, you'd have problems too. Often people say good things about us; we need to cultivate the presence of hearing and being encouraged by others. Nouwen says prayer is a way of listening to blessing. And we need to learn how to hear and how to say positive things about ourselves.

In the sacrament of Communion, after the bread is chosen and blessed, something else is necessary before it is passed out. The third step of Communion—and of life itself—is that the bread is broken. And paradoxically, we must also be broken before we can be given to others, before we have credibility and experience that will be useful to them. As human beings we have all been broken in different ways, we are all imperfect. Nouwen says, "Our brokenness reveals something about who we are. Each of us suffers in a way no other does...." He goes on to say, "Inner brokenness of the heart . . . is often most painfully experienced with respect to our sexuality" (Nouwen 1992, 87–90).

Something not widely known about Henri Nouwen is that he was gay, celibate because he was a priest, but he struggled throughout his life with his homosexuality. Perhaps there is a special appropriateness for discussing Nouwen on this Sunday following the Supreme Court's decision legalizing same-sex marriages throughout the United States.

We all experience brokenness. What do we do with this brokenness? Nouwen says that rather than deny or suppress our brokenness, we must accept it. As he says, "We must face it squarely and be-friend it . . . We must make our most feared enemy into a friend" (Nouwen 1992, 93). We thus put our brokenness "under the blessing." It is sometimes tempting to explain our brokenness as a confirmation of a curse we feel we are under, but we must realize that our brokenness can be a way of "being purified, pruned and disciplined" (Nouwen 1992, 99). One of the most profound things about Twelve Step programs in overcoming addiction is that the wounds of addiction are accepted as an essential part of the fabric of our lives that can be used to help others.

In Communion, only after the bread is broken, can it be passed out or given to others. Perhaps also only after we have been broken, do we have something worthwhile that can be given to others. As Nouwen says, life is "giving ourselves to others in our brokenness" (Nouwen 1992, 109). Thus, curiously we become bread or food for another, and are able to nurture them. Our life itself is our greatest gift: our "friendship, kindness, patience, joy, peace, forgiveness, gentleness, love, hope, trust. . . ." (Nouwen 1992, 14).

As I grow older, I have come to realize that life is never about not making mistakes. Being perfect, even if it was possible, is not all that it's cracked up to be. Instead, life is about being secure and happy, coming to love ourselves in what Nouwen terms our "brokenness." Nor do I need to be in the company of perfect people who have it all together. Because I don't think they exist, or if they did, they wouldn't be much fun. I remember the story about the man who was searching for the perfect woman. He went to his friend and said, "I found her. I found the perfect woman!" "Where is she?" the friend replied as he looked around. "She's out there looking for the perfect man," he replied.

Recently, Teresa and I had a conversation about getting along with people who are troubled and seem to have more than their share of problems. How do you relate to people that fall into this category? I think Henri Nouwen would have had an answer. Just as Nouwen said, we need to be-friend ourselves in our brokenness, I think he would say, we need to be-friend others in their brokenness. That is, after all, what makes them the most interesting. Kahlil Gibran said, "The only time a juggler appeals to me is when I see him miss the ball" (Gibran n.d.). We need to seek out and be-friend those who are eccentric and different, those who may annoy us, those even who can be troubling and disturbing.

Nouwen did this when he went to L'Arche Community and became the friend and chaplain to the handicapped and retarded. Christ did it when he met the Samaritan woman at the well, or touched blind men and lepers, or sat at the same table with prostitutes and tax collectors. And we can do it too. We can do it with others, even those within our own church who are different than we are. Let us learn how to be-friend them, as we learn to be-friend ourselves just as we are, in our brokenness and humanity. For, after all, this is the way God created us. And just for today—let us try not to say that we know better than God.

— 44 —

The Meaning of Pain[1]

GOOD MORNING, MY FRIENDS. It is six weeks to the day that Hurricane Irma paid us a visit. Pastor Kerby has dealt with this at length. The Sunday after the storm, we had a special service when we shared personal experiences and feelings. We have had a lot of cleanup to do at our homes and here at church, including repair of the steeple and clearing of fallen trees. Our church's back porch roof is still "missing in action." We have received remarkable help from others both inside and outside United Church of Christ, and our church has likewise made a significant contribution to the recovery of the Upper Keys.

In short, we have had the chance to start to get our lives and homes back together. As the mountains of trash start to recede, we begin to get back to normal. We now have the luxury and opportunity to reflect on the events of the last two months. We are in a position to take a deep breath and answer the question, "What happened?" I don't know how many of you watch Fareed Zakaria on CNN, but this is my chance to give you "My Take."

The first thing apparent after a storm like Irma in Florida—or Harvey in Houston or Maria in Puerto Rico—is that we have seen and felt the unleashed power of Nature or God, if you will. It is a true lesson in humility, of how limited and finite we are, and how powerful God and Nature are. Ultimately, there is little we can do in the face of that power. About all we can do, is get out of the way, and then return to pick up the pieces.

---

1. Sermon by the author at Coral Isles Church, Tavernier, Florida, on October 22, 2017. A video of this sermon as originally presented is available online: https://youtu.be/to4YscgL1-Q

As human beings, we respond with our emotions and minds, with our anxiety and our fears, and with our courage and our faith. One thing is clear for those of us in Florida, or Texas, or Puerto Rico: We have been deeply traumatized. We have experienced a form of PTSS (Post Traumatic Storm Syndrome). We have been reminded of our human frailty and vulnerability. As a result, we are a little less confident, a little less smug, a little less in control. And we are a lot more dependent on other people than we thought. We take their help and support less for granted. We become appreciative of simple things. We become friendlier and closer to our neighbors, and we become bonded to them in a special way. We become more conscious of our interdependence on each other.

Storms like Irma help us get in touch with deeper issues such as the meaning of pain and suffering. What do we mean by pain? The most important thing to say about pain is that it is not only physical. Pain can be mental, emotional, and spiritual as well. There can be the pain of not liking ourselves. There can be pain in not being liked, or cared for, or loved by others. There is pain of not being forgiven. There is pain of rejection, of being punished. There is the pain of loss from the hurricane. There is the pain of being alone.

We all experience emotional, even social pain early in life. We can react to pain by fight or flight. We become not only afraid, but angry. We want to "get even." We'll show them. They can't do this to us. They don't know who they're dealing with—especially the insurance companies. Opposite of fight is flight. We run away, we refuse to engage, we become passive-aggressive. Who needs them anyway? They can't treat us that way!

We may choose to be alone, feeling there is protection in isolation. Others will never get a chance to hurt me again. That won't happen to me again. I'll put my house on the market and move to the mountains in the Carolinas, far from hurricanes. Then we feel a different kind of pain, the pain of being alone and abandoned. The pain of isolation, of not being good enough.

We experience a deeper pain—fear. The fear of not being loved, and of not being lovable, the fear of being alone, even the fear of being lonely. Protected, but at what price? We become isolated from others. The fear is not of the bad things that have happened, but of the bad things that might happen in the future. Fear of losing our home, our stuff. We become depressed. Depression is pain turned inward, and some of us have experienced depression after the hurricane.

When the pain is constant, unrelenting, when it is not only physical but social, it becomes acute and mutates into suffering. We all experience pain; only some of us suffer. You may have heard the expression, "Pain is inevitable; suffering is optional." Some of us, however, become "experienced sufferers." I'm not going to forget Irma; I'm going to continue to relive it for years and years. I'll be a martyr!

What is religion's answer to all of this? Does Christianity have anything to say about pain and suffering? Actually, it does. In a sense, Christianity is as much about the human as the divine condition, and it is as much about the meaning of pain as the meaning of joy. Christianity is a religion that was designed originally for people who were oppressed, hopeless, and hurting, both socially and physically. In traditional Christianity, the emphasis has been about an "after-life" where regardless of the pain and suffering of this life, we will be rewarded with comfort and bliss for eternity.

Although this is not the view of most churches today, Christianity at its best has been about healing and recovery. Christ was noted for his miracles of healing: the blind man, the cripple, the leper, the story of the Good Samaritan, the hurting woman taken in adultery. He is remembered for his friendship with the outcast and rejected—the tax collectors, the Sadducees and Pharisees. As he declared, "Come to me, all who labor and are heavy laden, and I will give you rest" (Matt 11:28 RSV).

The story of Jesus' life is a story about healing people, of touching them and removing their pain—the man possessed by demons, the leper, the blind man, the cripple. Some of Jesus' most memorable sayings are about dealing with suffering: "He has appointed me to preach good news to the poor. He has sent me to proclaim release to the captives and recovering of sight to the blind" (Luke 4:18 RSV).

Christianity offers an even deeper moral about pain and suffering. Although I have reservations about the theology, I have heard this deeper moral expressed something like this: Even after creating man and woman, infinite and all-powerful God, still could not understand what it was really like to be human. The only way he could do this was to become human and fully vulnerable himself, which he did through Jesus. Being all-powerful, Christ could have avoided arrest and death and crucifixion. But choosing to become vulnerable, Jesus elected to suffer the pain of an outrageous death, so he could fully experience and understand what it was like to be one of us. That is a moving narrative.

Being human means being vulnerable, getting sick, hurting, feeling pain, and dying. It means experiencing hurricanes and storms, and earthquakes and wildfires and floods. But it also means growing, being courageous, not being defined by the pain, but miraculously rising above it. Kahlil Gibran puts it succinctly, "The deeper that sorrow carves into your being, the more joy you can contain" (Gibran 1942, 35). Pain deepens our capacity to care, to empathize with others. Through it we enter into fellowship with fellow sufferers. For the first time, we can truly understand and identify with them. We have paid the admission price; we have joined the human race.

We come to understand that "they" are "us." We transcend fear with faith. We finally realize, with Arnold Crompton, "All that God loves he constantly is healing, and when we are broken beyond the power of our love and skill to mend, the Divine hand is laid upon us and Lo, the unequal struggle ends and the peace that passes all understanding touches our weariness like all the mother love of the world, and he lifts us up in his wonderful arms and bears us across the waters of Remembrance" (Hudson 1962; Adapted from Fairless 1905, 24).

— 45 —

The Sun Also Rises (*Koinonia*)[1]

LAST WEEK WE TALKED about the reality and the meaning of hitting bottom in life. We referred to this by the Greek term *kenosis,* the experience of being emptied out. We said it is from this point that we begin to truly grow. We mentioned that this emptying out can sometimes feel like "The Dark Night of the Soul," as John of the Cross described it (John of the Cross 2003). But the good news is, as the title of Hemingway's book suggests, "the sun also rises" (Eccl 1:5 KJV).

Today we focus on another theological concept. It refers to the principal way that we become fulfilled and grow. We do this through God's love. And I believe we find God's love and presence in fellowship and community with one another. God's love through such fellowship is found in our churches, in recovery fellowships, in families, and in all close and loving relationships. And you will be happy to know there is another Greek term that refers to the empowerment of fellowship. Are you ready? It is *koinonia*. One of my mentors, Jim Van Yperen, considers the derivation of the word: "Community, communion, and communicate all come from the same Greek root word, *koinonia*, meaning to 'hold things in common,' or 'joint participation,' most commonly translated as 'fellowship'" (Van Yperen 2002, 203).

After creating man, God observed, "It is not good for the man to be alone" (Gen 2:18 NIV). Significantly, the only thing in all creation not good is man on his own. Trying to live in the image of God (imago

---

1. Sermon by the author at Coral Isles Church, Tavernier, Florida, on January 13, 2019. A video of this sermon as originally presented is available online: https://youtu.be/SBoV-kgxtkg

Dei) means being in relationship with each other: "The image of God is a relational image," Michael Hardin declares, "We, together, constitute the image of God. As isolated individuals, we are but a fracture of that image. To be made in the image of God is to be made in relationship" (Hardin 1994, 49).

When asked when the Kingdom of God was coming Jesus answered, "The kingdom of God is in the midst of you" (Luke 17:21 RSV). God is in relationship. In a mystical sense, he is relationship itself. This is a reason that Jesus gathered together a group of disciples. Fellowship was also significant to the apostle Paul, whose "band of brothers" included Prisca and Aquila, Urbanus, Timothy, Epaphroditus, Euodia, Syntyche, Clement, Epaphras, Tychicus, Archippus, and Phoebe.

Clearly, God is in community and fellowship. Gerald G. May, author of *Addiction and Grace,* testifies to the value of the "lasting steadiness" of communities of faith: "When I cannot pray, the prayer of countless others goes on. Where I am complacent, others are struggling. Where I am in conflict, others are at peace. Most important, when I cannot act in loving ways, there are those in my communities who can" (May 1991, 175).

An Episcopal clergyman, Samuel Shoemaker, testifies to the value of community in spiritual growth:

> From the first, Christ drew about Him a company. To join Him, you had also to join that company. The church has always been a scratch company of sinners. It is not the best people in the community gathered together for self-congratulation; it is the people who know they have a great need gathered to find its answer in worship toward God and fellowship with one another. The church is not a museum; it is a hospital. (Alcoholics Anonymous World Services 1957, 268)

From their inception, Twelve Step groups such as Alcoholics Anonymous intuitively grasped the value of fellowship. The Preamble of A.A. states, "Alcoholics Anonymous is a fellowship of men and women who share their experience, strength and hope with each other that they may solve their common problem and help others to recover from alcoholism" (*A.A. Grapevine* 2013). The book *Alcoholics Anonymous* offers this assurance:

> Life will take on new meaning. To watch people recover, to see them help others, to watch loneliness vanish, to see a fellowship grow up about you, to have a host of friends—this is an

experience you must not miss. We know you will not want to miss it. Frequent contact with newcomers and with each other is the bright spot of our lives. (Alcoholics Anonymous World Services 2001, 89)

In 1940, a New York philanthropist observed A.A.'s practice of abstinence and fasting from alcohol, daily meetings for prayer and edification, seeking God's will, breaking bread together, mutual encouragement, and fellowship. He declared flatly, "Why, this is first century Christianity" (Alcoholics Anonymous World Services 1984, 184).

So, too, we can find the fellowship we seek in our families, with our friends, and within the walls of our church. It is here that we are nourished, be-friended, and upheld. Here we find support and encouragement for living a life that sometimes demands more strength than we seem to have.

Perhaps one of the best contemporary illustrations of the importance of human community as a touchstone to the divine is found in the contemporary writer Henri Nouwen. Nouwen turned his back on the world of fame and teaching at Notre Dame, Yale, and Harvard. In a remarkable act of humility, he became a chaplain at L'Arche Community for mentally handicapped adults near Toronto.

A sensitive man who was gay, Nouwen had been deeply wounded by life and became a Jesuit priest. He had personally experienced alienation, separation, and loneliness. It was Nouwen's central premise that out of such wounds and scars, a loving and healing person can emerge who can best identify with and help others who are hurt. Such a person becomes what Nouwen referred to in the title of his book as a "Wounded Healer" (Nouwen 1972). As Nouwen says, "the emptiness of the past and future can never be filled by words but only by the presence of a man." Then one who suffers can feel that "Maybe, after all, someone is waiting for me. . . . Everyone who returns from a long and difficult trip is looking for someone waiting for him. . . . thousands of people commit suicide because there is nobody waiting for them tomorrow" (Nouwen 1972, 65–67). We can save the lives of others by becoming their tomorrow. Let us commit ourselves to becoming the tomorrow for those about us.

As we said last week, we confront who we are and what life is through adversity and the dark night of our souls. But this is not the end of the story. If we are blessed, we move on and find purpose and joy in the company of kindred spirits, in fellowship with one another. As Ecclesiastes says, "One generation passes away, and another generation cometh: but the earth abides forever. The sun also rises" (Eccl 1:4–5 KJV).

— 46 —

This Side of Eden[1]

Good morning, my friends. It is a pleasure to be back with you in this esteemed pulpit to cover for Kerby who is travelling this Sunday. It is an especially happy occasion for me to be able to celebrate the first Sunday of the New Year with you, and to share Communion.

As you can see, I have titled the sermon today, "This Side of Eden." Let's begin by talking about what the mythological Eden was like. It was perfect. The weather was great: it never got hot, it never flooded, and there was never a hurricane. There was sunshine all the time, and there were always beautiful clouds. At night, the stars were bright and clear. There was always a beautiful, full moon. Although it hardly ever rained, everything grew perfectly.

There were no wars. No one ever died. No one ever got sick. There were no doctors. There were no taxes, no fees, no hidden charges. There were no bills to pay. There were no laws to break. So, there were no police or judges or courts or prisons. God came to visit every day, you could ask him anything you wanted, and he would always give complete and truthful answers. Eve was beautiful. Adam was handsome and strong. They were always young, and they lived forever. Life was problem-free and perfect.

If that was what Eden was like, what is life like "this side of Eden" as the sermon title suggests? I'm afraid we know the answer to that, as well. It is not perfect. As a matter of fact, it is conspicuous for its imperfection.

---

1. Sermon given by the author at Coral Isles Church, Tavernier, Florida, on January 3, 2016. A video of this sermon as originally presented is available online at: https://youtu.be/IqNw4wGnskg

As human beings we are born, we get sick, we suffer. The one constant thing about life is change, and the change often seems to be for the worst. As humans, we are inherently vulnerable. We can be broken and hurt. We grow old, and we die. We are transitory, we are but visitors. Eventually, we must say "Good-bye" and leave.

Here in the Coral Isles Church, it seems that we have experienced many losses recently. We are reminded that our pastor for over twenty years and her husband left a year and a half ago and moved to Georgia. Other beloved members of our church have left the Keys and relocated elsewhere. Some of us have lost family members—some have lost partners; several have lost parents and fathers this past year. Many of us have suffered from illness: some have had cancer; some T.B.; several of us have had heart attacks; some have had extensive medical testing and uncertainty. Some of us have had surgeries and are experiencing long convalescences. Some have lost jobs. Some have had serious accidents and are still recovering from them.

Sometimes it seems that life "This Side of Eden" is about imperfection, vulnerability, and brokenness. When we get preoccupied with our limitations and overwhelmed by our losses, we have what I would call a fractured view of life. This failure to see the whole picture, this preoccupation with the negative side of life may be what sin is.

Now, I have never liked the Christian idea of sin very much, but in some recent study I have been doing I have come to understand it better. In the twenty-first century, sin has come to reference general attitudes and postures, more than specific behaviors. One commentator points out, "Sin is not primarily about behavior, morality, nor acts. Instead, it is about one's primary orientation, telos, direction" (Mercadante 1997, 39). A form of sin is being so overwhelmed by loss and negativity that we abandon our positive orientation toward self, others, and God. Sin has been defined as that which violates the self; it is an "attack of the self on the self" (Hardin 1994, 51).

This side of Eden, then, includes our vulnerability, our limitation and brokenness, but it also includes the presence of a God who loves us enough to have given us the good stuff in the first place, and despite our losses never leaves us alone. The bad news is that we had to leave Eden, but the good news is that God goes with us. Who is this God? I think this God has at least three qualities or characteristics. This sovereign God is characterized by omnipotence, generosity, and forgiveness.

First, God is omnipotent. The word "omnipotent" comes from the two Latin terms, *omni*, "all," and *potens*, "powerful," meaning "all-powerful." We see such a God throughout history. God brings his people out of Egypt with "great power" (Ex 32:11, Deut 4:37 RSV). Job declares that God's "wisdom is profound, his power is vast" (Job 9:4 NIV). Gabriel reassures Mary, "For with God nothing will be impossible" (Luke 1:37 RSV). Jesus says, "with God all things are possible" (Matt 19:26 NIV), and Paul counsels, "Finally, be strong in the Lord and in his mighty power" (Eph 6:10 NIV).

The second characteristic of God is his generosity and abundance. Throughout history, the theme of plenty and hospitality plays out. In Genesis, God created all that we need: light, water, land, vegetation, birds, fish, and animals, even a wife for Adam. In the Old Testament, God's promise is consistently one of plenty and increase. Following the story of Creation is what is referred to as the Great Mandate: "Be fruitful and increase in number; fill the earth and subdue it" (Gen 1:28 NIV), and after the Flood we are told that God will make Israel and humankind "as numerous as the stars in the sky" (Deut 10:22 NIV).

In the New Testament, the theme of sufficiency continues with the Great Invitation: "Come to me, all you who are weary and burdened, and I will give you rest" (Matt 11:28 NIV). Jesus sent his disciples forth in anticipation of generosity when he told them, "Take nothing for the journey—no staff, no bag, no bread, no money, no extra shirt. Whatever house you enter, stay there until you leave that town. If people do not welcome you, leave their town and shake the dust off your feet" (Luke 9:3–5 NIV). In the feeding of the 5,000, Christ exemplified the principle of plenty when he determined not to send people away hungry and instead multiplied the loaves and fish (Luke 9:10–17). Christ's actions at the Last Supper embodied the spirit of hospitality and sufficiency when he washed his disciples' feet (John 13) and gave them bread and wine (Matt 26:17–30). The sacrament of Communion continues to be a reminder of God's provision and blessing. And the story of the Good Samaritan presents an unforgettable example of extravagant generosity and provision (Luke 10: 30–37).

The third characteristic of God I would mention this morning is his forgiveness and grace in giving us a second chance, an attribute found in both the Old and New Testaments. Moses murdered a man, but God chose him to lead his people. David committed adultery with Bathsheba and had her husband killed, but became "a man after . . . [God's] own heart" (1 Sam 13:14 NIV). Peter denied Christ and ran away, but turned out to be the leader of the church. Paul persecuted early Christians, but became an apostle and author of much of the New Testament. The Prodigal Son illustrates that we have never fallen too low to be welcomed back to God's grace. The Prodigal Son is the story of a man lost in the world—perhaps even caught up in addiction—who "came to his senses" (Luke 15:17 NIV) and returned home. As such, it is a portrayal of "nostos" or homecoming, the theme immortalized in Homer's *Odyssey* written in the eighth century B.C.

So, looking at life from "This Side of Eden," we have seen not only human limitation, vulnerability, and brokenness, but we have seen the power, abundance, and forgiveness of a God who loves us. My friends, I know that we often experience life in its adversity and struggle, and sometimes live in "the dark night of the soul," to borrow the phrase from St. John of the Cross (John of the Cross 2003). We were never meant to be completely satisfied, and as St. Augustine said, "our hearts find no peace until they rest" in God (Augustine 1961, 21).

Gerald G. May, psychologist and author, concluded:

> We must not only accept and claim the sweetly painful incompleteness within ourselves, but also affirm it with all our hearts. Somehow we must come to fall in love with it. . . . It is a willing, wanting, aching venture into the desert of our nature, loving the emptiness of that desert because of the sure knowledge that God's rain will fall and the certainty that we are both heirs and co-creators of the wonder that is now and of the Eden that is yet to be. (May 1991, 181–82)

— 47 —

Where Is God?[1]

GOOD MORNING, MY FRIENDS. As I have mentioned before, sermons are autobiographical. Of course, they are about the subject that is announced, but they are as much about the minister. I would like to acknowledge and affirm individual differences in the views of our congregation. Differences of opinion and belief among members of our congregation should be recognized and honored.

Therefore, today when I preach about what or where God is, I am telling you about my own beliefs. I am disclosing my deepest self. And we know that self-disclosure is difficult, because there's only one of me, and if you don't like what I share, there is not another version I can trot out. It's the only one I've got.

At a recent meeting of the Upper Keys Ministerial Association, our chairman, Phil Underwood, raised an interesting question about whether God is king or friend. We concluded he should have the power of a king, but have the affection and love of a friend. I observed that perhaps the best metaphor for God is that of a parent, who has power and authority, yet is loving and supportive.

In doing my doctoral dissertation, I identified three characteristics of God. The first is power. The second quality is generosity. And the third characteristic is forgiveness wherein God gives us a second chance.

We probably agree most on the first attribute of God, his power. What good is having a God unless he has power? The word *omnipotence*

---

1. Sermon by the author at Coral Isles Church, Tavernier, Florida, on July 2, 2017. This sermon restates some of the characteristics of God found in the earlier presentation, "This Side of Eden." A video of this sermon as originally presented is available online: https://youtu.be/j3kg6_Qiw5w

comes from the two Latin terms—*omni*, "all," and *potens*, "powerful," or "all-powerful." The Bible is a chronicle of God's power. God brings his people out of Egypt with "great power" (Exod 32:11 NIV) and "great strength" (Deut 4:37 NIV). Job declares that God's "wisdom is profound, his power is vast" (Job 9:4 NIV). Gabriel reassures Mary, "For with God nothing will be impossible" (Luke 1:37 RSV). Jesus says, "With God all things are possible" (Matt 19:26 NIV), and Paul counsels, "Finally, be strong in the Lord and in his mighty power" (Eph 6:10 NIV).

The second characteristic of God is his generosity. What good is his power if he's not willing to share it with us, if he doesn't have our welfare at heart? In the Bible, the message of Christianity is one of God's extravagant generosity and bountiful provision. In Genesis, the story of Creation is one of God as the perfect host providing the world as a place for us to be comfortable and to prosper. To this end, he created all that we need: light, water, land, vegetation, birds, fish, and animals, even a wife for Adam. In the Old Testament, God's promise is consistently one of plenty and increase.

In the New Testament, the theme of abundance and hospitality continues with the "Great Invitation:" "Come to me, all you who are weary and burdened, and I will give you rest" (Matt 11:28 NIV). Jesus sent his disciples forth in anticipation of generosity when he told them, "Take nothing for the journey—no staff, no bag, no bread, no money, no extra shirt. Whatever house you enter, stay there until you leave that town. If people do not welcome you, leave their town and shake the dust off your feet" (Luke 9:3–5 NIV). In the feeding of the 5,000, Christ exemplified the principle of sufficiency when he determined not to send people away hungry and instead multiplied the loaves and fish (Luke 9:10–17). Christ's actions at the Last Supper embodied the spirit of hospitality and sufficiency when he washed his disciples' feet (John 13:1–17) and gave them bread and wine (Matt 26:26–29). The sacrament of Communion continues to be a reminder of God's provision and blessing. The commandment of "Double Love" portrays the principle of love that has no limits (Mark 12:30–31). The story of the "Good Samaritan" is an unforgettable example of extravagant generosity and provision (Luke 10: 30–35). The theology of God's sufficiency and plenty is not a frill, an embellishment, or an "add-on" to Christianity. It is the essence of the Christian faith, a faith based upon a God of radical generosity.

The third characteristic of God is his forgiveness. Moses murdered a man, but God chose him to lead his people. David committed adultery with Bathsheba and had her husband killed, but became "a man after ... [God's] own heart" (1 Sam 13:14 NIV). Peter denied Christ and ran away, but turned out to be the leader of the church. Paul persecuted early Christians but became an apostle and author of much of the New Testament. Jesus knew that the Samaritan woman at the well had several husbands, but he befriended her. Christ said to the woman caught in adultery, "Then neither do I condemn you" (John 8:11 NIV). The allegory of the Prodigal Son illustrates that we have never fallen too low to be welcomed back to God's grace. The Prodigal Son is the story of a man lost in the world—perhaps even caught up in addiction—who "came to his senses" (Luke 15:17 NIV) and returned home.

As human beings, we are best known for our propensity to make mistakes, for messing up. We often need a chance to start over. Fortunately, life is full of second chances. We need a God who forgives us—and we need to cut ourselves some slack until we finally "get it right."

We need to forgive others, to give them the same chance and consideration we want for ourselves. "To forgive is divine." As humans, we are not all powerful; we do not have endless opportunities and resources, but at least we can emulate God in forgiving others—thus paradoxically giving them new power and another chance. Our main job on earth is to forgive and love others.

God exists, then, in that we can seek his power, his generosity, and his forgiveness. We don't have as much of a problem with who this God might be. Where we sometimes get stuck is, where is this God? Sometimes the usual answers of "within us" or "everywhere" don't seem like enough.

Life experiences and my recent studies have confirmed something I have thought for some time. For me, God is in relationships, in fellowship, and in human community. After creating man, God observed, "It is not good for the man to be alone" (Gen 2:18 NIV). Significantly, the only thing in all creation that is not good is man on his own. Trying to live in the image of God (*imago Dei*) means being in relationship with each other. "The image of God is a relational image," Michael Hardin asserts, "We, together, constitute the image of God. As isolated individuals, we are but a fracture of that image. To be made in the image of God is to be made in relationship" (Hardin 1994, 49).

Where do we find God? When asked where the Kingdom of God was, Jesus answered, "The kingdom of God is in the midst of you" (Luke 17:21 RSV). We find God in human community, in families, in churches, in friendships, and in the fellowship of Twelve Step programs. As the Scripture reading this morning from Matthew reminded us, when we give food and drink and clothing to those who suffer, we do it to God: ". . . whatever you did for one of the least of these brothers and sisters of mine, you did for me" (Matt 25:40 NIV). When God decided to play "Hide-and-Go Seek" with us, he didn't make it very hard to find him.

I am not here to tell you whether you should believe in God or not, or to try to tell you what kind of God you should believe in. I'm here to encourage you to avail yourself of God—and let him use you. Give life a second chance. Kahlil Gibran said, "Hate is a dead thing. Who of you would be in a tomb" (Gibran 2008, 56)? When Teresa and I were in Rome, we went into the catacombs where Christian martyrs were buried. It was interesting, but I was sure glad to climb out into the fresh air again! Dare to climb out, to live, and to love again.

So, you've been hurt, and you're afraid? Believe me, you're not alone. As Christians we need to find the power, to tap the resource of forgiveness. As Christians we need the willingness to live and suffer, and take yet another chance on life.

— 48 —

Wings Like a Dove[1]

RELIGION TRIES TO ANSWER many different questions. It tells us who or what God is. It speaks about the nature of man, and the role of Christ. It teaches about prayer and the sacraments. And perhaps most important, it tells us how to live a good and loving life, a subject that you and I talk about frequently. Religion also has a view about what happens to you after you die, about heaven and hell. A chief teaching of traditional Christianity is the resurrection of Christ and our own resurrection and afterlife. This morning I would like to discuss the topic of death and give some of my views on immortality.

Some years ago when I was visiting my son in Upstate New York, I was out walking and on impulse turned into the lobby of a Lutheran Church. Just inside the door on the wall was a memorial plaque with a beautiful picture of a dove in flight. The plaque was in memory of a church member's husband who was in the hospital in a coma and close to death. As the wife sat by his bedside holding his hand, she prayed that God would send her a sign that his soul would find peace. Then she heard a strange sound for a quiet hospital room, a tapping noise. Several taps, quiet, then several more taps. She looked everywhere in the room, then she looked out the window. There on the windowsill she saw a beautiful dove, tapping against the glass with its beak. Then the dove spread is lovely white wings and flew away. She turned back to her husband at the same moment that he took his last peaceful breath. At the bottom of

---

1. Sermon delivered by the author at the Coral Isles Church, Tavernier, Florida, on June 1, 2014.

the plaque, was a verse from Psalm 55: "O that I had wings like a dove! I would fly away and be at rest" (Psa 55:6 RSV).

We all have had experience with death. I am no exception. My parents died about 25 years ago. My first German Shepherd dog, Ruby, died 15 years ago. As you probably know, my current dog and friend, Maxwell, died three weeks ago. It is a difficult experience to lose someone you are close to and love. After the return of Maxwell's ashes, Teresa and I came to the church and Bonnie did a short service of blessing the ashes in commemoration of Maxwell's life. Somehow, all I could think of were the words from a poem: "If tears could build a stairway and memories a lane, I'd walk right up to heaven and bring you home again" (Lugo 2019).

What are we to think about death and immortality? Twelve Step recovery groups are more "spiritual" than "religious" in the traditional sense, and they have a saying: "church is for people who are afraid of going to hell. A.A. is for people who have already been there." I have heard it expressed another way, "Religion is for people who live and die and go to heaven. Spirituality is for people who live as though they are already in heaven."

Returning to our question, what are we to think about death and immortality? My faith is in God. I believe in him and trust him, and that when I die, I will somehow be closer to him. Henri Nouwen put it beautifully: "the One who sent me on the mission is waiting for me to come home and tell the story of what I have learned" (Nouwen 1992, 110). Some of you may have a more traditional faith about immortality and afterlife. From my days as a pastor, I learned never to dispute, or repudiate anyone's idea of immortality. My conviction was that the time of bereavement is a time for support and providing comfort, not taking advantage of people's vulnerability by challenging their beliefs.

Let me tell you what I believe. I do not think there is anything to fear about death. The 23rd Psalm is a classic statement about walking through the valley of the shadow of death yet fearing no evil. We are told that God will lead us beside still waters, and that he will restore our souls. The Psalm draws a beautiful and comforting word picture. Over and over in the New Testament, Jesus admonishes us to "Fear not. . . ." (Luke 2:10 KJV).

The nineteenth century American orator Robert Ingersoll spoke about death without fear:

> Why should we fear that which will come to all that is? We cannot tell, and we do not know, which is the greater blessing—life or death. We cannot say that death is not a good. We do not know whether the grave is the end of this life, or the

door of another, or whether the night here is not somewhere else a dawn. . . . No man, standing where the horizon of a life has touched the grave, has any right to prophecy a future filled with pain and tears. May be that death gives all there is of worth to life. If those we press and strain within our arms could never die, perhaps that love would wither from the earth. May be this common fate treads from out the paths between our hearts the weeds of selfishness and hate. And I had rather live and love where death is king, than have eternal life where love is not. (Ingersoll 1911, 116)

When Maxwell died, or whenever I have lost someone else who was close, I could not grasp the idea that they suddenly and arbitrarily "ceased to exist." That for me was incomprehensible, even disrespectful. I preferred to think that they have left upon their journey. But I suspect it is closer to the truth to say that they are now with me in a different, deeper way; that when they die their spirit becomes more permanently embedded in my consciousness than before. Someone once said, "Death is an anchor to love." I like how Boris Pasternak expressed it in his book *Dr. Zhivago*: "You have always been in others and you will remain in others. What does it matter to you if later on that is called your memory? This will be you—the you that enters the future and becomes a part of it" (Hughes 1974, 117).

This intense and lasting presence is what I consider heaven and immortality to be. Notice how consistent this is with what Jesus told his followers, "Behold, the kingdom of God is within you" (Luke 17:21 KJV). I believe that we have immortality in the hearts of those we have influenced and loved. Harriet Beecher Stowe, the transcendentalist poet, spoke of this kind of immortality when she wrote of her feelings about God and someone close whom she lost:

> Still, still with thee, when purple morning breaketh,
> When the bird waketh and the shadows flee;
> Fairer than morning, lovelier than the daylight,
> Dawns the sweet consciousness, I am with thee.
>
> Alone with thee, amid the mystic shadows,
> The solemn hush of nature newly born;
> Alone with thee in breathless adoration,
> In the calm dew and freshness of the morn. . . .

> When sinks the soul, subdued by toil, to slumber,
> Its closing eye looks up to thee in prayer;
> Sweet the repose beneath thy wings o'ershading,
> But sweeter still to wake and find thee there.
>
> So shall it be at last, in that bright morning
> When the soul waketh and life's shadows flee:
> O in that hour, fairer than daylight dawning,
> Shall rise the glorious thought, *I am with thee*. (Stowe n.d., italics hers)

Next, I am enough of a pantheist to see God and signs of those I have lost in the world about me: in the wind, the sunset, the moon, a dove, even a butterfly. I spent several days with my Uncle Wayne, who was ninety-five years old, when he was unconscious in a hospice at Port St. Lucie. After sitting with him several hours on the last morning, I took an hour break to walk in the garden. There were beautiful flowers, but I noticed something unusual for South Florida, there were no butterflies. Just as I was ready to return to the hospice room, I saw it—a grand monarch butterfly on a flower that spread his wings and gracefully flew away. At that very moment, they called me from the hospice ward and told me that Uncle Wayne had just died. Juanita De Long expressed a sense of union with the natural world in her poem:

> I will look up at you from the eyes of little children;
> I will bend to meet you in the swaying boughs of bud-thrilled trees,
> And caress you with the passionate sweep of storm-filled winds. . . .
> I will flood your soul with the flaming radiance of the sunrise,
> And bring you peace in the tender rose and gold of the after-sunset.
> All of these have made me happy;
> They are part of me;
> I shall become a part of them. (DeLong n.d.)

Finally, we may think of death as not something alien, but as part of life by which we refuse to be diminished or defeated. We may think of it as a part of the process of life, a moment in Universal Love. Here is nothing monstrous or out-of-the-way, but something of a piece with the setting sun and the falling leaf, which binds all being to the throne of God. St. Francis, who embraced all animals and plants with affectionate sympathy, included death as a part of nature in his infinite goodwill. "Welcome Sister Death," he said, as he felt his end drawing near.

So also, Tennyson declared in his poem, "Ulysses":

Come, my friends
'Tis not too late to seek a newer world.
Push off, and sitting well in order smite
The sounding furrows; for my purpose holds
To sail beyond the sunset, and the paths
Of all the western stars, until I die.
It may be that the gulfs will wash us down;
It may be that we shalt touch the Happy Isles,
And see the great Achilles, whom we knew;
Tho' much is taken, much abides; and tho'
We are not now that strength which in old days
Moved earth and heaven; that which we are, we are;
One equal temper of heroic hearts,
Made weak by time and fate, but strong in will
To strive, to seek, to find and not to yield. (Tennyson 2019)

— 49 —

A Cure for Tocharianism[1]

I DOUBT IF MANY of you have ever heard of Tocharianism. You may not know who the Tocharians were. But more about that later.

§

Today is World Communion Sunday. All over the world, Christian churches are celebrating Communion, and we will join with them when we observe Communion later in our service here at the Coral Isles Church. This Sunday gives us a chance to reflect on what church means in our lives. It is my contention that church, church life, and the ceremonies that we observe are an integral part of our lives as human beings—and have their roots in family and friendship affiliations we have had throughout our lives.

§

I would like to begin by telling you about my background with churches going back as far as I can recall. I must confess that I am older than I look. I was born before World War II. When that war came, my father was assigned to Fort Belvoir in Alexandria, Virginia. My mom, my brother, and I moved to Virginia. Shortly afterwards, my father was transferred to Europe, and we stayed in Virginia and waited for him to return. World War II was a traumatic time for the whole world, and it was for me also. I was only eight years old, and inexplicably my father was

---

1. Sermon delivered by the author at Coral Isles Church, Tavernier, Florida, on October 6, 2019.

taken away. My memories are remarkably intact about this period. There was great uncertainty and fear about what it all meant. In Virginia, I went to a small country school where I was in third grade. Because we were from Chicago, my classmates labelled me a "Damned Yankee!" Now, I had no idea about what World War II was about—let alone the Civil War, and I felt alone and frightened. One war at a time!

Prior to this time my parents had not been active in a church, but in Virginia they started attending a small Lutheran church in the country. I have a clear memory of sitting close to the front on the left side of the church directly in front of the pulpit, where we could easily see and hear the minister when he gave his sermons. Of course, I don't remember details, but I do remember how impressed I was. I thought that someday it would be nice to be a preacher! I attended Vacation Bible School one summer, where we made tabletop wooden crosses, and where we played softball—I was even more impressed because the minister came out and pitched to us.

I spent a lot of time by myself, exploring in the woods near our home. I remember finding a small clearing in the forest and making a giant cross out of fallen trees—thus creating my own little chapel area where I knelt and prayed. A hymn that made a great impression me at the time was one that Loretta Lynn made famous:

> There's a church in the valley by the wildwood
> No lovelier spot in the dale
> No place is so dear to my childhood
> As the little brown church in the vale
> Oh, come, come, come, come
> Come to the church by the wildwood
> Oh, come to the church in the vale
> No spot is so dear to my childhood
> As the little brown church in the vale (O'Donnell 2019)

Even today, I keep a picture on my bedroom wall of a little brown church in the woods.

We all have our memories and stories of what our early contact with a church was like. As with our families, churches often became an expression of a deep need for affiliation and comfort, acceptance, and protection—particularly in a depersonalized and troubled world. I have always thought that religion was very personal. The kind of church we are drawn to is frequently autobiographical—it says much about our own needs, our longings, our hopes and fears, about who we are and what our needs are for love and belonging.

When adults "shop" for a church, it is much the same as looking for a life partner. What we chose says as much about us and our past as it says about the church we are considering.

§

It is no coincidence that we refer to "our church home and church family." Fellow members are our brothers and sisters. Sometimes we look upon the pastor as a parental figure. Small Sunday School rooms are hopefully not where children sleep, but where they have special ownership. There is a kitchen and dining room, and we regularly share meals. We celebrate Communion, or breaking bread together, as we will this morning. The candles on the altar give warmth like a fire in the fireplace. Christening and foot-washing services are reminiscent of bathing. Our church office is like a study or library. Sometimes our choir wears special robes. We even have a big-screen TV. We happily invite our friends to come on over and visit. We then encourage them to "join our church family."

Some of us come from families and homes where we were well nurtured and cared for. In our church families we seek to celebrate and reinforce that memory. Some of us come from families of origin where there was a deficiency in caring, where there was insufficient trust and warmth—perhaps even where there was addiction or domestic violence. Our churches become our surrogate families, where we can compensate for previous deficiencies, where we can re-experience life, and hopefully get it right this time.

The kind of church home we desire, the kind we have chosen is in part a product of our past, and in part our hope for the future. So, Jews go to synagogues (and we will be blessed to have Rabbi Rich Agler from the Keys Jewish Community Center with us next Sunday). Protestants go to churches, and Catholics go to Mass or Confession. Catholics are quite overt in their use of family symbolism—Father, Mother of God, Sister, Brother. When Teresa and I were in Rome a year and a half ago, we had the privilege of an audience with Pope Francis, who gave us a blessing. It was special because he asked us to take it with us and pass it on to others. So, I pass the Blessing of Francis on to you this World Communion Sunday. "God Bless you. Amen."

A Cure for Tocharianism

§

Oh . . . I almost forgot to tell you about Tocharianism. You probably have never heard of Tocharians. The Tocharians were an ancient civilization that inhabited an area known as the Tarim Basin in Central Asia. They were a highly intelligent and very successful culture—that suddenly ceased to exist, and completely disappeared from the face of the earth.

PART IV

Prayers and Readings

— 50 —
Invocations and Opening Words

From the busy paths of this ever-moving world we have turned aside with reverent footsteps, with ears open for echoes, be they ever so faint, from the hills and valleys of our own experience: echoes suggesting to us the vast mysterious setting of our lives which we too seldom recollect. We turn aside from the daily road we follow, seeking the hidden springs of life, hearing their murmurs through the harsher noises of our short day. May we stoop and drink of their living waters, and rise refreshed and strengthened.

—A. Phillip Hewett (Hudson 1962)

§

To know the worth of love and beauty, and grace and form,
and not to store the treasure but increase it by your own life span
for all the world to see and know—isn't that a pleasant prospect?
And, you know, it just might be true.

—Albert Frederick Ziegler (Howe 2001)

§

Truth has no special time of its own. Its hour is now, always, and indeed then most truly when it seems most unsuitable to actual circumstances.

—Albert Schweitzer (Schweitzer 1947, 30)

Part IV: Prayers and Readings

§

The ethic of Reverence for Life is the ethic of love widened into universality. It is the ethic of Jesus, now recognized as a logical consequence of thought....

—Albert Schweitzer (Schweitzer 1990, 235)

§

In the midst of winter, I finally discovered that there was in me an invincible summer.

—Albert Camus (Marquet 1972, 5)

§

This is the temple of the aspiring human spirit. Here entertain high hopes and noble aspirations. Let not your heart and mind be marred by mean or ignoble objectives but seek after the sublime significance of life.

—Attributed to Alfred J.N. Henriksen (Hudson 1962)

§

Touch not my lips with the white fire from the glowing altar of some peaceful shrine. Thrust not into my hand the scroll of wisdom gleaned through the patient toil of centuries. Give me no finished chart that I may follow without effort or the bitter taste of tears. I do not crave the comfort of the ancient creeds nor the sheltered harbor where the great winds cease to blow. But winnow my heart and torture my soul with doubt. Let me feel the clean gales of the open sea until thy creative life is my life and my joy, one with the miracle of spring and the blowing grain, the yearning of all humankind, and the endless reach of the stars.

—Alfred S. Cole (Hudson 1962)

§

We come into this home of homes to celebrate the life of all our lives. Here we rejoice in the sun and the movement of the stars. Here we feel our kinship with every living thing on this green and pleasant earth: the fish and the many creatures of the sea, the birds which make the air their home, and all the animals that move upon the surface of the earth. All these are born and live and die, and in this elemental fact are one with us. And we who are conscious of this force—this life within us, this inherited determination to exist and leave the world enriched with our own kind—raise our eyes in wonder at it all.

—Adapted from Arnold Farrow Westwood (Hudson 1962)

§

To have discovered in this moment some melody which only the ears of the soul hear; to have found in oneself some lurking power, often dormant, but right now lifting one beyond himself; to have learned that no loneliness is absolute, and no darkness is engulfing; to have seen a sparkle (or a tear) in another's eye and felt as if it were one's own; to have decided that there is much more to be known, but the truth is not confined to mere scientific demonstration; to have become oneself blessedness, peace, gratitude and love, and one more, therefore, to stand in awe—this is to worship.

—Attributed to Arthur Boyd Jellis

§

Infuse yourself with action. Don't wait for it to happen. Make it happen. Make your own future. Make your own hope. Make your own love. And whatever your beliefs, honor your creator, not by passively waiting for grace to come down from upon high, but by doing what you can to make grace happen . . . yourself, right now, right down here on Earth.

—Bradley Whitford (Whitford 2019)

Part IV: Prayers and Readings

§

Even as we find ourselves confused by the evils of the past that we have not solved, we are faced with the frightening problems of the future than are thrust upon us. We know that our fears and failures have caused us to doubt our abilities and despair of our ideals. We reflect so much the winds of our time and so little the climate of truth. We long to be free, to be unafraid, to live with courage, to be creative. May we be inspired in our search for truth and with resolute courage demonstrate that our free spirits can prevail.

—Attributed to Carl V. Bretz (Hudson 1962)

§

O God, thy sea is so great and my boat is so small.

—Winfred Ernest Garrison (Garrison 1965)
(Plaque on the desk of John F. Kennedy)

§

The sea moves always, the wind moves always,
They want and want and there is no end to their wanting.
What they sing is the song of the people.
Man will never arrive, Man will always be on the way.
It is written he shall rest but never for long.
The sea and the wind tell him he shall be lonely, meet love,
Be shaken with struggle, and go on wanting.

—Carl Sandburg (Sandburg 2016)

§

If we fill our lives with things, and yet more things, if we feel that we must fill every moment that we have with activity, when will we have time to make the long slow journey across the burning desert, as did the wisemen? Or sit and watch the stars as did the shepherds? Or brood over the coming of the child as did Mary? For each of us there is a desert to cross, a star to discover and follow, and a being within ourselves to bring to life.

—Anonymous (Hudson 1962)

§

Go placidly amid the noise and the haste, and remember what peace there may be in silence. As far as possible without surrender, be on good terms with all persons. Speak your truth quietly and clearly; and listen to others, even the dull and ignorant; they too have their story. . . . Be yourself. Especially do not feign affection. Neither be cynical about love: for in the face of all aridity and disenchantment it is perennial as the grass. Take kindly the counsel of the years, gracefully surrendering the things of youth. Nurture strength of spirit to shield you in sudden misfortune. But do not distress yourself with imaginings. Many fears are born of fatigue and loneliness. Beyond a wholesome discipline, be gentle with yourself. You are a child of the universe no less than the trees and the stars; you have a right to be here. And whether or not it is clear to you, no doubt the universe is unfolding as it should. Therefore, be at peace with God, whatever you conceive Him to be, and whatever your labors and aspirations, in the noisy confusion of life keep peace with your soul. With all its sham, drudgery and broken dreams, it is still a beautiful world. Be cheerful. Strive to be happy.

—*Desiderata* (Ehrmann 1952)

§

I am only one, but I am one. I cannot do everything, but I can do something. And I will not let what I cannot do interfere with what I can do.

—Edward Everett Hale (Hale 2019)

§

This church practices union; has no creed, seeks to make religion as intellectual as science, as appealing as art, as vital as the day's work, as intimate as home, and as inspiring as love.

—Edward Scribner Ames (Hudson 1962)

§

And though around our path some form of mystery ever lies,
And life is like the calm and storm that checker earth and skies,
Through all its mingling joy and dread, permit us, Holy One,
By faith to see the golden thread of thy great purpose run.

—Edwin Hubbell Chapin (Chapin 1856, 635)

§

We men of Earth have here the stuff
Of Paradise—we have enough!
We need no other stones to build
The temple of the Unfulfilled—
No other ivory for the doors—
No other marble for the floors—
No other cedar for the beam
And dome of man's immortal dream.
Here on the paths of every-day—
Here on the common human way
Is all the stuff the gods would take
To build a Heaven, to mold and make
New Edens. Ours is the task sublime
To build Eternity in time!

—Edwin Markham (Trine n.d., 102–3)

§

Man's giant thought in ever daring flight explores the universe, the ancient night, and finds infinity even in the flower. Yet, the greatest wonder of all is man's heroic will which gives him power to live and to perish for his dreams.

—Attributed to Edwin Markham (Hudson 1962)

§

Come to worship in gentleness and humility, conscious of our own weaknesses but also grateful for the gifts of grace and wisdom, of love and courage, that are the marks of the spirit of man.

Invocations and Opening Words

In the spirit of seeking and sharing, of giving and receiving, let us worship together in the truth and in peace.

—Eugene A. Luening (Hudson 1962)

§

Why dost thou wonder, O man, at the height of the stars or the depth of the sea? Enter into thine own soul and wonder there.

—Francis Quarles (Hudson 1962)

§

Week by week in this familiar and beloved place, we renew within our souls the knowledge of eternal realities, that here at least we may acknowledge no sovereignty less than the highest nor worship in any shrine save that of our noblest and loftiest ideals. May the ministry of these hours become so strong influence upon our lives that we shall go forth from this place cleansed and renewed in spirit, with hope that no disappointment can destroy and with convictions mightier than every doubt.

—Attributed to Frederick May Eliot (Hudson 1962)

§

Our prayer is for the readiness of mind that is quick to perceive the truth that comes to us from unexpected sources, that is not closed against new and strange ideas merely because they are unfamiliar, nor reluctant to see the enduring value of truths which were first discovered many years or centuries ago. We would understand the timelessness of truth, its independence of circumstance or place. . . . For we know how prone we are to set up false limits of our own, making truth the slave of fashion or of personal needs or private whims. May we catch a glimpse of the august and the humbling face of that truth which is no respecter of persons, which is eternal, in the heavens; and may we find our own stumbling efforts to know the meaning of that truth undergirded by the infinite and unassailable power of the God in whom truth abideth. So, shall we go onward, day by day, meeting the experiences of our common human life with quiet and resolute courage, and looking forward to the days ahead with faith that grows stronger and happier with the years.

—Attributed to Frederick May Eliot (Hudson 1962)

§

Be ye lamps unto yourselves;
Be your own confidence.
Hold to the truth within yourself
As to the only lamp.

—Adapted from Gotama Buddha (Hudson 1962)

§

The spirit of Love will be intensified to Godly proportions when reciprocal love exists between the entire human race and each of its individual members. That love must be based upon mutual respect for the differences in color, language and worship, even as we appreciate and accept with gratitude the differences that tend to unite the male and female of all species. We do not find those differences obstacles to love.

—George de Benneville (de Bennville 2012)

§

Here we are, you and I, and the millions of men and animals about us: the innumerable atoms which make our bodies, blown as it were by mysterious processes together, so that there has happened, just now, for every one of us, the wonder of wonders, we have come to life. And here we stand, with our senses, our keen intellects, our infinite desires, our nerves quivering to the touch of joy or pain: beacons of brief fire, burning between two unexplored eternities.

—Robert Killam (Seaburg 1998, 309)

Invocations and Opening Words 225

§

One would suppose that intelligent human beings living on this wandering island in the sky, on the outskirts of the universe where the nearest fixed star is millions of light-years away, would in the nature of the case be humble when they try to formulate the truth about life as they see it. And one would suppose that such humility would be forced on them when they see their successive theologies shifting and changing as their social cultures alter, never absolute and final, but always relative to the current situation. This is as true for the radicals as for the conservatives, and such liberalism as I have achieved has sprung in part from the honest endeavor to take account of it. All these theological systems and all others that will follow them are partial, tentative, contemporary formulations of great matters. To take the best insights in them all, to see the incompleteness and falsity in them all, [to] trust none than our tentative conditioned explanation—this seems to me wisdom.

—Harry Emerson Fosdick (Hudson 1962)

§

Life consists not simply in what heredity and environment do to us but in what we make out of what they do to us.

—Harry Emerson Fosdick (B., Dick 1992, 65)

§

Nothing else matters much . . . not wealth, not learning, not even health . . . without this gift: the spiritual capacity to keep zest in living. To this the creed of creeds, the final deposit and distillation of all important faiths: that you should be able to believe in life.

—Harry Emerson Fosdick (Fosdick n.d.)

§

Why should not we also enjoy an original relation to the universe? Why should not we have a poetry and philosophy of insight and not of tradition, and a religion by revelation to us, and not the history of theirs. Embosomed for a season in nature, whose floods of life stream around and through us, and invite us, by the powers they supply to action proportioned to nature, why should we grope among the dry bones of the past, or put the living generation into masquerade out of its faded wardrobe? The sun shines today also. There is more wool and flax in the fields. There are new lands, new men, new thoughts. Let us demand our own works and laws and worship.

—Ralph Waldo Emerson (Emerson n.d.)

§

We come together from our busy lives to find something of quietness and peace, something of purpose and direction. We pause to let our deepest feelings and highest thoughts emerge. We open ourselves to truth in word, and love in others.

We know that our lives often fall short. But there are those who love us, and they are here with us now. May we learn to be kinder, quicker to forgive and slower to condemn. We rekindle the fires of affection within us to provide warmth for others. Amen.

—Author

§

We come together through the winding streets and wandering roads of many different lives. We have come each of us from a land where no other man has set foot.

We have struggled across different deserts, climbed different mountains, found our way through different forests. We come with different pain and fears.

We have seen smooth sands of different deserts, we have seen the clouds crown different mountains, we have seen flowers carpet the floors of different forests. Each of us comes with his own memories and dreams.

As we have come, so too, we will go different ways. Each has his own path before him. Each sees a horizon bounded by different needs and visions.

Yet, in this place and at this hour, our paths cross and our lives converge. We sit with each other by the well's side to quench our thirst and rest in the shade. May there be something here to quench all our thirsts. May there be something here to expose our fears, recall our dreams, and fulfill our visions. Amen.

—Author

§

If we agree in love, there is no disagreement that can do us any injury, but if we do not, no other agreement can do us any good.
Let us endeavor to keep the unity of the spirit in the bonds of peace.

—Hosea Ballou (Ibrahim 2019, 113)

§

Two things fill the mind with ever new and interesting admiration and awe, the more often and steadily we reflect upon them: the starry heavens above me and the moral law within me.

—Immanuel Kant (Humanists UK, 2019)

§

Here may no man be altogether stranger, no honesty of thought ignored, no depth of feeling easily dismissed. May whatever clarity of heart and mind we may achieve be treasured—and may our failures be accepted also in that forgiveness each man needs to give and to receive.

—Attributed to J. Donald Johnston (Hudson 1962)

§

In the midst of chaos, distress, and confusion, we repair to the sanctuary of the temple as our fathers have done. We do well to be here, for this is one of the natural ways by which we nourish our goodness and wisdom and give of these to one another. May contrition for our shortcomings and compassion for all who suffer draw us together as comrades in a dedicated quest.

—Adapted from Jack Mendelsohn (Hudson 1962)

§

Wisdom, be thou more precious than possessions without end. Truth, be now more sacred than the pleasing of a friend. Courage, be thou our strength to gain the distant goal. Beauty, send out a cleansing wonder through our souls. Goodness, be thou our guide upon life's way. Peace, be thou the benediction of our day.

—Attributed to Jacob Trapp and Donald S. Harrington (Hudson 1962)

§

A new commandment I give unto you, That ye love one another; as I have loved you, that ye also love one another.

—John 13:34 KJV

§

The gifts of life are free to all who will open their hearts unto life. The lonely shall find companions; the sorrowing shall find comfort; the fearful shall find peace. A bridge of love shall be built between the generations, and the bridge shall be open to all.

—John M. Kolbjornsen (Hudson 1962)

§

We have come together in the solitariness of each to seek the fellowship of all. Here the spirit is joined with spirit that we may express with single voice the worth of life. May there rise within us an increased faithfulness to all that we know is good, a steady devotion to the true and the just, a dedication to the removal from this earth of all that curses it with hate and greed and enmity. And when we depart from this place, may there have been added significance to the meaning of life, the power to sustain us in the long hours when we are absent one from the other.

—Attributed to John Winthrop Brigham (Hudson 1962)

Invocations and Opening Words

§

O Thou fountain of all our spirits, blessed be that love of thine, from which we come, in which we are upheld all the days of our life, and into whose infinite peace at last we return. In these moments we are met here, our hearts are open to one another and to Thee. Help us to know ourselves and the deep things of life better and clearer. Amen.

—Attributed to Josiah R. Bartlett (Hudson 1962)

§

Look to this day:
For it is life, the very life of life.
In its brief course
Lie all the verities and realities of your existence
The bliss of growth,
The glory of action,
The splendor of achievement
Are but experiences of time.
For yesterday is but a dream
And tomorrow is only a vision;
But today well-lived, makes
Yesterday a dream of happiness
And every tomorrow a vision of hope.
Look well therefore to this day;
Such is the salutation to the ever-new dawn!

—Kalidasa (Shapiro 2005)

§

This is the vision of a great and noble life: to endure ambiguity and make light shine through it; to stand fast in uncertainty; to prove capable of unlimited love and hope.

—Karl Jaspers (Stern 1998, 112)

§

Let us worship with our eyes and ears and fingertips;
Let us love the world through heart and mind and body....
Life comes with singing and laughter,
With tears and confiding,
With a rising wave too great to be held in the mind
And heart and body,
To those who have fallen in love with life.
Let us worship, and let us learn to love.

—Kenneth L. Patton (Patton n.d.)

§

Ours, O men, has been yesterday, and ours will be today and tomorrow. Ours is the world, the universe, and life, if we will make it ours by the largeness and strength of our love. Ours is the commonwealth of man, now and tomorrow, building and yet to be built.

—Kenneth L. Patton (Patton 1944, 233)

§

We arrive out of many singular rooms, walking over the branching streets. We come to be assured that brothers and sisters surround us, to restore their images on our eyes. We enlarge our voices in common speaking and singing. We try again that solitude found in the midst of those who with us seek their hidden reckonings. Our eyes reclaim the remembered faces; their voices stir the surrounding air. The warmth of their hands assures us, and the gladness of our spoken names. This is the reason of cities, of homes, of assemblies in the houses of worship. It is good to be with one another. Amen.

—Attributed to Kenneth L. Patton (Hudson 1962)

Invocations and Opening Words

§

What is it a man desires? A child to live after him, a mate to share his days. A friend who will not think strange the thoughts of his mind. Something that will use all of him in a great doing.

—Kenneth L. Patton (Hudson 1962)

§

We come to celebrate life—to enter with reverence upon the deep thoughts of birth and death, of meaning and purpose. We come to celebrate life—to rejoice in the tides of life about us and within, to sing in gladness for the companionship of man. We come to celebrate life—recalling in a bright procession of memory the great and good who have blessed mankind; giving thanks that no less noble men still arise with minds for knowledge and hearts for righteousness.

—Kenneth L. Patton, W. R. Holloway, and Robert Ingersoll (Hudson 1962)

§

If you have come this morning to hear old answers to old questions: You will be disappointed. We have already dismissed the old answers; now we must ask the new questions.

—Lawrence M. Hamby (Hudson 1962)

§

Come again into this circle where we seek to grow in love and justice. Come in calmness to be deeply thoughtful; deeply grateful to all that has made us. Come that at this point between birth and death each one of us, and all within our reach may grow mightily toward surpassing goodness and adequacy for our day.

—Lewis Lester Clark (Hudson 1962)

§

For every one that asketh receiveth; and he that seeketh findeth; and to him that knocketh it shall be opened.

—Matthew 7:8 KJV

§

I brought my spirit to the sea
I stood upon the shore.
I gazed upon infinity
I heard the waters roar.

And then there came a sense of peace
Some whisper calmed my soul.
Some ancient ministry of stars
Had made my spirit whole.

I brought my spirit to the trees
That stood against the sky.
I touched each wand'ring careless breeze
To know if God were nigh.

And then I felt an Inner Flame
That fiercely burned my tears.
Upright, I rose from bended knee
To meet the asking years.

—Max A. Kapp (Hudson 1962)

§

My mission in life is not merely to survive, but to thrive, and to do so with some passion, some compassion, some humor, and some style.

—Maya Angelou (Hudson 1962)

§

Though our knowledge is incomplete, our truth partial, and our love imperfect, we believe that new light is ever waiting to break through individual hearts and minds to enlighten the ways of men, that there is mutual strength and willing cooperation, and that the bonds of love keep open the gates of freedom.

—Napoleon W. Lovely (Hudson 1962)

§

We are gathered together that we may seek those things which make life larger and better, and that we may learn to avoid those things which diminish and degrade us.

—Attributed to Paul B. Henniges (Hudson 1962)

§

Let the words of my mouth, and the meditation of my heart, be acceptable in thy sight, O Lord, my strength, and my redeemer.

—Psalm 19:14 KJV

§

There is no hell for any of us to fear outside of ourselves.

—Quillen Hamilton Shinn (Owen-Towle 1993, 43)

§

Where the mind is without fear
And the head is held high,
Where knowledge is free
Where the world has not been broken up into fragments by narrow
    domestic walls.
Where words come out from the depth of truth,
Where tireless striving stretches its arms toward perfection.
Where the clear stream of reason has not lost its way
Into the dreary desert sand of dead habit.

Where the mind is led forward by Thee
Into ever-widening thought and action.
Into that heaven of freedom, my Father,
Let my country awake!

—Rabindranath Tagore (Paul 2006, 162)

§

It is easy in the world to live after the world's opinion; it is easy in solitude to live after our own; but the great man is he who in the midst of the crowd keeps with perfect sweetness the independence of solitude.

—Ralph Waldo Emerson (Emerson 1987, 31)

§

Life is inconvenient, no doubt about it.
It's messy.
It is mystery wrapped in an enigma and surrounded by a quandary, all in the shape of a question mark.
It is often more question than answer, more doubt than faith.
It is defined by contradiction, paradox, ambivalence and oxymoron.
That is why human beings invented religion—to figure it all out.

—Richard S. Gilbert (Gilbert 2019a)

§

Life is too transient to be cruel with one another;
It is too short for thoughtlessness,
Too brief for hurting.
Life is long enough for caring,
It is lasting enough for sharing,
Precious enough for love.
Be gentle with one another.

—Richard S. Gilbert (Gilbert n.d.)

§

Strengths and weakness,
Arrogance and humility,
Confidence and fear
Live together in each one,
Reminding us that we share a common humanity.
We are all more human than otherwise.

—Richard S. Gilbert (Gilbert 2019b)

§

Swinging through the universe on the invisible chord of existence, we experience moments of profound searching, trying with our thoughts and feelings to reach the mystery, the reason why, the ultimate source of existence itself. We find ourselves human beings in a tiny corner of a vast universe upon a planet which one day will disappear. Our search is for meaning. And our search is for the right.

—Adapted from Robert Nelson West (Hudson 1962)

§

We lift our eyes from the swiftly moving scenes about us by which we are often confused, that we may see again the wisdom and power and love sufficient for all our necessities. May we walk in the light, share in wisdom, rest upon love that we may be ready to play our part in the life of our times. May we think surely, act kindly, love wisely that we may leave the world better for having lived.

—Attributed to Robert T. Dick (Hudson 1962)

§

Part angel, part beast. Human. Perfect in imperfection.

—Michael Johnson
(personal communication, September 1992)

§

For, lo, the winter is past, the rain is over and gone; the flowers appear on the earth; the time of the singing of birds is come, and the voice of the turtle dove is heard in our land.

—Song of Solomon 2:11–12 KJV

§

Here beyond the striving and confusion of the world
Is a pathway to peace and power
Where departed visions may be regained
And wearied faith renewed.
Within these stately walls,
Through quiet meditation and communion,
May be found the soul of all beauty,
The source of all good,
And the eternal spirit resident in all sanctuaries of love.

—Rollins College Chapel Tablet (Hudson 1962)

§

Be ours a religion which, like sunshine, goes everywhere; its temple, all space; its shrine, the good heart; its creed, all truth; its ritual, works of love; its profession of faith, divine living.

—Theodore Parker (Parker 2019)

§

Into this house of light we come to seek that which is just and to find that which is good, and here we remember those whose lives are darkened by the greed and wrong of others. We have not purged the commerce of our times of those harsh ways that thwart the hopes and dreams of many. In this house of peace we remember wars and rumors of wars; we have made but feeble effort to understand the peoples of the world and to foster peace among the nations. In this house of joy we remember all sorrowing and troubled folk. Let us here be gathered into a common power of goodwill which shall issue in lasting peace and larger right.

—Von Ogden Vogt (Vogt 2011)

Invocations and Opening Words

§

Whoever you are! You are he or she for whom the earth is solid and liquid,
You are he or she for whom the sun and moon hang in the sky,
For none more than you are the present and the past,
For none more than you is immortality.

—Walt Whitman (Whitman 1902, 249)

§

My spirit has passed in compassion and determination around the whole earth; I have looked for equals and lovers, and found them ready for me in all lands; I think some divine rapport has equalized me with them. . . . I see ranks, colors, barbarisms, civilizations—I go among them—I mixed indiscriminately, and I salute all the inhabitants of the earth.

—Walt Whitman (Whitman 1902, 191)

§

I say the whole earth, and all the stars in the sky, are for religion's sake.
I say no man has ever yet been half devout enough;
None has ever yet adored or worship'd half enough;
None has begun to think how divine he himself is, and how certain the future is.

—Walt Whitman (Whitman 1902, 6)

§

I know that the past was great, and the future will be great,
And I know that both curiously conjoint in the
present time, in myself and yourself,
And that where I am, or you are, this present day,
There is the center of all days, all races,
And there is the meaning, to us, of all that has ever
Come of races and days, or ever will come.

—Walt Whitman (Whitman 1902, 133)

§

We dedicate this hour to that which is highest—recognized by us in our bodies as health, in our minds as intelligence and zest for learning, in our hearts as love and loyalty, in our society as freedom and justice, and in the universe around us as beauty and order. . . .

—Adapted from William D. Hammond (Hudson 1962)

§

Let not this house be desecrated by a religion of show. Let it not degenerate into a place of forms. . . . Do not come here to take part in lethargic repetitions of sacred words. Do not come from a cold sense of duty, to quiet conscience with the thought of having paid a debt to God. . . . Come to worship in spirit and in truth, that is intelligently, rationally, with clear judgment . . . not prostrating your understandings, not renouncing the divine gift of reason, but offering an enlightened homage, such as is due to the Fountain of intelligence and truth.

—William Ellery Channing (Channing 1894, 420)

§

There is no choice but to immerse oneself in the stream of history, accept one's time-location, breathe in—with shared memories and hopes—the contamination of tradition, become defined as the man of this cause, this party, this emergency. Failure to accept responsibility, refusal to take a stand on vital issues, timid rejection. . . . These are denials of life—in effect they are deeds of death. To understand the times in which we live, to add our weight to the scales on the side of brotherhood and equality within valid difference, this is "life with shape and character"—the one eternity worth having.

—Attributed to William Ernest Hocking (Hudson 1962)

— 51 —

Readings and Songs

My husband and I had been at a small hotel in Bergen for two days before we discovered the stairway.

    We had known it was there, of course. We had seen the sign, if not the thing itself. But we used the elevator. Saved time, we thought, and the energy we needed for exploring that charming Norwegian town on misty October days.

    After breakfast on the third day, when the elevator seemed slow in arriving, my husband decided to walk up. He was waiting at the elevator door when I—and the elevator—arrived on the fourth floor. "Let me show you something," he said, and led me back down the stairs he had just come up.

    I was dazzled. Instead of the sterile, institutional look of most hotel stairways, this one had the warm beauty of an art-lovers home. There were bright paintings on all the walls, and at each landing a rug in jeweled tones, a table with fresh flowers, and exquisite chair or two. When we reach the first floor, we walked up again, filled with energy, drinking in the beauty.

    "We might have missed this," I said.

    "Have to be careful about saving time and losing life," he said.

—"The Unexpected Stairway"
by Barbara Rohde (Montgomery 2001, 15–16)

§

There was once a fellow who, with his father, farmed a little piece of land. Several times a year they'd load up the ox-cart with vegetables and drive to the nearest city. Except for their name and the patch of ground, father and son had little in common. The old man believed in taking it easy, and the son was the go-getter type. One morning they loaded the cart, hitched up the ox and set out. The young fellow figured that if they kept going all day and night, they'd get to the market by next morning. He walked alongside the ox and kept prodding it with a stick.

"Take it easy," said the old man. "You'll last longer."

"If we get to the market ahead of the others," said his son, "we have a better chance of getting good prices."

The old man pulled his hat down over his eyes and went to sleep on the seat. Four miles and four hours down the road, they came to a little house.

"Here's your uncle's place," said the father, waking up. "Let's stop in and say hello."

"We've lost an hour already," complained the go-getter.

"Then a few minutes more won't matter," said the father. "My brother and I live so close, yet we see each other so seldom."

The young man fidgeted while the two old gentlemen gossiped away an hour. On the move again, the father took his turn leading the ox. By and by they came to a fork in the road. The old man directed the ox to the right. "The left is the shorter way," said the boy.

"I know it," said the old man, "but this way is prettier."

"Have you no respect for time?" asked the impatient young man.

"I respect it very much," said the old fellow. "That's why I like to use it for looking at pretty things."

The young man was so busy watching the sun sink he didn't notice how lovely the sunset was. Twilight found them in what looked like one big garden.

"Let's sleep here," said the old man.

"This is the last trip I take with you," snapped his son. "You're more interested in flowers than in making money."

"That's the nicest thing you've said in a long time," smiled the old fellow.

A minute later he was asleep. A little before sunrise, the young man shook his father awake. They hitched up and went on. A mile and an hour away they came upon a farmer trying to pull his cart out of a ditch.

"Let's give him a hand," said the father. "And lose more time?" exploded the son.

"Relax," said the old man. "You might be in a ditch sometime yourself."

By the time the other cart was back on the road, it was almost eight o'clock.

Suddenly a great flash of lightning split the sky. Then there was thunder. Beyond the hills the heavens grew dark.

"Looks like a big rain in the city," said the old man.

"If we had been on time, we'd be sold out by now," grumbled his son.

"Take it easy," said the old gentlemen, "You'll last longer."

It wasn't until late in the afternoon that they got to the top of the hill overlooking the town. They looked down at it for a long time. Neither of them spoke. Finally, the young man who had been in such a hurry said, "I see what you mean, father."

They turned their cart and drove away from what had once been the city of Hiroshima.

—FROM *READER'S DIGEST* BY BILLY ROSE (ROSE N.D.)

§

I, Charles Lounsbury, being of sound and disposing mind and memory, do hereby make and publish this my Last Will and Testament, in order, as justly as may be, to distribute my interests in the world among succeeding men.

That part of my interests which is known in law and recognized in the sheep-bound volumes as my property, being inconsiderable and of no account, I make no disposition of in this, my Will. My right to live, being but a life estate, is not at my disposal, but, these things excepted, all else in the world I now proceed to devise and bequeath.

ITEM: I give to good fathers and mothers, in trust to their children, all good little words of praise and encouragement, and all quaint pet names and endearments; and I charge said parents to use them justly, but generously, as the deeds of their children shall require.

ITEM: I leave to children inclusively, but only for the term of their childhood, all, and every, the flowers of the field, and the blossoms of the woods, with the right to play among them freely according to the custom of children, warning them at the same time against the thistles and the thorns. And I devise to the children the banks of the brooks and the golden sands beneath the waters thereof, and the odors of the willows that dip therein, and the white clouds that float high over the giant trees. And I leave the children the long, long days to be merry in a thousand ways, and the night and the moon and the train of the Milky Way to wonder at, but subject, nevertheless, to the rights hereinafter given to lovers.

ITEM: I devise to boys jointly all the idle fields and commons where ball may be played, all pleasant waters where one may swim, all snow-clad hills where one may coast, and all streams and ponds where one may fish, or where, when grim winter comes, one may skate, to have and to hold the same for the period of their boyhood. And all meadows, with the clover-blossoms and butterflies thereof; the woods with their appurtenances; the squirrels and birds and echoes and strange noises, and all distant places, which may be visited, together with the adventures there to be found. And I give to said boys, each his own place at the fireside at night, all pictures that may be seen in the burning wood, to enjoy without hindrance and without any incumbrance of care.

ITEM: To lovers, I devise their imaginary world, with whatever they may need, as the stars of the sky, the red roses by the wall, the bloom of the hawthorn, the sweet strains of music, and anything else they may desire to figure to each other the lastingness and beauty of their love.

ITEM: To young men jointly, I devise and bequeath all boisterous inspiring sports of rivalry, and I give to them the disdain of weakness and undaunted confidence in their own strength. Though they are rude, I leave them to the powers to make lasting friendships, and of possessing companions, and to them exclusively I give all merry songs and brave choruses to sing with lusty voices.

ITEM: And to those who are no longer children, or youths, or lovers, I leave memory, and bequeath to them the volumes of the poems of Burns and Shakespeare, and of other poets, if there be any, to the end that they may live the old days over again, freely and fully without tithe or diminution.

ITEM: To the loved ones with snowy crowns, I bequeath the happiness of old age, the love and gratitude of their children until they fall asleep.

—"Last Will and Testament"
by Charles Lounsbury (Lounsbury n.d.)

Note: In the pocket of an old ragged coat belonging to an elderly man in Chicago, there was found, after his death, this will. According to Barbara Boyd, in the *Washington Law Reporter*, the man had been a lawyer, and the will was written in a firm clear hand on a few scraps of paper. So unusual was it, that it was sent to another attorney; and so impressed was he with its contents, that he read it before the Chicago Bar Association and a resolution was passed ordering it probated. It is now on the records of Cook County, Illinois.

§

We stand with eyes toward the east, awaiting the rising of the star, we pray that love shall become flesh and dwell among us; And that compassion shall be born in human hearts. We celebrate the discovery of fact in the garment of legend. Let every cradle be visited by the three good kings of Faith, Hope and Love. Then Christmas is with us always, and every birth is the birth of God among us, and every child is the Christ Child, and every song is the song of angels. To celebrate Christmas is to attest the power of love to remake humankind. May we be renewed in the love which can save the world.

—Edward L. Ericson (Ericson 2009)

§

The problem we face here is that what is most obvious is the easiest to forget and overlook. Man, as we know him today, seems able to go on living year after year without ever pausing to gape in wonder at the sheer miracle of existence itself. He lives as if all the world around him were simply a matter of course, a thing to be taken for granted, a part of humdrum familiarity that is nothing to get excited about. We exist, he says, so what?

Such strange forgetfulness of basic reality, such terrible insensitivity to the miraculous, may well be called a Fall, or original sin, as mythological language would have it. Man forgets to such an extent that he runs around like a squirrel chasing its own tail.

He is born and brought up; he goes to school and college; he matures and reaches adulthood; he works at a job in order to go on working; he gets married in order to bear children who will go through the same thing all over again; he dies. What is all this about? Where are we going and why? We do not ask ourselves such questions, for they are subversive and disturb the social order. We feel it is better to keep our minds on the trivial chores of the day, on the worries and economic problems of the next few years; and that it is not wise for us to brood too much about the fact that the world will one day come to an end and that long before that happens man as a race will be extinct. We prefer to forget that, and our subconscious orders us to forget it. Such thoughts seem to us morbid and inevitably to lead to the mental clinic.

Healthy-minded people, we believe, do not think such thoughts. Above all things we like to see ourselves as healthy-minded. When we turn over the brightly colored pages of *Life* or *The Saturday Evening Post* we see everybody in the advertisements riding in cars; cooing over washing machines; and exulting in sanforized shirts. Everyone is happy; everyone smiles; and everyone is fifteen to thirty years old, healthy, ruddy-cheeked, having a swell time, and preserved from grief by Monuments of Eternity and air foam mattresses. Occasionally an old timer, leaning on a stick, stands aside to watch the crowd, but only occasionally. The end of it all is carefully and decorously hidden. It is comfortable and snug. But it is not secure. A second look is enough to convince us that the happy life so advertised is sheer, unadulterated boredom. It is a charge account world in which the future is anchored down only by installments and the present is in the hands of the repair man. Yet we seem strangely able to forget that the whole fascination of life lies in our ability to live on a thin crust laid over a fathomless abyss of mystery.

—Frederic Spiegelberg (Hudson 1962)

§

I went to the woods because I wished to live deliberately, to front only the essential facts of life, and see if I could not learn what it had to teach, and not, when I came to die, discover that I had not lived. I did not wish to live what was not life, living is so dear; nor did I wish to practice resignation, unless it was quite necessary. I wanted to live deep and suck out all the marrow of life....

Our life is frittered away by detail. An honest man has hardly need to count more than his ten fingers, or in extreme cases he may add his ten toes, and lump the rest. Simplicity, simplicity, simplicity! I say, let your affairs be as two or three, and not a hundred or a thousand; instead of a million count half a dozen, and keep your accounts on your thumb-nail. In the midst of this chopping sea of civilized life, such are the clouds and storms and quick sands and thousand-and-one items to be allowed for, that a man has to live, if he would not founder and go to the bottom and not make his port at all, by dead reckoning, and he must be a great calculator indeed who succeeds. Simplify, simplify. Instead of three meals a day, if it be necessary eat but one; instead of a hundred dishes, five; and reduce other things in proportion. Our life is like a German Confederacy, made up of petty states, with its boundary forever fluctuating, so that even a German cannot tell you how it is bounded at any moment.... Men think that it is essential that the *nation* have commerce, and export ice, and talk through a telegraph, and ride thirty miles an hour....

Why should we live with such hurry and waste of life.... Hardly a man takes a half-hour's nap after dinner, but when he wakes he holds up his head and asks, "What's the news?" as if the rest of mankind had stood his sentinels. Some give directions to be waked every half-hour, doubtless for no other purpose; and then, to pay for it, they tell what they have dreamed....

Shams and delusions are esteemed for soundest truths, while reality is fabulous. If men would steadily observe realities only, and not allow themselves to be deluded, life, to compare it with such things as we know, would be like a fairy tale and the Arabian Nights' Entertainments. If we respected only what is inevitable and has a right to be, music and poetry would resound along the streets. When we are unhurried and wise, we perceive that only great and worthy things have any permanent and absolute existence, that petty fears and petty pleasures are but the shadow of the reality....

Time is but the stream I go a-fishing in....

—*WALDEN* BY HENRY DAVID THOREAU (THOREAU 1992, 86–89)

§

Last Christmas Eve, we had received orders to be prepared for a surprise attack against the Russians. Our trenches had been under heavy fire for days; we had either to retreat or to advance, and those who plan the moves of war decided on an advance. We had been waiting for hours, crouching against the walls of our trenches, when the word came, "Go."

We crept out into the snow, countless silent dark shapes against the whiteness, and ran to the sunken road which lay between our lines and the mountainside where the Russian trenches were. Shells screamed overhead and burst behind us, drowning out all noise we might have made, and when we reached the road, whispered orders from the Captain scurried down the line like mice: "Advance along the road. Don't dare make a sound or strike a light."

We tramped in knee-deep snow, skirting the friendly hillside that sheltered us from the fire, stealing toward the Russians. And then, just ahead of me I saw a boy kneel in the snow before a wayside crucifix and light a candle. It flickered in the still air, casting a feeble light on the image of Christ above it. "Oh, Lord," the man next to me sighed, reaching into his knapsack for a candle. Others had seen the glowing light, and as I looked around, I saw that more and more candles were lighted all around. A whisper spread, like the order from the Captain from mouth to mouth, only this was not an order from the Captain. "Light a candle for Christmas Eve," men whispered, and their very words seemed to turn into tiny stars as dozens and dozens, then hundreds of candles came forth from the knapsacks to be lighted and stuck in the snow. The hillside now was one glow of light and the crucifix was bright with an unearthly brightness. We were a target for the Russian guns, but we never gave it a thought. For a little while we were lost in prayer, until one of the men cried: "They have stopped firing. Look!"

Across the valley, on the hillside where the Russians were entrenched, a few small flames began to tremble, then more and more. Candles, hundreds of them, thousands, one for every gun that was now silent. Around me men began to sing "Holy Night, Silent Night" and from across the valley the song came back to us a thousand-fold. Behind the lines so facing each other, the guns had ceased to roar and no more shells were screaming between men and the stars. Perhaps the Christ Child had walked between the lines and while He walked, peace had stayed the guns.

—Adapted from *The Singing Tree* by Kate Seredy (Seredy 1990, 200–201)

§

Humility is perpetual quietness of heart. It is to have no trouble. It is never to be fretted or vexed, or irritable, to wonder at nothing that is done to me.... It is to be at rest when nobody praises me, and when I am blamed or despised. It is to have a blessed home within myself where I can go in and shut the door, and kneel to my Father and be at peace, as in a deep sea of calmness, when all around seems trouble.

—Andrew Murray (Murray 2011)
(Plaque on the desk of Dr. Bob Smith, co-founder of A.A.)

§

Christ climbed down
from His bare Tree
this year
and ran away to where
there were no rootless Christmas trees
hung with candy canes and breakable stars

Christ climbed down
from His bare Tree
this year
and ran away to where
there were no gilded Christmas trees
and no tinsel Christmas trees
and no tinfoil Christmas trees
and no pink plastic Christmas trees
and no gold Christmas trees
and no black Christmas trees
and no powder blue Christmas trees
hung with electric candles
and encircled by tin electric trains
and clever cornball relatives

Christ climbed down
from His bare Tree
this year
and ran away to where
no intrepid Bible salesmen
covered the territory
in two-tone Cadillacs
and where no Sears Roebuck crèches
complete with plastic babe in manger
arrived by parcel post
the babe by special delivery
and where no televised Wise Men
praised the Lord Calvert Whiskey

Christ climbed down
from His bare Tree
this year
and ran away to where
no fat handshaking stranger
in a red flannel suit
and a fake white beard
went around passing himself off
as some sort of North Pole saint
crossing the desert to Bethlehem
Pennsylvania
in a Volkswagen sled
drawn by rollicking Adirondack reindeer
with German names
and bearing sacks of Humble Gifts
from Saks Fifth Avenue
for everybody's imagined Christ child

Christ climbed down
from His bare Tree
this year
and ran away to where
no Bing Crosby carolers
groaned of a tight Christmas
and where no Radio City angels
ice skated wingless
thru a winter wonderland
into a jingle bell heaven
daily at 8:30
with Midnight Mass matinees

Christ climbed down
from His bare Tree
this year
and softly stole away into
some anonymous Mary's womb again
where in the darkest night
of everybody's anonymous soul
He awaits again

an unimaginable
and impossibly
Immaculate Reconception
the very craziest
of Second Comings

—*A Coney Island of the Mind*
by Lawrence Ferlinghetti (Ferlinghetti 1958, 69–70)

§

Whoso would be a man must be a nonconformist. He who would gather immortal palms must not be hindered by the name of goodness, but must explore if it be goodness. Nothing is at last sacred but the integrity of your own mind. Absolve you to yourself, and you shall have the suffrage of the world. . . .

What I must do is all that concerns me, not what the people think. This rule, equally arduous in actual and in intellectual life, may serve for the whole distinction between greatness and meanness. It is the harder, because you will always find those who think they know what is your duty better than you know it. It is easy in the world to live after the world's opinion; it is easy in solitude to live after our own; but the great man is he who in the midst of the crowd keeps with perfect sweetness the independence of solitude. . . .

A foolish consistency is the hobgoblin of little minds, adored by little statesmen and philosophers and divines. With consistency a great soul has simply nothing to do. He may as well concern himself with his shadow on the wall. Speak what you think now in hard words, and to-morrow speak what to-morrow thinks in hard words again, though it contradict everything you said to-day.—"Ah, so you shall be sure to be misunderstood?"—Is it so bad, then, to be misunderstood? Pythagoras was misunderstood, and Socrates, and Jesus, and Luther, and Copernicus, and Galileo, and Newton, and every pure and wise spirit that ever took flesh. To be great is to be misunderstood. . . .

We lie in the lap of immense intelligence, which makes us receivers of its truth and organs of its activity. When we discern justice, when we discern truth, we do nothing of ourselves, but allow a passage to its beams. If we ask whence this comes, if we seek to pry into the soul that causes, all philosophy is at fault. Its presence or its absence is all we can affirm.

And now at last the highest truth on this subject remains unsaid; probably cannot be said; for all that we say is the far-off remembering of the intuition. That thought, by what I can now nearest approach to say it, is this. When good is near you, when you have life in yourself, it is not by any known or accustomed way; you shall not discern the footprints of any other; you shall not see the face of man; you shall not hear any name; the way, the thought, the good, shall be wholly strange and new. It shall exclude example and experience. . . .

We are afraid of truth, afraid of fortune, afraid of death, and afraid of each other. . . .

Our housekeeping is mendicant, our arts, our occupations, our marriages, our religion, we have not chosen, but society has chosen for us. We are parlor soldiers. We shun the rugged battle of fate, where strength is born. . . .

Nothing can bring you peace but yourself. Nothing can bring you peace but the triumph of principles.

—"Self Reliance"
by Ralph Waldo Emerson (Emerson 1987, 29–34)

§

Starr King Carol

Wake little babe, a shepherd is here
A lamb in his arms has he
He gives you his lamb
And he gives you his staff
For you too a shepherd shall be.

Wake little babe for three Kings are here
With gifts in their arms for thee
They give you a crown, a robe and a ring
For you too a King shall be.

Sleep little babe—we watched through the night
And here are our gifts for thee
We give you our hearts
We give you our love
And these are our gifts to thee.

—Al Harmon (personal communication, December 1960) Written and first performed at the Starr King School, Berkeley, California

§

Well, so that is that. Now we must dismantle the tree,
Putting the decorations back into their cardboard boxes—
Some have got broken—and carrying them up to the attic.
The holly and the mistletoe must be taken down and burnt,
And the children got ready for school. There are enough
Left-overs to do, warmed-up, for the rest of the week—
Not that we have much appetite, having drunk such a lot,
Stayed up so late, attempted—quite unsuccessfully—
To love all of our relatives, and in general
Grossly overestimated our powers. Once again
As in previous years we have seen the actual Vision and failed
To do more than entertain it as an agreeable
Possibility, once again we have sent Him away,
Begging though to remain His disobedient servant,
The promising child who cannot keep His word for long.
The Christmas Feast is already a fading memory,
And already the mind begins to be vaguely aware
Of an unpleasant whiff of apprehension at the thought
Of Lent and Good Friday which cannot, after all, now
Be very far off. But, for the time being, here we all are,
Back in the moderate Aristotelian city
Of darning and the Eight-Fifteen, where Euclid's geometry
And Newton's mechanics would account for our experience,
And the kitchen table exists because I scrub it.
It seems to have shrunk during the holidays. The streets
Are much narrower than we remembered; we had forgotten
The office was as depressing as this. To those who have seen
The Child, however dimly, however incredulously,
The Time Being is, in a sense, the most trying time of all. . . .
There are bills to be paid, machines to keep in repair,
Irregular verbs to learn, the Time Being to redeem
From insignificance. . . .

—Adapted from "For the Time Being: A Christmas Oratorio"
by W. H. Auden (Auden n.d.)

– 52 –

Prayers and Meditations

Among all the chances and changes of our lives there are never-ending opportunities to do the wrong thing. We undertake tasks we never should have assumed. Tasks that need to be done and that are in our power to do, we refuse to do. We say things we never meant to say. We leave unsaid words that ought to have been spoken. Others wrong us just as we wrong them. It is a curious thing, in life so short, how much we can do to offend others, how much we can do that makes us feel guilt and shame inside. Mindful of our shortcomings, our prayer in this quiet and holy hour is for forgiveness: forgiveness that comes from the ability to see in others' errors our own mistakes; forgiveness finds life too short to nurture animosity; forgiveness that recognizes the universal need for a second chance, for new beginnings. But most of all we pray for the ability to forgive ourselves. When in the hour of our great despair, we flay ourselves and "all alone beweep our outcast state" let us have the courage and the calm to pray, "Forgive us our trespasses, even as we forgive those who trespass against us." And let us, in the spirit of forgiveness, which is the final and greatest act of love, know the being we would be shall yet come within us. Amen.

—Attributed to Arnold Farrow Westwood (Hudson 1962)

§

The life of man is a long march through the night, surrounded by invisible foes, tortured by weariness and pain, towards a goal that few can hope to reach, and where none may tarry long.

One by one, as they march, our comrades vanish from our sight.... Very brief is the time in which we can help them, in which their happiness or misery is decided. Be it ours to shed sunshine on their path, to lighten their sorrows by the balm of sympathy, to give them the pure joy of a never-tiring affection, to strengthen failing courage, to instill faith in times of despair. Let us not weigh in grudging scales their merits and demerits, let us think only of their need—of the sorrows, the difficulties, perhaps the blindness that makes the misery of their lives. Let us remember that they are fellow sufferers in the same darkness, actors in the same tragedy with ourselves. And so, when their day is over, when their good and their evil have become eternal by the immortality of the past, be it ours to feel that where they suffered, where they failed no deed of ours was the cause; but wherever spark of the divine fire kindled in their hearts, we were ready with encouragement, with sympathy, with brave words, in which high courage glowed.

—Bertrand Russell (Russell 1923, 25–27)

§

This is our aspiration: that we may live in a world made better by the efforts of our own hands. That we may come to understand the secret, hidden places of the human soul and fulfill its urgent needs. That we may seek freedom for the human spirit as a flying bird strokes his way through the unwalled air. That we may savor the delights of living, the rewards of loving, the expectations of dreaming, the fulfillment of giving ourselves, which only the youthful of heart, the strong of purpose, the confident of will can know. That we may measure ourselves against the possibility of what we ought to be. That we may comfort the weary and discover that our own weariness is comforted. That we may free the slave and behold that our own bonds are loosened. That we may cheer the lonely and find that our own loneliness is overcome. That we may grieve for the injured and rejoice that our own injury is healed. That we may love those who have never learned to love in return and perceive that our own hatred is vanquished. Amen.

—Attributed to Edward L. Ericson (Hudson 1962)

§

God make me brave for life; Oh, braver than this!
Let me straighten after pain, as a tree straightness after the rain,
Shining and lovely again.
God make me brave for life; much braver than this.
As the blown grass lifts, let me rise
From sorrow with quiet eyes,
Knowing Thy way is wise.
God make me brave, life brings
Such blinding things.
Help me to keep my sight;
Help me to see aright
That out of the dark, comes light!

—Grace Noll Crowell (Hudson 1962)

§

Life is full of opportunities for a second chance, a new beginning. Despite our shortcomings, there is hope that we may try again.

We think of the many ways that we long to do better. We will try harder with our children. We would try again with our marriages. We would not forget our parents. We would be more honest in our dealings with others. We would do our part to make this world a place of justice and peace.

We would try to be better persons just for ourselves. We would be filled with joy, although we cannot deny life's hardships. We would be open to beauty, although we cannot deny the difficulties of existence. We would open the springs of our creative power to nourish the wastelands of our being.

We seek forgiveness for past shortcomings. We seek the forgiveness of others, of those we have wronged. Yet in continuing to know and love us, they have forgiven us. Hardest of all, we would forgive ourselves, for in that moment we forgive ourselves we overcome what we have been and are freed to become greater persons.

Life may be blessed and holy. When we find peace within, our souls may be freed to soar in usefulness and joy. Amen.

—Author (Hudson 1962)

Prayers and Meditations

§

We would know the presence of peace.

Our lives are twisted into nonsense. We have learned how to swim through the ocean like fish, how to fly through the sky like birds—but we have forgotten how to walk on the earth like men. We would pause in the meadows of quiet; we would let the gentle breeze dry our tears; we would breathe the clean, fresh air; we would let sunshine fill our hearts.

In the hush of this place, we reach out for balance. We constantly weigh what we were and what we will be against what we are. May we not find ourselves wanting in the balance. Yet if we are wanting, may our inadequacies not embitter us. May we find peace within ourselves somewhere between our aspirations and our limitations. May we keep from crucifying ourselves on the cross of frustration between the thieves of regret for yesterday and fear of tomorrow. Amen.

—AUTHOR (HUDSON 1962)

§

It is evening—that gentle moment between day and night. We have left behind the noise and confusion of the day. The angel of night would enfold us in her wings of silence and peace.

It is twilight—the glare of day has been left behind. The depth of night has not yet enveloped us. It is a special time, not a time of noise and confusion, but a time of quietness and calm, a time of awareness and serenity.

It is twilight; it is evening.

—AUTHOR, 1956, STAR ISLAND (HUDSON 1962)

§

Few are the moments in which we can free ourselves to be whole, poised with love and courage for the adventure of life. We come here to confront our consciences, to recognize the wrongs and ills of this anguished world, to rededicate our hearts and hands to righting those wrongs.

We pause in grateful remembrance of those who are no longer with us, whose lives have enriched and enlarged us. Their example and instruction will always be an inspiration to us.

We patiently seek the paths which lead to our tomorrows. This is a place of quiet and of peace. There is gentleness here: in the wood, in the music, and in the presence of those about us. This is a place where we come to look into ourselves—and to look beyond ourselves.

We come here frenzied and rushed. We do many things, not doing any one very well. We do some things we don't need to, and leave undone many things that should be done.

We see ourselves as we once were, as we are now, and as we will be. May we accept what we have become, and may we have faith in what we will be. May we see the past and future converge in the present moment, which is eternal. Amen.

—Author (Hudson 1962)

§

Thou art the confidence of those who go down to the sea in ships, we also seek confidence and courage. We must venture forth on the seas of life. Some may simply stand on the shore and tremble at the thunder of the sea. But for us, it is not enough to remain in the secure harbor of past accomplishment. There is within us the impulse to reach toward the horizon, to better ourselves: just as in the mariner there is a restless urge to see the strain of canvas in the wind, to feel the rolling deck underfoot, and smell the salt air.

Nor, once under sail, can we wander aimlessly over the seas of life. We must choose a star, a goal, and set sail in that direction. We men of earth will never reach that star, earth-bound are we, but it will lead us as far as we can go. And we are limited to earth, to the limitation of being human. May we accept this. May we resign ourselves to necessary imperfection yet strive to do our best.

Storms beset us. We struggle with problems. Yet from each storm, we somehow pick ourselves up, wring the tears from our garments, and face life surer and stronger than before. We may be lashed about for many days by the elements, but we do not give up.

After the storm, the sun scatters the storm clouds, the sea stops striving. Not only do the elements cease to hamper us, however, they may cease to help us. When the world about us fails, we must reach within for strength, and pull on oars of determination and integrity.

Some day we may return to the port from which we sailed. Those we once knew, who stayed behind, who cringed in the corners of indecision, will hardly recognize us. We will be tall, sun-bronzed. Our hands will be rope-burned and calloused from our work. We will have about us the way of the sea, the way of life: the breath of the ocean, the freedom of the wind, the clarity of the sky, and the beauty of the sunset. Amen.

—Author (Hudson 1962)

§

Man, take off your hat and make yourself at home.
This is the end of the line.
This is where you get off.
This is your earth, where you belong.
Smell the air; it's good.
It's your air.
Your lungs grew in the breathing of it.
Take a drink of cool water.
It's yours to bubble through every cell of your being.
Stand in the wind and sun.
Breathe deep.
Let yourself go.
You're at home, boy.
Look at your dog running crazy through the grass.
He's glad to be alive in a world of smells and sounds and sunlight.
He isn't worrying about heaven and hell.
Take off your hat;
Let down your hair;
Make yourself at home.
It's all yours,
the fields, the clouds, the sky.
The same life that is in you runs through all the earth.
Pull a slender blade of grass.
Nibble the white tip.
Take life into your living body.
Run down the hill.
Jolt your bones a little.
Stretch your muscles.
Heave the air in and out of your lungs.
You are an animal.
It's good to be an animal.

You are not so far from all this.
The mother dog nursing her puppies is very close to the Madonna with
    the child at her breast.
The male robin feeding worms to his gaping young
Is very close to man bringing home the paycheck to his family....
Get next to yourself, fellow;
This is the end of the line.
This is where you get off.
Take off your hat and make yourself at home.
You belong!

—Kenneth Leo Patton (Hudson 1962)

§

In this quiet moment let each of us summon to remembrance those particular joys and burdens which we bring to this our common assembly. Let moments of special happiness be recalled in all their intensity, that we may rejoice in each other's joy. Let the burdens of frustration, of the little sacrifices which must be daily made without complaining, of the pain and grief and apprehension we all must sometimes bear—let these be placed upon the living altar of our common devotion. Let us recall those moments of which we are not proud, that here in this company of kindred spirits we may feel the cleansing and sustaining power of fellowship. Let us open our hearts to the ministrations of love, our eyes to the vision of beauty, our minds to the fullness of the truth. So, may we find strength and poise and wisdom for every time of need. Amen.

—Attributed to Max D. Gaebler (Hudson 1962)

§

We pray to God, the unconquerable spirit in man, that we may think of needs beyond our own. We pray that those who know pain may find relief, that those touched by the sorrow of death will find consolation. We pray that there will be meaning in all that man suffers.

    We pray for those in public office that they may seek only to do the common good. We pray for those who buy and sell, that they may seek no advantage for themselves that would hinder the good of all. We pray for all who work in fields or factory, for all who toil beneath the earth or fly the pathways of the air; for all who go down to the sea in ships; that they may have joy and gladness in their work.

We pray for this embittered broken world of ours, that somehow its leaders will find understanding; that somehow we can do our part to make it whole and safe again.

"Whatsoever things are true, whatsoever things are honest, whatsoever things are just, whatsoever things are pure, whatsoever things are lovely, whatsoever things are of good report; if there be any virtue, and if there be any praise, think on these things." Amen.

—Author and Phil 4:8 KJV

§

Our true life lies at a great depth within us. Our restlessness and weaknesses are in reality merely stirring on the surface. That is why we must each day retire in silence far into the quiet depths of our spirit and experience the real life within us. If we do this, our words and actions will come to be real also. May we learn the way to gently enter another's sorrow by sympathy, into another's joy by gladness, into another's hopes by faith and trust, into another's need by understanding and a sense of shared dignity. May we be to other souls the strength that abides and the spirit that is remembered with gladness.

—Attributed to Rabindranath Tagore (Hudson 1962)

§

God grant me the serenity
to accept the things I cannot change;
courage to change the things I can;
and wisdom to know the difference.

Living one day at a time;
enjoying one moment at a time;
accepting hardship as the pathway to peace;
taking, as He did, this sinful world
as it is, not as I would have it;
trusting that He will make all things right
if I surrender to His Will;

that I may be reasonably happy in this life
and supremely happy with Him
forever in the next.
Amen.

—Attributed to Reinhold Niebuhr (Wing 2009)

§

Lord, we thank Thee for this place in which we dwell;
For the love that unites us;
For the peace accorded us this day;
For the hope with which we expect the morrow;
For the health, the work, the food, and the bright skies,
That make our lives delightful;
And for our friends in all parts of the earth.
Let peace abound in our small company.
Purge out of every heart the lurking grudge.
Give us grace and strength to forbear and to persevere.
Give us the grace to accept and to forgive offenders.
Forgetful of ourselves, help us to bear cheerfully
the forgetfulness of others.
Give us courage and gaiety and the quiet mind.
Spare to us our friends, soften to us our enemies.
Bless us, if it may be, in all our innocent endeavors.
If it may not, give us the strength to encounter
that which is to come,
That we be brave in peril, constant in tribulation,
temperate in wrath,
And in all changes of fortune, and, down to the gates of death,
loyal and loving one to another.

—Robert Louis Stevenson (Stevenson n.d.)

§

Swinging through the universe on the invisible cord of existence, we experience moments of profound searching ... trying with our thoughts and feelings to reach the mystery, the reason why, the ultimate source of existence itself—where one day we ourselves will be at home.

We find ourselves human beings in a tiny corner of a vast universe upon a planet which one day will disappear. Our search is for meaning. And our search is for the right. In moments of painful awareness, we see our duty as unfulfilled creatures—our duty to strive for greater love, for courage to overcome our secret fears, but above all for wisdom and understanding.

We strive to attain that fullness of being of which we are so grandly capable. May we open ourselves to receive the truth which is around us and gird ourselves to assume the responsibility which does rest upon us. We would strive toward fulfilling the best within ourselves and every human being. . . . To make the best of life we have and to the share that life with others—in small ways, in great ways, but always with genuine love and intelligence and understanding.

—Robert Nelson West (Hudson 1962)

§

Out of the mystery of life, out of the mystery of the universe we came. We awoke to consciousness . . . In this strange world . . . surrounded by love, cared for by those who gave their lives for us. We found our way had been prepared through many generations by those who, forgetting themselves, had lived for humanity, and built homes and cities, and states, had banded together for the spiritual life, that the finer things as they appeared in human life might be ours also. . . . So, our prayer is not a prayer to a power far off, but a prayer to that power which is within us, that life of the eternal manifest through us, that spirit of peace and love about us, beyond our comprehension and yet a part of us. So, may we be joined together in this household of love. So, we would gather together all gracious memories and all high hopes and all real desires, feeling we are uttering that which is most human and that which is most divine.

—Attributed to Samuel McChord Crothers (Hudson 1962)

§

Lord, make me an instrument of Thy peace;
where there is hatred let me sow love;
where there is injury, pardon;
where there is doubt, faith;
where there is despair, hope;
where there is darkness, light;
and where there is sadness, joy.

O Divine Master,
grant that I may not so much seek to be consoled, as to console;
to be understood, as to understand;
to be loved, as to love;
for it is in giving that we receive,
it is in pardoning that we are pardoned,
and it is in dying that we are born to eternal life.

—St. Francis of Assisi (Francis n.d.)

§

Let us hold in our thoughts and in our love all persons with whom we live and work and play. We need one another in our purposes, in our happiness and in our achievements. We need one another when in trouble and the help or understanding word brings us hope and assurance. In the hours of feverish illness, the hand and voice of another is our comforting medicine. We need one another in our defeats, when with encouragement we must strive again; and in the hours of triumph we would have others rejoice with us in our joy. All our lives we are the sharing of one another. And we live most when we bring to each other understanding, encouragement, and love.

—Attributed to Todd J. Taylor (Hudson 1962)

§

It is not for comfort and solace for which we pray; rather we pray that we may be sensitive to wrong, conscious of injustice, troubled by falsity. Where there is poverty let us be poor, where there are prisons let us be prisoners. We do not pray for immunity from the world's ills; rather we pray for full knowledge of those ills to the enlargement of our powers for the cure of souls. We pray to be first to know wrong that we may be first to set it right. Where there is joy let us share it; where there is love let us partake of it. This we pray that all peoples may come to live in harmony in a world fit for human habitation.

—Attributed to Edward Ericson (Hudson 1962)

— 53 —
Benedictions and Closing Words

Truth has no special time of its own. Its hour is now, always, and indeed then most truly when it seems most unsuitable to actual circumstances.

—Albert Schweitzer (Schweitzer 1947, 30)

§

Come, my friends,
'Tis not too late to seek a newer world.
Push off, and sitting well in order smite
The sounding furrows; for my purpose holds
To sail beyond the sunset, and the paths
Of all the western stars, until I die.
It may be that the gulfs will wash us down:
It may be we shall touch the Happy Isles,
And see the great Achilles, whom we knew.
Tho' much is taken, much abides; and tho'
We are not now that strength which in old days
Moved earth and heaven, that which we are, we are;
One equal temper of heroic hearts,
Made weak by time and fate, but strong in will
To strive, to seek, to find, and not to yield.

—Alfred Lord Tennyson (Tennyson 2019)

§

Your fear will tell you that you are lost in the forest. Your love will tell you that you are the forest.

—Michael Johnson (personal communication, September 1992)

§

A lonely planet this is, in a vast, vast sky. But on this . . . tiny sphere, men love, and in their loving make all the belongingness we need.

—Arnold Farrow Westwood (Hudson 1962)

§

May peace dwell within our hearts,
And understanding in our minds;
May courage steel our wills,
And the love of truth forever guide us.

—Arthur Foote II (Foote n.d.)

§

Now, therefore, since the struggle deepens, since evil abides and good does not yet prosper, let us gather what strength we have, what confidence and valor, that our small victories may end in triumph, and the world awaited be a world attained.

—Barrows Dunham (Dunham 1947)

§

May life bless and keep you always, may your wishes all come true. May you always do for others, and let others do for you. May you build a ladder to the stars, and climb on every rung. May you stay forever young. May you grow up to be righteous, may you grow up to be true. May you always know the truth, and see the light surrounding you. May you always be courageous, stand upright and be strong, may you stay forever young.

Benedictions and Closing Words

May your hands always be busy, may your feet always be swift, may you have a strong foundation, when the winds of changes shift. May your heart always be joyful, may your song always be sung. May you stay, forever young.

—Bob Dylan (Dylan n.d.)

§

May the strength of the wind and the light of the sun, the softness of the rain and the mystery of the moon reach you and fill you. May beauty delight you and happiness uplift you, May wonder fulfill you and love surround you. May your step be steady and your arm be strong, May your heart be peaceful and your word be true. May you seek to learn, may you learn to live, May you live to love, and may you love—always.

—Celtic Blessing (Celtic Blessing n.d.)

§

When we come to realize the nature of the conflict and the issues that are at stake, we too will know that we have still to fulfill our promise to mankind. We will know that now, more truly than when Lincoln spoke, "we shall nobly save or meanly lose the last, best hope of mankind."

—Henry Steele Commager (Commager 1951, 42)

§

And, now may the courage of the early morning's dawning,
The strength of eternal hills and open fields,
The joy of silent streams and of the gentle wind,
The beauty of flowered gardens and the song of birds,
And the faith of youth be in your hearts:
And the love of God, that alone can build happiness
That makes family love flourish with the radiance of great joy,
Be with you always:
And the peace of a quiet evening's ending
And of the midnight,
Be yours now and forever. Amen.

—Irish Blessing (Wedding in Paradise n.d.)

§

May the spirit of Christmas which is peace, the beauty of Christmas which is hope, and the blessing of Christmas which is joy, be ours today and always. Amen.

—Author (Hudson 1962)

§

May the road rise to meet you,
May the wind be always at your back.
May the sun shine warm upon your face,
The rains fall soft upon your fields.
And until we meet again,
May God hold you in the palm of his hand.

May God be with you and bless you;
May you see your children's children.
May you be poor in misfortune,
Rich in blessings,
May you know nothing but happiness
From this day forward.

May green be the grass you walk on,
May blue be the skies above you,
May pure be the joys that surround you,
May true be the hearts that love you.

—Irish Blessing (Irish Blessing n.d.)

§

May you always have walls for the winds, a roof for the rain, and tea beside the fire. Laughter to cheer you, those you love near you, and all your heart might desire. May the sun shine all day long, everything go right, and nothing wrong. May those you love bring love back to you, and may all the wishes you wish come true. May luck be your friend, in whatever you do. And may trouble be always, a stranger to you.

—Traditional Irish Blessing (Hudson 1962)

Benedictions and Closing Words

§

Seek ye the Lord while he may be found, call ye upon him while he is near.... For ye shall go out with joy, and be led forth with peace: the mountains and the hills shall break forth before you into singing, and all the trees of the field shall clap their hands.

—Isa 55: 6,12 KJV

§

Go your ways, knowing not the answers to all things, yet seeking always the answer to one more thing than you know. Be searching with your fellow men; be adventurers in ways untrod. Hold the hope of discovery high within you—sharing the hope, and whatever discovery may come, with others.

—Attributed to John Winthrop Brigham (Hudson 1962)

§

Thus the spirit separates itself from the body . . . passing like clouds over the valleys of sorrow and mountains of happiness and returns to its starting place, the endless ocean of love and beauty which is God.

—Kahlil Gibran (Hudson 1962)

§

May we be tired of pain, hateful of hate, intolerant of intolerance, at war with war. May we know that life is how we fumble through our days, hurt and hurting, feared and fearing. Let us be struck now with the urgent need to serve life so that pain will cease to plague our world in that tomorrow that always comes.

—Max Alden Coots (Hudson 1962)

§

The Lord bless thee, and keep thee:
The Lord make his face shine upon thee, and be gracious unto thee:
The Lord lift up his countenance upon thee, and give thee peace. Amen.

—Num 6:24–26 KJV

§

Here unto you has been spoken the truth,
Because of this truth you shall stand.
Here, declared is the truth!
Here in this place has been shown you the truth;
Therefore, arise, go forth in its strength. Amen.

—Omaha Indian Ceremony ("Naming Indian Children" 2018)

§

May the truth that makes us free, and the hope that never dies, and the love that casts out fear, lead us forward together, until the dayspring breaks and the shadows flee away. Amen.

—Hymns of the Spirit (Patheos 2017)

§

Let the horizon of our minds include all men: the great family here on earth with us; those who have gone before and left to us the heritage of their memory and of their work; and those whose lives will be shaped by what we do or leave undone.

—Attributed to Samuel McChord Crothers (Fewkes 1999)

§

Go, and be happy. You are born into the dazzling light of day. Go, and be wise. You are born upon an earth which needs new eyes. Go, and be strong. You are born into a world where love rights wrong. Go, and be brave. Possess your soul; that you alone can save.

—Siegfried Sassoon (Sasson n.d.)

§

Preach the Gospel at all times. Use words if necessary.

—Attributed to St. Francis (Zimmerman 2002)

§

May our experience be enlightened by understanding, our love ennobled by service, and our faith strengthened by knowledge.

—T. Conley Adams (Adams 1963)

§

There is no single punchline, but many. And actually no happy endings, because there is no ending.

—Wendy Starr Hudson (Hudson 1962)

§

Thank you for being there with us in the midst of our troubles. Help us lean on you when trouble strikes and not to fear anything, because of your promises and love. When I was in trouble, I called out to You, Lord, and You answered me. Amen.

—Deborah Joy Schultheiss (Hudson 1962)

PART V

Special Services

– 54 –

Membership

Leader: One of the most precious values a human being has to give to the world in which he lives is his loyalty, for it expresses what is deepest and most powerful in his attitude toward life. There is no substitute for sincere, intelligent devotion to universal human ideas. Nor is any man's life complete without a vital relationship to a living institution into which are built the values and satisfactions a man deems highest in human living.

Congregation: We unite to affirm the principles of freedom of belief, the preservation of personal integrity, the search for truth through critical inquiry, the use of the democratic process in human relations, and devotion to the greater good of mankind. We welcome you among us; by your increase we are stronger; by your addition is the free faith more able to plan mightily and achieve greatly. We welcome you among us, brothers and sisters; new seekers after truth and good.

—Anonymous (Hudson 1962)

§

Leader: We welcome you into our membership. We need your courage and skill, as being human you need our supporting fellowship. May you find here both happiness and wisdom for daily living. We would place our hands in yours and have you share our perspectives, our satisfactions, and our certainty that our finest hopes may here be realized.

Congregation: We welcome you as new friends in the search for truth. We share your confidence in the ultimate triumph of goodwill and justice in the world, and your belief that a living church can foster the coming of that victory. We would join our strengths and talents with yours, believing that humankind can be liberated from the age-old fetters of fear and superstition, poverty, and hate.

New Members: We join the fellowship of this church, not to seek escape from duty, nor refuge from the struggle of this world, but to add our portion great or small, to the common riches of humanity. We would cherish truth more than comfort and security. We would lend aid to the weak and disheartened, that together we may help to build a society, united, full and free.

—Anonymous (Hudson 1962)

§

Minister: As a minister of this congregation, I am privileged to welcome new members to a growing community. In doing so I speak now with those who constitute our present congregation, of all who have labored with us in the past and who shall benefit from our fellowship in the future.

Congregation: We are eager to share fellowship and our vision. We are strengthened and encouraged by the desire of these new members to join our church community.

New Members: We count it a privilege to share the joys and responsibilities of this church. May the ties that bind us together be strengthened day by day and year by year, and may the whole world be enriched by what we have to give.

Minister: This is a free church. It has no creed. It requires a member to think through his own beliefs and apply them in his life. It is a church of all peoples and all faiths, that welcomes every seeker of truth, beauty and goodness regardless of sect, class, nation, faith, race, or sexual preference.

New Members: We pledge ourselves to serve this community and all our fellowmen. We shall take pride in the freedom of the pulpit and the pew. We shall accept differences among us as opportunities for the growth of love and understanding, and for the enrichment of our religious life. We shall strive to be unselfish in our service to the common good.

All: As members of a beloved community, cherishing freedom, truth and love, we pledge our lives anew to the building of the church universal, which shall make of all sexes, classes, nations and races, one fellowship of all, and bring equality and peace on earth at last.

—Anonymous (Hudson 1962)

§

When you join this church, as we hope you will, you will not be asked to subscribe allegiance to any form of belief, nor to pledge fidelity to this church as an institution. To require the former would be to do violence to the principles of free inquiry and spiritual liberty upon which our fellowship is founded, while to request the latter would be to doubt the sincerity of your intentions. In short, you will enter as a free person into a free church; and we take it for granted that your sense of honor will cause you to fulfill the obligations of freedom, even as your intelligence will be clear to you what these obligations are.

It is in this friendly spirit, pervaded by freedom, sensitive to responsibility, and characterized by mutual respect, that we welcome you into active, voting membership, with all the rights, privileges and moral obligations pertaining thereto.

—Christopher G. Raible (Hudson 1962)

§

We gladly walk with those who like to travel with us. If you have more truth than we have found, we need your light; if you found less, you are in need of our fellowship. If the way is lonely and the quest seems endless, you will at least have understanding, companionship and affection. . . . So, we welcome you to the way not only of the trained mind but also of the educated heart.

—George Patterson (Hudson 1962)

§

Love is the doctrine of this church,
The quest of truth is its sacrament,
And service is its prayer.
To dwell together in peace,
To seek knowledge in freedom,
To serve mankind in fellowship,
To the end that all souls shall grow into harmony with the Divine—
Thus do we covenant with each other and with God.

—Compiled by L. Griswold Williams (Williams n.d.)

§

This is the church of the free spirit which welcomes every honest seeker after truth. Its membership is open to all who, accepting its methods and sharing its principles, would join with others in common cause. We can offer you no titles to celestial real estate, but we can offer you ground to stand upon today. We can offer you no non-cancelable fire insurance for future protection, but we can be volunteer firemen with you to extinguish current flames. We can offer no bound book of God's final revelation, but we will share with you the loose-leaf pages of the ever-growing Bible of human inspiration. Joining this church neither saves nor sells your soul, but it can bring nourishment to your spirit. Joining this church does not weaken your ties with society; it strengthens your bonds with the cause of freedom.

—Marin County Church Newsletter (Hudson 1962)

§

Minister: As minister of this congregation, I am privileged to welcome new members to our growing community. In doing so, I speak not only for those who constitute our present congregation, but for all who have shared with us in the past and I trust for those who shall participate with our fellowship in the future.

Congregation: We would share our fellowship and our vision. We are strengthened and encouraged by the desire of the new members to join our community.

New Members: We would share in the joys and responsibilities of this church. May the ties that bind us together be strengthened day by day and year by year, and may the whole world community be enriched by what we have to give.

Minister: This is a free church. It has no creed. It requires a member to think through his own beliefs and to apply them in his life. It is a church of all people and all faiths, welcoming every seeker of truth, beauty and goodness, regardless of his sect, class, nation, faith or race.

New members: We pledge ourselves to serve our community and all of society. We shall take pride in the freedom of the pulpit and of the pew. We shall accept all differences among us as opportunities for the growth of love and understanding, and for the enrichment of our religious life. We shall strive to be unselfish in our service of the common good.

All: As members of a beloved community we unite in the free quest of the high values of religion and life. Cherishing freedom, truth and love, we pledge our lives anew to the building of the church universal, which shall make of all sects, classes, nations and races, one fellowship of all people to dwell on the face of the earth.

—Marin County Church (Hudson 1962)

§

Minister: Fellow members, by joining this liberal church, you reaffirm your wish to find fellowship, work, and worship in our society of free faith. Here you may discover the measure of your beliefs through the dedication of your better selves. Here with your help may we find the renewal of our faith in the worthfullness of life and the wonder of the universe.

Congregation: We, the members of May Memorial Unitarian church, welcome you into this church and pledge you our friendship, as we strive for the common purposes that bring us here.

New Members and Congregation: Together we dedicate ourselves anew to the high calling of truth, the urgent needs for human service, the responsibilities of freedom, and the larger living of worship.

—May Memorial Unitarian Church (Hudson 1962)

— 55 —
Weddings and Commitments

INVOCATION

Dearly beloved, we are gathered together to unite this man and this woman in marriage, which is an institution ordained by God in the very laws of our being, for the happiness and welfare of mankind, and made honorable by the faithful keeping of good men and women in all ages.

To be true, this outward act must be but a symbol of that which is inner and real—a sacred union of hearts which the church may bless, and the state may make legal, but which neither can create or annul.

To be happy, there must be a consecration of each to the other, and the both to the noblest ends of life.

PRAYER

In the quiet of this hour, let each of us bring an offering of penitence, if not of purity; of love, if not of holiness; of teachableness, if not of wisdom; of devout obedience for the time to come, if not the fruits of well doing in the time that is past.

"Whatsoever things are true, whatsoever things are honest, whatsoever things are just, whatsoever things are pure, whatsoever things are lovely, whatsoever things are of good report; if there be any virtue, and if there be any praise, think on these things" (Phil 4:8 KJV).

VOWS

Will you, _____, have _____ to be your wedded wife/husband, to love and to cherish, to hold and to comfort, in sickness or in health, in sorrow or in joy, forsaking all others, from this day forth?

Who gives this woman to be married?

Will you please join hands and repeat after me: I _____ take thee _____, to be my wedded wife/husband, to have and to hold from this day forward, for better for worse, for richer for poorer, in sickness and in health, to love and to cherish, all the days of our lives.

RINGS

What do you offer as a token of these vows?

The circle is the symbol of the sun and the earth and the universe. In these rings is the symbol of unity in which your lives are joined in one unbroken circle, in which wherever you go, you will always return to one another.

Repeat after me: With this ring I thee wed.

PRONOUNCEMENT

Forasmuch as this man and woman have taken the solemn vows of matrimony, and in token have given and received rings, by virtue of the authority vested in me by the State, I do pronounce them husband and wife.

§

ALTERNATIVE WEDDING CEREMONY

To everything there is a season, and a time to every purpose under the heaven: a time to be born, and a time to die; a time to plant, and a time to pluck up that which is planted; a time to kill, and a time to heal; a time to break down, and a time to build up; a time to weep, and a time to laugh; a time to mourn, and a time to dance . . . a time to rend, and a time to sew; a time to keep silence, and a time to speak; a time to love, and a time to hate; a time of war, and a time of peace (Eccl 3:1–8 KJV).

BLESSING OF RINGS

The circle is the symbol of the sun and the earth and the universe. In these rings is a symbol of unity, in which your lives are joined in one unbroken circle, in which wherever you go, you will always return unto one another.

WEDDING PRAYER

Eternal one, we pray rich blessings upon this couple, who in thy presence and in the sight of this company have pledged unto each other all that mind and heart and hand can give. May they ever remain faithful to the vows taken this day. In serenity of spirit, may they learn to face with courage and patience whatever afflictions may be visited upon them and on those whom they love. May the love which they have for one another grow in meaning and strength until its beauty is made manifest in a common devotion to all that is compassionate and life-giving. Learning to serve one another in a partnership of love, may they learn to serve the highest ends of humanity itself, and thus become constant witnesses to Thy living presence in the midst of each common day. Amen.

VOWS

I take you to be the wife/husband of my days, to be the mother/father of my children, to be the companion of my house; we shall keep together what share of trouble and sorrow falls upon us, and we shall share together our store of goodness and plenty and love.

PRONOUNCEMENT

Now you will feel no rain, for each of you will be a shelter to the other. Now you will feel no cold, for each of you will be warmth to the other. Now there is no more loneliness, for each of you will be companion to the other. Now you are two bodies, but there is one life before you. Go now to your dwelling place, to enter into the days of your togetherness. And may your days be good and long upon the earth.

—Apache Wedding Prayer Blessing (Apache 2019)

§

May you be friends forever and ever
When the hills are all flat
And the rivers run dry
When the trees blossom in winter
And the snow falls in summer
When heaven and earth mix
Not till then will you part from each other.

—Chinese Blessing ("Jacob Marries" n.d.)

§

May God be with you and bless you
May you see your children's children
May you be poor in misfortunes, rich in blessings
May you know nothing but happiness
From this day forward. Amen.

—Irish Wedding Prayer (Emerald Heritage n.d.)

§

There was a man in Jambunada who was to be married the next day, and he thought, "Might the Buddha, the Blessed One, be present at the wedding." And the Blessed One passed by his house and met him, and when he read the silent wish in the heart of the bridegroom, he consented to enter. . . . The Blessed One was pleased to see so many guests full of good cheer and he quickened them and gladdened them with words of truth, proclaiming the bliss of righteousness: "The greatest happiness which a mortal man can imagine is the bond of marriage that ties together two loving hearts. But there is a greater happiness still: it is the embrace of truth. Death will separate husband and wife, but death will never affect him who has espoused the truth. Therefore, be married unto the truth and live with the truth in holy wedlock. The husband who loves his wife and desires for union that shall be everlasting must be faithful to her so as to be like truth itself, and she will rely upon him and revere him and minister to him. And the wife who loves her husband and desires a union that shall be everlasting must be faithful to him so as to be like truth itself; and he will place his trust in her, he will honor her, he will provide for her. Verily, I say unto you, their wedlock will be holiness and bliss, and their children will become like unto their parents and will bear witness to their happiness. Let no man be single, but everyone be wedded in holy love to the truth. And when Mara, the destroyer, comes to separate the visible forms of your being, you will continue to live in the truth.... For the truth is immortal.

—"Marriage Feast in Jambunada" by Gotama Buddha (Buddha 1894, 180–82)

§

How do I love thee? Let me count the ways.
I love thee to the depth and breadth and height
My soul can reach, when feeling out of sight
For the ends of Being and ideal Grace.
I love thee to the level of every day's
Most quiet need, by sun and candle-light.
I love thee freely, as men strive for Right;
I love thee purely, as they turn from Praise.
I love thee with the passion put to use
In my old griefs, and with my childhood's faith.
I love thee with a love I seemed to lose
With my lost saints—I love thee with the breath,
Smiles, tears, of all my life!—and, if God choose,
I shall but love thee better after death.

—Elizabeth Barrett Browning (Browning 1908, 43)

§

May your joys be as bright as the morning,
Your years of happiness as numerous as the stars in the heavens,
And your troubles but shadows that fade in the sunlight of love.

—Old English Blessing (Old English Blessing n.d.)

§

Though I speak with the tongues of men and of angels, and have not charity, I am become as sounding brass, or a tinkling cymbal. And though I have the gift of prophecy, and understand all mysteries, and all knowledge; and though I have all faith, so that I could remove mountains, and have not charity, I am nothing. And though I bestow all my goods to feed the poor, and though I give my body to be burned, and have not charity, it profiteth me nothing. Charity suffereth long, and is kind; charity envieth not; charity vaunteth not itself, is not puffed up. Doth not behave itself unseemly, seeketh not her own, is not easily provoked, thinketh no evil; Rejoiceth not in iniquity, but rejoiceth in the truth; beareth all things, believeth all things, hopeth all things, endureth all things. Charity never faileth: but whether there be prophecies, they shall fail; whether there be tongues, they shall cease; whether there be knowledge, it shall vanish away. For we know in part, and we prophesy in part. But when that which is perfect is come, then that which is in part shall be done away. When I was a child, I spake as a child, I understood as a child, I thought as a child: but when I became a man, I put away childish things. For now we see through a glass, darkly; but then face to face: now I know in part; but then shall I know even as also I am known. And now abideth faith, hope, charity, these three; but the greatest of these is charity.

—1 Cor 13:1–13 KJV

— 56 —

Christenings and Dedications

Do you parents commit yourselves to this child, promising to share with him/her your love and understanding, helping him/her grow into the person he/she potentially is?
 Do you friends here gathered dedicate yourselves to this child, promising from this day forward to assume responsibility for his/her well-being as the need arises?
 What is the name of this child?
 With the pedals of this rose, a symbol of promise and beauty, I dedicate your thoughts and vision and speech to the work of all humanity. May you find life to be the wonderful adventure of goodness and happiness that it can be. Amen.

—Author

§

In the great religions of the world—Christianity, Buddhism, and Confucianism—the birth of a baby plays a very important part. The reason the birth of a baby is central to these religions is that they have realized instinctively that regardless of their mysteries and miracles, there is no miracle greater than the birth of a baby.
 There's nothing that brings people together as does the birth of a child—as the three wisemen demonstrated. And as has been said, "a baby is very powerful, more powerful than the forces of violence because if people have feelings they answer and respond to a baby and the baby's needs, and they wonder at how he came from such a small beginning."

Christenings and Dedications

We come together to dedicate this child and to dedicate ourselves to him/her. I dedicate you to that which is lovely and true. I commend to parents and to us such love and wisdom that this small one will become a fully loving person. We shall provide the support and limitations necessary, and we shall offer the welcoming acceptance that enables this child to delight us in his/her growth and achievement. "The invincible shield of caring is a weapon from the sky against being dead." (Lao-Tse)

—Horton G. Colbert (Hudson 1962)

§

Families begin in love. They grow and deepen in meaning as a man and woman work and play and plan, sharing joy and sorrow. And just as the family celebrates their marriage, the family can gain strength and friendship in sharing the wonder and delight of children.

With these parents, we look back with thanks on the way they have come: their trials and their triumphs, their hopes realized and hopes disappointed, but even in disappointment deepening the bonds of affection and understanding. For all of us, this is a moment in which we pledge ourselves to be the friends of these parents and this child, whose coming into our circle we celebrate. Our aim for this child is, in Channing's words:

> Not to stamp our minds irresistibly on the young, but to stir up their own; not to make them see with our eyes, but to look inquiringly and steadily with their own; not to give them a definite amount of knowledge, but to inspire a fervent love of truth; not to form an outward regularity, but to touch inward springs. (Channing 1894, 449)

For you parents, this is a moment of rededication to the high purpose of your marriage for your growing family. Upon you who bring this child rests the high duty and the sacred joy of nurturing him/her with your understanding care. To you is trusted the weighty and wonderful privilege of helping to shape a new life, whose ultimate promise no one may guess. And from time out of mind, this happy occasion has been taken also as the fitting one for the bestowal of a child's name. For the name we bear is first the loving gift of our parents, echoing their hopes, honoring those whose life has made it precious.

It is our prayer that the name we now bestow may, through this child's growing life, come to be, by what he/she is and becomes, a symbol of what is lovely and of good report. _____, with the petals of this rose, symbol of promise and of beauty, I dedicate your thoughts, your vision, and your speech for the work of all humanity. May you serve with all your mind and soul and strength the ideals of truth and beauty, and may you put on nobility of purpose day by day.

We lift up our hearts in gratitude for this gift of new life. May this child, now accepted into our community of friendship and into the greater community of humanity, receive abundantly the blessings of health, love, knowledge and wisdom, and give back richly of these into the common heritage whence they receive them.

—Josiah R. Bartlett (Hudson 1962)

§

When parents asked me to dedicate their children, they are neither asking to cleanse them from some imaginary guilt, nor attempting to make them one of an elect and favored few. Rather, in dedicating a child we are recognizing him/her as an individual personality; we are acknowledging the sanctity of his/her own selfhood; and we are pledging him/her our aid that their high and noble hopes may find fulfillment....

Parents bring their children . . . not that they may be prematurely committed to doctrines and practices of whose meaning they can for years have no understanding; not that their own rightful choice in mature religious allegiance may be prejudiced; but in order that in their upbringing they may be surrounded with the love and care of an organized liberal religious fellowship.

—Robert T. Weston (Hudson 1962)

§

Dearly beloved, we bow our heads in silence a moment and seek God in our hearts, that He may be with us in what we do. O thou who art always in our midst, in time of joy and in time of happiness, and who needest only our open hearts to come, be with us in the joy of this hour, and by thy presence make our happiness supreme. It is in recognition of Thee, good giver of life and joy, who has given to man and woman a little child to keep, that we are gathered here. Make us feel thy presence, Lord. Make this thy holy place. Amen.

—Anonymous (Hudson 1962)

§

And to God, on whose name we have not called in vain, let us now dedicate this child. In the spirit of Jesus, who loved little children and found in their simplicity the Kingdom of Heaven, let us dedicate this child to the faith of his life and our inheritance. But still more, let us dedicate ourselves to this day. May this water of purification, so little heeded on this innocent brow, work its miracle in our hearts.

—Anonymous (Hudson 1962)

§

Go, and be happy. You are born into the dazzling light of day. Go, and be wise. You are born upon an earth which needs new eyes. Go, and be strong. You are born into a world where love rights wrong. Go, and be brave. Possess your soul; that you alone can save.

—Siegfried Sassoon (Sasson n.d.)

§

You may be Christ or Shakespeare, little child, a Savior or a sun to our lost world. There is no babe born but may carry furled strength to make bloom the earth's disastrous wild.

—James Oppenheim (Oppenheim 1907)

— 57 —

Funerals and Memorials

MEMORIAL SERVICE

We are met in a brief service of memory and of love, to mark the dignity and the mystery of what we call death, and each in his own way and in his own heart to cherish with honor and affection one who has passed from among us. It is not right that I should try to tell you about him/her. Rather that each in their own thoughts remember and honor the living personality and the fine qualities that were his/hers.

We know that these good things are not lost to us.

This is true of the memories we cherish. They will come flooding in to comfort us, ever more richly as the days go by.

This is true also in the sense of what the great teachers of mankind have called "ideal immortality," of which George Eliot wrote so beautifully in "The Choir Invisible":

> O may I join the choir invisible
> Of those immortal dead who live again
> In minds made better by their presence!

The good influences which from this life touched other lives, through them again affects others. So, the good things of this earth are created and handed on, and so from living person to person the Kingdom of God is perpetuated and enriched, in a reality over which death has no dominion.

It is true in an even more intimate way. As we grow older we find, as one of the most wonderful discoveries in life, that the dead are not lost to us so long as we love them, that they are forever part of us not only, but that they are with us and within us, themselves our comforters, themselves bringers of love and joy. The frailties and imperfections of their day-by-day existence, and our own imperfections in relation to them, now vanish from sight or become transmuted into something steadfast and beautiful. They shine like stars in the firmament of our lives and are often present in our thoughts more constantly and helpfully than when they were with us on this earth. They themselves deepen our faith and renew our courage. They are indeed "a choir invisible whose music is the gladness of the world."

The temple of clay which for a time the bright spirit inhabited now lies untenanted. But the spirit lives on, in us, and is its own reality.

There is for us at first a sense of utter lost in this change. But the benediction, the peace and the love of the departed are with us. And the spiritual is a reality which stands outside of and above time.

In this lofty faith we salute the passing of our friend lovingly and with profound respect; and commit to God's grace the soul that dwelt beautifully among us.

—Anonymous (Hudson 1962)

§

This world is the threshold of a vast life—the first stepping-stone in the boundless expanse of possibility. The universe is not a stage set for tragedy, but a highway which leads toward a life of hope and beauty.

All that God loves he constantly is healing, and when we are broken beyond the power of our love and skill to mend, the divine hand is laid upon us and Lo the unequal struggle ends and the peace that passes all understanding touches our weariness like all the mother love of the world, and he lifts us up in his wonderful arms and bears us across the waters of remembrance.

—Arnold Crompton (Hudson 1962)

§

Nothing is here for tears, nothing to wail
Or knock the breast, no weakness, no contempt
Dispraise, or blame, nothing but well and fair,
And what may quiet us in a death so noble

—John Milton (Milton 1853, 521)

§

The symbol of perpetual youth, the grass blade, like a long green ribbon, streams from the sod. . . . Lifting its spear of last year's hay with the fresh life below. . . . So our human life but dies down to its root, and still puts forth its green blade to eternity.

—Henry David Thoreau (Thoreau 1992, 292)

§

We would be undaunted by the thought of our mortality. Life is ours, rich in hope and rich in memory. Its glory is not that it endures forever, but that it for a time incarnates so much that is beautiful. We do not demand from the flower that it shall never wither, the sunset that it shall never fade, the song that it shall never cease. Nor would we rail at life because at length its beauty shall be ashes, its music silence, and all its laughter and all its tears forgotten. Life, the reality, is ours. We would shape it as nobly as we can. We would not linger, like a timid mariner in port, but live dangerously, devoting ourselves with abandon to what seems to us the good, the beautiful, the true.

—Curtis W. Reese (Hudson 1962)

§

We are drawn together this afternoon by our love of one who has stepped forth from this circle of earth into the luminous mystery of the ongoing universe. We are met, not for grief, but for the joy we have in him/her. Ours is a service, not a farewell, but of thanksgiving for the best part of him/her which remains with us, and which love can never lose.

Funerals and Memorials

Except that all parting is painful, this is not an occasion for tears; neither he/she nor we would have it so. We have not come to say farewell, except in an outer, transitory sense. Our purpose is higher: to look into our hearts for the spirit of one who is indeed already part of us, one whose deeds and thoughts have lasting value. We take this time to recall what he/she has meant to us, the principles he/she tried to live by, so we may take firmer hold on them, and be faithful to him/her by making them more truly our own.

—Josiah R. Bartlett (Hudson 1962)

§

His life was gentle,
And the elements mixed so well in him
That Nature might stand up and say to all the world
"This was a man."

—William Shakespeare (Shakespeare 1992, 209)

§

What a world it would be if nobody died! How old-fashioned, and conservative, and bigoted it would become! The very babies would be born old-fashioned children, and no man would be permitted to marry until a thousand years old, nor allowed to vote until one-and-twenty hundred.... God be thanked that we are born, and also that in due time we pass out of this world, and carry to that brighter sphere a few grains of goodness gathered here.

—Theodore Parker (Hudson 1962)

§

Something there is,
Something there is more immortal even than the stars,
Something that shall endure longer even than lustrous Jupiter
Longer than sun or any revolving satellite,
Or the radiant sisters the Pleiades.

—Walt Whitman (Whitman 2019)

§

The name of death was never terrible
To him that knew how to live.

—Attributed to Ralph Waldo Emerson (Emerson 2015)

§

The time of my departure has come. I have fought the good fight, I have finished the race. I have kept the faith. Henceforth there is laid up for me the crown of righteousness, which the Lord, the righteous judge, will award to me at that Day. . . .

—2 Tim 4:6–8 RSV

§

How strange is the lot of us mortals! Each of us is here for a brief sojourn; for what purpose he knows not, though he sometimes thinks he senses it. But without deeper reflection one knows from daily life that one exists for other people—first of all for those upon whose smiles and well-being our own happiness is wholly dependent, and then for the many, unknown to us, to whose destinies we are bound by the ties of sympathy. A hundred times every day I remind myself that my inner and outer life are based on the labors of other men, living and dead, and that I must exert myself in order to give in the same measure as I have received and am still receiving.

—Albert Einstein (Einstein 2019)

§

There is an ancient story about people who went to a tomb, seeking their dead friend. But the tomb was empty, and the people heard these words: "Why seek ye the living among the dead? He is not here."

He/she has returned to the silent mystery that is our common origin and our common destiny. His/her death, I know, has plowed your hearts and minds, turning up relics of past moments, and preparing for new harvests made possible by his/her life.

—Greta W. Crosby (Hudson 1962)

§

Nothing happens to any man that he is not formed by nature to bear.

—Marcus Aurelius (Aurelius 2019)

§

Blessed are the poor in spirit: for theirs is the kingdom of heaven. Blessed are they that mourn: for they shall be comforted. . . . Blessed are they which do hunger and thirst after righteousness: for they shall be filled. Blessed are the merciful: for they shall obtain mercy. Blessed are the pure in heart: for they shall see God.

—Matt 5:3–8 KJV

§

Come unto me, all ye that labour and are heavy laden, and I will give you rest. Take my yoke upon you, and learn of me; for I am meek and lowly in heart: and ye shall find rest unto your souls. For my yoke is easy, and my burden is light.

—Matt 11:28–30 KJV

§

He that goeth forth and weepeth, bearing precious seed, shall doubtless come again with rejoicing, bringing his sheaves with him.

—Ps 126:6 KJV

§

I have loved the stars too fondly to be fearful of the night.

—Adapted from Sarah Williams (Williams 2019)

§

For to fear death, my friends, is only to think ourselves wise without being wise: for it is to think we know what we do not know. For aught that we can tell, death may be the greatest good that can come to men: but they fear it as if they knew that it is the greatest of evils. . . . Believe this as a truth, that no evil can happen to a good man, either in life, or after death.

—Socrates (Socrates 1880, 49–50)

§

Were it not for friendship and love,
There would be little sorrow.
And were it not for sorrow
There would be less love.
Were it not for pain
There would be less joy and sympathy.
For the light makes the shadows possible
And the shadows reveal the light.

The passing of a true and noble life
Brings grief,
But no other experience makes the
Good life so precious,
Or the immortal hope so strong.

—Christopher R. Eliot (Eliot 1919, 233)

§

That life is more than death can halt our words which hope throughout all the ages has been whispering to love. The miracle of thought we cannot understand. The mystery of life and death we cannot comprehend. This chaos called "world" has never been aptly explained. The golden bridge of life from gloom emerges, and on shadow rests. Beyond this we do not know. Fate is speechless; destiny is dumb, and the secret of the future has never yet been told. We love; we wait; we hope. Sometimes the more we love the more we fear. Upon the tenderest heart the deepest shadow falls. All paths, whether filled with thorns or flowers, point to this. Here success and failure are all the same. The rag of wretchedness and the purple robe of power lose all differences and distinctions in this democracy of death. Love is immortal: goodness lives, and something of the personality survives.

—Robert G. Ingersoll (Hudson 1962)

§

Though I speak with the tongues of men and of angels, and have not charity, I am become as sounding brass, or a tinkling cymbal. And though I have the gift of prophecy, and understand all mysteries, and all knowledge; and though I have all faith, so that I could remove mountains, and have not charity, I am nothing. And though I bestow all my goods to feed the poor, and though I give my body to be burned, and have not charity, it profiteth me nothing. Charity suffereth long, and is kind; charity envieth not; charity vaunteth not itself, is not puffed up. Doth not behave itself unseemly, seeketh not her own, is not easily provoked, thinketh no evil; Rejoiceth not in iniquity, but rejoiceth in the truth; beareth all things, believeth all things, hopeth all things, endureth all things. Charity never faileth: but whether there be prophecies, they shall fail; whether there be tongues, they shall cease; whether there be knowledge, it shall vanish away. For we know in part, and we prophesy in part. But when that which is perfect is come, then that which is in part shall be done away. When I was a child, I spake as a child, I understood as a child, I thought as a child: but when I became a man, I put away childish things. For now we see through a glass, darkly; but then face to face: now I know in part; but then shall I know even as also I am known. And now abideth faith, hope, charity, these three; but the greatest of these is charity.

—1 Cor 13:1–13 KJV

§

David therefore besought God for the child; and David fasted, and went in, and lay all night upon the earth. And the elders of his house arose, and went to him, to raise him up from the earth: but he would not, neither did he eat bread with them.

And it came to pass on the seventh day, that the child died. And the servants of David feared to tell him that the child was dead: for they said, Behold, while the child was yet alive, we spake unto him, and he would not hearken unto our voice: how will he then vex himself, if we tell him that the child is dead?

But when David saw that his servants whispered, David perceived that the child was dead: therefore, David said unto his servants, Is the child dead? And they said, He is dead. Then David arose from the earth, and washed, and anointed himself, and changed his apparel, and came into the house of the Lord, and worshipped: then he came to his own house; and when he required, they set bread before him, and he did eat.

Then said his servants unto him, What thing is this that thou hast done? Thou didst fast and weep for the child, while it was alive; but when the child was dead, thou didst rise and eat bread. And he said, While the child was yet alive, I fasted and wept: for I said, Who can tell whether God will be gracious to me, that the child may live? But now he is dead, wherefore should I fast? Can I bring him back again? I shall go to him, but he shall not return to me.

—2 Sam 12:16–23 KJV

§

The Lord is my shepherd; I shall not want.

He maketh me to lie down in green pastures: he leadeth me beside the still waters.

He restoreth my soul: he leadeth me in the paths of righteousness for his name's sake.

Yea, though I walk through the valley of the shadow of death, I will fear no evil: for thou art with me; thy rod and thy staff they comfort me.

Thou preparest a table before me in the presence of mine enemies: thou anointest my head with oil; my cup runneth over.

Surely goodness and mercy shall follow me all the days of my life: and I will dwell in the house of the Lord forever.

—23 Ps KJV

§

Say not they die, those splendid souls
Whose lives are winged with purpose fine;
Who leave us, pointing to the goals;
Who learn to conquer and resign.

Such cannot die; they vanquish time,
And fill the world with growing light,
Making the human life sublime
With memories of their sacred might.
They cannot die whose lives are part
Of that great life—Humanity;
Whose hearts beat with the world's great heart,
And throb with its high destiny.
These souls are great, who, dying gave
New a gift of greater light to man;
Death stands abashed before the brave;
They own a life death cannot ban.

—Anonymous (Remembrances and Celebrations 1999, 254)

§

To laugh often and love much; to win and hold the respect of intelligent persons and the affection of little children; to earn the approbation of honest critics and to endure without flinching the betrayal of false friends; to appreciate beauty always, whether in earth's creations or man's handiwork; to have sought for and found the best in others, and to have given it oneself; to leave the world better than one found it, whether by a healthy child, a garden patch, a cheery letter, or a redeemed social condition; to have played with enthusiasm, laughed with exuberance, and sung with exaltation; to go down to dust and dreams, knowing that the world is a wee bit better, and that even a single life breathes easier because we have lived well, this is to have succeeded.

—Ralph Waldo Emerson (Emerson 2019)

§

You are anxious about whether you will rise from the dead or not, but you rose from the dead when you were born and you didn't notice it.... You have always been in others and you will remain in others. And what does it matter to you if later this is called your memory? This will be you—the you that enters the future and becomes a part of it.

—*Dr. Zhivago* by Boris Pasternak (Pasternak 1991, 68)

Part V: Special Services

§

The wheel turns.
The wheel comes to a standstill.
The wheel waits.
The wheel turns.
"Something began me
And it had no beginning;
Something will end me
and it has no end."

—*The People Yes* by Carl Sandburg (Sandburg 1970, 88–89)

§

Chuang-Tse, of the Tao faith, tells the story of how he once dreamed that he was a butterfly fluttering around gaily here and there. He was completely unaware of being a man any longer. Then, suddenly, he awoke and found himself lying in bed, still a human being. However, Chuang-Tse then had to ask: "Was I then a man and dreaming I was a butterfly, or am I now a butterfly dreaming I am a man?"

—Chuang-Tse (Ross and Hills 1954, 102)

§

Some time at eve when the tide is low,
I shall slip my moorings and sail away,
With no response to a friendly hail
Of kindred craft in the busy bay.
In the silent hush of the twilight pale,
When the night stoops down to embrace the day,
And the voices call in the waters' flow—
Some time at eve when the tide is low,
I shall slip my moorings and sail away.
Through the purpling shadows that darkly trail
O'er the ebbing tide of the Unknown Sea,
I shall fare me away, with a dip of sail
And a ripple of waters to tell the tale
Of a lonely voyager, sailing away
To the Mystic Isles, where at anchor lay
The crafts of those who have sailed before
O'er the Unknown Sea to the Unseen Shore.

A few who watched me sail away
Will miss my craft from the busy bay;
Some friendly barks that were anchored near,
Some loving souls that my heart held dear,
In silent sorrow will drop a tear—
But I shall have peacefully furled my sail
In mooring sheltered from the storm or gale,
And greeted the friends who had sailed before
O'er the Unknown Sea to the Unseen Shore.

—Elizabeth Clark Hardy (Hardy 1965, 273–74)

§

Think of death not as inevitable merely, but as something divine; a process of the universal Love, a moment in the universal life. Here is nothing monstrous or out-of-the-way. . . . But something of a piece with the setting sun or the waning moon and the falling leaf—a part of the great order, a necessary link in the universal chain which binds all being to the throne of God. St. Francis, who embraced all nature, brute and plant as well as men, with affectionate sympathy, included death also, as a part of nature, in his infinite goodwill. "Welcome, sister death," he said, as he felt his end draw near.

—Frederic Henry Hedge (Hedge 1866, 148–49)

§

[Adam Bebe] had not outlived his sorrow—had not felt it slip from him as a temporary burden and leave him the same man again. Do any of us? God forbid! It would be a poor result of all our anguish and wrestling, if we won nothing but our old selves at the end of it—if we could return to the same blind loves, the same self-confident blame, the same light thoughts of human suffering, the same frivolous gossip over blighted human lives, the same feeble sense of that Unknown towards which we have sent forth irrepressible cries in our loneliness. Let us rather be thankful that our sorrow lives in us as an indestructible force, only changing its form, as all forces do, and passing from pain into sympathy—that one poor word which includes all our best insight and our best love.

—George Eliot (Eliot 1900, 492)

§

Oh, may I join the choir invisible
Of those immortal dead who live again
In minds made better by their presence
In pulses stirred to generosity,
In deeds of daring rectitude, and scorn
For miserable aims that end with self,
In thoughts sublime that pierce the night like stars,
And with their mild persistence urge man's search
To vaster issues,—so to live in heaven:
To make undying music in the world.

—GEORGE ELIOT (ELIOT 1895, 217)

§

With you a part of me hath passed away;
For in the peopled forest of my mind
A tree made leafless by this wintry wind
Shall never don again its green array.
Chapel and fireside, country road and bay,
Have something of their friendliness resigned;
Another, if I would, I could not find,
And I am grown much older in a day.
But yet I treasure in my memory
Your gift of charity, and young hearts ease;
And the dear honour of your amity;
For these once mine, my life is rich with these.
And I scarce know which part may greater be,
What I keep of you, or you rob of me.

—GEORGE SANTAYANA (SANTAYANA 1998)

§

The life of mortals in this world is troubled and brief and combined with pain. For there is not any means by which those that have been born can avoid dying; after reaching old age there is death; of such a nature are living beings. As ripe fruits are early in danger of falling, so mortals when born are always in danger of death. As all earthen vessels made by the potter end in being broken, so is the life of mortals. Both young and adult, both those who are fools and those who are wise, all fall into the power of death; all are subject to death....

So, the world is afflicted with death and decay, therefore the wise do not grieve, knowing the terms of the world. In whatever manner people think something will come to pass, it is often different when it happens, and great is the disappointment; see, such are the terms of the world. Not from weeping or from grieving will anyone obtain peace of mind; on the contrary, his pain will be the greater and his body will suffer. He will make himself sick and pale, yet the dead are not saved by his lamentation. People pass away, and their fate after death will be according to their deeds. If a man live one hundred years, or even more, he will at last be separated from the company of his relatives and leave the life of this world. He who seeks peace should draw out the arrow of lamentation, and complaint, and grief. He who has drawn out the arrow and has become composed will obtain peace of mind. He who has overcome all sorrow will become free from sorrow and be blessed.

—Gotama Buddha (Buddha 1894, 187–89)

§

A Hindu mother gave birth to a son. When the boy was able to walk by himself, he died. The young mother carried the dead child clasped to her bosom, and went from house to house, asking if anyone could give her medicine for it. Some regarded her as mad; but a wise man said: "I cannot cure your son, but I know one who can attend to it. You must go to him: he can give medicine."

Then she went to him, and said, "Lord and Master, do you know any medicine that will be good for my boy?" He answered, "I know of some." She asked, "what medicine do you require?" The sage replied, "I require a handful of mustard seed taken from the house were no son, husband, parent, or servant has died." The mother then went about with her dead child, asking for the mustard seed. The people said, "Here is some mustard seed: take it." Then she asked, "In my friend's house has there died a son, a husband, a parent, or servant?" They replied: "What is this you say? The living are few, but the dead are many."

Then she went to other houses; but one said, "I have lost my son;" another, "I have lost my parent;" until at last she said: "This is a heavy task I have undertaken. I am not the only one whose son is dead. In the whole country, children are dying, parents are dying."

The woman went and laid her child down in the forest, and then came to the teacher. He said to her "Have you received the handful of mustard seed?" She answered, "I have not: the people of the village told me, the living are few, but the dead are many." Then he said, "You thought that you alone had lost a son; the law of death rules all." Then the mother devoted herself to helping others.

—Gotama Buddha (Hudson 1962)

§

I have an understanding with the hills
At evening when the slanted radiance fills
Their hollows, and the great winds let them be,
And they are quiet and look down at me.
Oh, then I see the patience in their eyes
Out of the centuries that made them wise.
They lend me hoarded memory and I learn
Their thoughts of granite and their whims of fern,
And why a dream of forests must endure
Though every tree be slain: and how the pure,
Invisible beauty has a word so brief
A flower can say it or a shaken leaf,
But few may ever snare it in a song,
Though for the quest a life is not too long.
When the blue hills grow tender, when they pull
The twilight close with gesture beautiful,
And shadows are their garments, and the air
Deepens, and the wild veery is at prayer,
Their arms are strong around me; and I know
That somehow I shall follow when you go
To the still land beyond the evening star,
Where everlasting hills and valleys are:
And silence may not hurt us any more,
And terror shall be past, and grief, and war.

—Grace Hazard Conkling (Conkling 2019)

§

Still, still with Thee, when purple morning breaketh,
When the bird waketh, and the shadows flee;
Fairer than morning, lovelier than daylight,
Dawns the sweet consciousness, I am with Thee.
Alone with Thee, amid the mystic shadows,
The solemn hush of nature newly born;
Alone with Thee in breathless adoration,
In the calm dew and freshness of the morn. . . .
When sinks the soul, subdued by toil, to slumber,
Its closing eye looks up to Thee in prayer;
Sweet the repose beneath thy wings o'ershading,
But sweeter still to wake and find Thee there.
So shall it be at last, in that bright morning,
When the soul waketh and life's shadows flee;
O in that hour, fairer than daylight dawning,
Shall rise the glorious thought, I am with Thee.

—Harriet Beecher Stowe (Stowe 1856, 356–57)

§

There is never a moment when the new dawn is not breaking over the earth, and never a moment when the sunset ceases to die. It is well to greet serenely even the first glimmer of the dawn when we see it, not hastening towards it with undue speed, nor leaving the sunset without gratitude for the dying light that once was dawn.

—Havelock Ellis (Ellis 1910, 641–42)

§

The day is done, and the darkness
Falls from the wings of Night,
As a feather is wafted downward
From an eagle in his flight.

I see the lights of the village
Gleam through the rain and the mist,
And a feeling of sadness comes o'er me
That my soul cannot resist:

A feeling of sadness and longing,
That is not akin to pain,
And resembles sorrow only
As the mist resembles the rain.

Come, read to me some poem,
Some simple and heartfelt lay,
That shall soothe this restless feeling,
And banish the thoughts of day.

Not from the grand old masters,
Not from the bards sublime,
Whose distant footsteps echo
Through the corridors of Time.

For, like strains of martial music,
Their mighty thoughts suggest
Life's endless toil and endeavor;
And to-night I long for rest.

Read from some humbler poet,
Whose songs gushed from his heart,
As showers from the clouds of summer,
Or tears from the eyelids start;

Who, through long days of labor,
And nights devoid of ease,
Still heard in his soul the music
Of wonderful melodies.

Such songs have power to quiet
The restless pulse of care,
And come like the benediction
That follows after prayer.

Then read from the treasured volume
The poem of thy choice,
And lend to the rhyme of the poet
The beauty of thy voice.

And the night shall be filled with music
And the cares that infest the day,
Shall fold their tents, like the Arabs,
And as silently steal away.

—HENRY WADSWORTH LONGFELLOW (LONGFELLOW N.D.)

§

Tell me not, in mournful numbers,
Life is but an empty dream!
For the soul is dead that slumbers,
And things are not what they seem.

Life is real! Life is earnest!
And the grave is not its goal;
Dust thou art, to dust returnest,
Was not spoken of the soul.

Not enjoyment, and not sorrow,
Is our destined end or way;
But to act, that each to-morrow
Find us farther than to-day.

Art is long, and Time is fleeting,
And our hearts, though stout and brave,
Still, like muffled drums, are beating
Funeral marches to the grave.

In the world's broad field of battle,
In the bivouac of Life,
Be not like dumb, driven cattle!
Be a hero in the strife!

Trust no Future, howe'er pleasant!
Let the dead Past bury its dead!
Act,—act in the living Present!
Heart within, and God o'erhead!

Lives of great men all remind us
We can make our lives sublime,
And, departing, leave behind us
Footprints on the sands of time;

Footprints, that perhaps another,
Sailing o'er life's solemn main,
A forlorn and shipwrecked brother,
Seeing, shall take heart again.

Let us, then, be up and doing,
With a heart for any fate;
Still achieving, still pursuing,
Learn to labor and to wait.

—Henry Wadsworth Longfellow (Longfellow 2019)

§

There are many fruits that never turn sweet until the frost has laid upon them; there are many nuts that never fall from the bough of the tree of life 'til the frost has opened and ripened them; and there are many elements of life that never grow sweet and beautiful until sorrow touches them. Then they are like autumn colors, and all men behold and admire them.

—Henry Ward Beecher (Beecher 2018)

§

So, I am glad not that my friend has gone,
But that the earth he laughed and lived upon was my earth too;
That I had closely known and loved him,
And that my love I'd shown.
Tears over his departure?
Nay, a smile—
That I had walked with him a little while.

—William Shakespeare (Hamlet n.d.)

§

When, by nobler culture, by purer experience, by breathing the air of a higher duty, vitality at length creeps into the soul, the instincts of immortality will wake within us. The word of hope will speak to us a language no longer strange. We shall feel like the captive bird carried accidentally to its homeland, when hearing for the first time the burst of kindred song from its native woods, it beats instinctively the bars of its cage in yearning for the free air that is thrilled with so sweet a strain. . . .

A single instant of the Divine life, spread over all that is simultaneous, is worth an eternity of ours, which at least begins by taking all things one by one. And in proportion as we emerge from this childhood of the mind, and claim our approach towards union with God, will the contents of our experience enrich themselves, and its area correct its evanescence; till a mere moment may become worth a millennium before; and the Transient may be to the large soul more than the Everlasting to the little: and then whether our Time be long or short by Sun and Moon may well remain indifferent, since the life that is beyond time in nature is vivid within us.

When, therefore, in higher moments brought by the sorrows of life, the tensions of duty, or the silence of thought, you catch some faint tones of a voice diviner than your own, know that you are not alone, and who it is that is with you. Stay not in the cold monologue of solitary meditation, but fling yourself into the communion of prayer. Fold not the personal shadows round you; lie open to the gleam that pierces them; confide in it as the brightest of realities—a path of heavenly light streaking the troubled waters of your being, and leading your eye to the orb that sends it.

—JAMES MARTINEAU (HUDSON 1962)

§

Man that is born of a woman is of few days and full of trouble. He cometh forth like a flower, and is cut down: he fleeth also as a shadow, and continueth not. . . .

For there is hope of a tree, if it be cut down, that it will sprout again, and that the tender branch thereof will not cease. Though the root thereof wax old in the earth, and the stock thereof die in the ground; yet through the scent of water it will bud, and bring forth boughs like a plant. But man dieth, and wasteth away: yea, man giveth up the ghost, and where is he? As the waters fail from the sea, and the flood decayeth and drieth up: So man lieth down, and riseth not: till the heavens be no more, they shall not awake, nor be raised out of their sleep.

Then Job arose, and rent his mantle, and shaved his head, and fell down upon the ground, and worshipped, and said, naked came I out of my mother's womb, and naked shall I return thither: the Lord gave, and the Lord hath taken away; blessed be the name of the Lord.

—JOB 14:1–2, 7–14; 1:20–21 KJV

§

So marvelous are thou, O spirit of man! So godlike in thy very nature! Thou dost reap death, and in return thou sowest the dream of everlasting life. In revenge for thine evil fate thou dost fill the universe with an all-loving God.

We bore our part in his creation, all we who are now dust; we who sank down into the dark like flames gone out; we wept, we exalted, we felt the ecstasy and the agony, but each of us, from the negro setting up the first mark above the grave of his dead to the genius raising the pillars of the temple toward heaven. We bore our part, from the poor mother praying beside a cradle, to the hosts that lifted their songs of praise high up into boundless space.

Honor to thee, O Spirit of man. Thou givest a soul to the world, thou settest a goal, thou art the hymn that lifts it into harmony; therefore turn back into thyself, lift high thy head and meet proudly the evil that comes to thee. Adversity can press thee, death can blot thee out, yet thou are still unconquerable and eternal.

—Johan Bojer (Hudson 1962)

§

No man is an island,
Entire of itself,
Every man is a piece of the continent,
A part of the main.
If a clod be washed away by the sea,
Europe is the less.
As well as if a promontory were.
As well as if a manner of thy friend's
Or of thine own were:
Any man's death diminishes me,
Because I am involved in mankind,
And therefore never send to know for whom the bell tolls;
It tolls for thee.

—John Donne (Donne n.d.)

§

Death this year has taken men
Whose kind we shall not see again.
Pride and skill and friendliness,
Wrath and wisdom and delight,
Are shining still, but shining less,
And clouded to the common sight.
Time will show them clear again.
Time will give us other men
With names to write in burning gold when they are great and we are old.
But these were royal-hearted, rare.
Memory keeps with loving care
Deeds they did and tales they told.
But living men are hard to spare.

—John Haynes Holmes (Hudson 1962)

§

Those we love truly never die,
Though year-by-year the sad memorial wreath, a ring of flowers, types
    of life and death, are laid upon their graves.
For death the pure life saves,
And life all pure is love;
And love can reach from heaven to earth,
And nobler lessons teach than those by mortals read.
Well blessed is he who has a dear one dead:
A friend he has whose face will never change—
A dear communion that will not grow strange;
The anchor of a love is death.
The blessed sweetness of a loving breath
Will reach our cheek all fresh through weary years.
For her who died long since, Ah! Waste not tears.
She's thine unto the end.

—John Boyle O'Reilly (O'Reilly n.d.)

§

A thing of beauty is a joy forever:
Its loveliness increases; it will never
Pass into nothingness; but still will keep
A bower quiet for us, and a sleep
Full of sweet dreams. . . .

—John Keats (Keats 2015)

§

Do not come when I am dead
To sit beside a low green mound.
Or bring the first gay daffodils
Because I love you so,
For I shall not be there.
You cannot find me there.
I will look up at you from the eyes
Of little children;
I will bend to meet you in the swaying boughs
Of bud-thrilled trees,
And caress you with the passionate sweep
Of storm-filled winds;
I will give you strength in your upward tread
Of everlasting hills;
I will cool your tired body in the flow
Of the limpid river;
I will warm your work-glorified hands through the glow
Of winter fire;
I will soothe you into forgetfulness to the drop, drop
Of the rain on the roof;
I will speak to you out of the rhymes
Of the Masters;
I will dance with you in the lilt
Of the violin,
And make your heart leap with the bursting cadence
Of the organ;
I will flood your soul with the flaming radiance
Of the sunrise,

And bring you peace in the tender rose and gold
Of the after-sunset.
All these have made me happy;
They are part of me;
I shall become part of them.

—Juanita De Long (De Long n.d.)

§

You would know the secret of death.
But how shall you find it unless you seek it in the heart of life?
The owl whose night-bound eyes are blind unto the day cannot unveil the mystery of light.
If you would indeed behold the spirit of death, open your heart wide unto the body of life.
For life and death are one, even as the river and the sea are one.

In the depth of your hopes and desires lies your silent knowledge of the beyond;
And like seeds dreaming beneath the snow your heart dreams of spring.
Trust the dreams, for in them is hidden the gate to eternity.
Your fear of death is but the trembling of the shepherd when he stands before the king. . . .
Is the shepherd not joyful beneath his trembling, that he shall wear the mark of the king?
Yet is he not more mindful of his trembling?

For what is it to die but to stand naked in the wind and to melt into the sun?
And what is it to cease breathing, but to free the breath from its restless tides,
That it may rise and expand and seek God unencumbered?
Only when you drink from the river of silence shall you indeed sing.
And when you have reached the mountain top, then you shall begin to climb.
And when the earth shall claim your limbs, then shall you truly dance.

—Kahlil Gibran (Gibran 1942, 90–91)

§

Walking in a barren land
I came upon a weeping beast.
It put its head into my hand
And rubbed against my breast.
It spoke as soft as woman might;
in weary voice it said,
"I would be shut of day and night.
Please cut off my head."
Pitying I drew my sword.
As I watched it die
it turned into a white bird
and flew into the sky.

Many things I might have been,
a leaf upon a tree,
A tall purple hollyhock,
the buzzing of a bee,
a woodland bird,
its song unheard,
the windy sky
Been mine to fly;
May it own me
when I die;
many things, if I had been
something else than me,
a drop of rain, a lazy moth,
a whitecap on the sea.
I know but whispers in the wind
I am their very brother,
and death will unite us all again
in the bosom of our mother.

—KENNETH LEO PATTON (HUDSON 1962)

§

We know not what it is, dear, this sleep so deep and still; the folded hands, the awful calm, the cheek so pale and chill; the lids that will not lift again, though we may call and call; the strange, white solitude of peace that settles over all.

We know not what it means, dear, this desolate heart-pain—this dread to take our daily way, and walk in it again. We know not what other sphere the loved who leave us go; Nor why we're left to wonder still; nor why we do not know.

But this we know: our loved and dead, if they should come this day—should come and ask us, "What is life?" not one of us could say. Life is a mystery as deep as ever death can be; Yet, O, how sweet it is to us, this life we live and see!

They might say—these vanquished ones—and blessed is the thought!—So death is sweet to us, beloved, though we may tell you naught. We may not tell it to the quick—reveal the mystery of death—Ye may not tell us, if ye would, the mystery of breath. The child who enters life comes not with knowledge or intent, so these who enter death must go as little children sent. Nothing is known. But I believe that God is overheard; and as life is to the living, so death is to the dead.

—Mary Mapes Dodge (Dodge 2015)

§

When I am alone I sit and dream
And when I dream the words are missing
Yes I know that in a room so full of light
That all the light is missing
But I don't see you with me, with me
Close up the windows, bring the sun to my room
Through the door you've opened
Close inside of me the light you see
That you met in the darkness
Time to say goodbye
Horizons are never far
Would I have to find them alone
Without true light of my own with you
I will go on ships overseas
That I now know
No, they don't exist anymore
It's time to say goodbye
When you were so far away
I sit alone and dream of the horizon
Then I know that you are here with me, with me
Building bridges over land and sea
Shine a blinding light for you and me

To see, for us to be
Time to say goodbye
Horizons are never far
Would I have to find them alone
Without true light of my own with you
I will go on ships overseas
That I now know
No, they don't exist anymore
It's time to say goodbye
So with you I will go
On ships overseas
That I now know
No, they don't exist anymore
It's time to say goodbye
So with you I will go. . . .
I love you

—Lucio Quarantotto and Frank Peterson (Brightman 2019)

§

This is the glory of earth-born men and women,
not to cringe, never to yield, but standing,
take defeat implacable and defiant,
and die unsubmitting. . . . On this star,
in this hard star-adventure, knowing not
what the fires mean to right and left, nor whether
a meaning was intended or presumed,
men can stand up, and look up blind, and say:
in all these turning lights I find no clue,
only a masterless night, and in my blood
no certain answer, yet is my mind my own,
yet is my heart a cry towards something dim
in the distance, which is higher than I am
and makes me emperor of the endless dark even in seeking!

—Maxwell Anderson (Anderson 1973, 90)

§

The messenger you sent to tell me of the death of my little daughter missed his way. But I heard of it through another.

I pray you let all things be done without ceremony or timorous superstition. And yet let us bear our affliction with patience. I do know very well what a loss we have had; but if you should grieve overmuch, it would trouble me still more. She was particularly dear to you; and when you call to mind how bright and innocent she was; how amiable and mild, then your grief must be peculiarly bitter. For not only was she kind and generous to other children, but even to her very playthings.

But should the sweet remembrance of those things which so delighted us when she was alive only afflict us now, when she is dead? Or is there danger that, if we cease to mourn, we shall forget her? Since she gave us so much pleasure that we had her, so ought we to cherish her memory, and make that memory a glad rather than a sorrowful one. And such reasons as we would use with others, let us try to make effective with ourselves. As we put a limit to all riotous indulgence in our pleasures, so let us check the excessive flow of our grief. It is well, both in action and dress, to shrink from an over-display of mourning, as well as to be modest and unassuming on festal occasions.

Let us also call to mind the years before little daughter was born. We are now in the same condition as then, except that the time she was with us is to be counted as an added blessing. Let us not ungratefully accuse Fortune for what was given us, because we could not also have all that we desired. What we had, and while we had it, was good, though now we have it no longer.

Remember also how much of good you still possess. Because one page of your book is blotted, do not forget all the other leaves whose reading is fair and whose pictures are beautiful. We should not be like misers, who never enjoy what they have, but only bewail what they lose.

And since she is gone where she feels no pain, let us not indulge in too much grief. The soul is incapable of death. And she, like a bird not long enough in her cage to become attached to it, is free to fly away to a purer air.

—"Consolatory Letter to His Wife"
by Plutarch (Hudson 1962)

§

O Lord, thou hast searched me, and known me. Thou knowest my downsitting and mine uprising, thou understandeth my thought afar off. . . . Such knowledge is too wonderful for me; it is high, I cannot attain unto it. Whither shall I go from thy spirit? Or whither shall I flee from thy presence? If I ascend up into heaven, thou art there: if I make my bed in the grave, behold, thou are there. If I take the wings of the morning, and dwell in the uttermost parts of the sea; even there shall thy hand lead me, and thy right hand shall hold me. If I say, surely the darkness shall cover me; even the night shall be light about me. Yea the darkness hideth not from thee; but the night shineth as the day: the darkness and the light are both alike to thee.

—Ps 139:1–12 KJV

§

I have but a few words to say: my ministry is now ended. I am going to my cold and silent grave; my lamp of life is nearly extinguished. I have parted with everything that was dear to me in this life for my country's cause and abandoned another idol I adored in my heart, the object of my affections.

My race is run. The grave opens to receive me, and I sink into its bosom. I am ready to die. I have not been allowed to vindicate my character. I have but one request to ask at my departure from this world: it is the charity of its silence. Let no man write my epitaph, for as no man who knows my motives dare not vindicate them, let not prejudice or ignorance asperse them. Let them rest in obscurity and peace, my memory be left in oblivion and my tomb remain uninscribed, until other times and other men can do justice to my character. When my country takes her place among the nations of the earth, then, and not till then, let my epitaph be written.

I have done.

—Robert Emmet (Haverty 1868, 246)

§

This song of mine will wind its music around you,
My child, like the fond arms of love.
This song of mine will touch your forehead
Like a kiss of blessing.
When you are alone it will sit by your side and
Whisper in your ear, when you are in the crowd
It will fence you about with aloofness.
My song will be like a pair of wings to your dreams,
It will transport your heart to the verge of the unknown.

It will be like the faithful star overhead
When dark night is over your road.
My song will sit in the pupils of your eyes,
And will carry your sight into the heart of things.
And when my voice is silent in death,
My song will speak in your living heart.

—Rabindranath Tagore (Tagore 2019)

§

Next to the encounter of death in our own bodies, the most sensible calamity is the death of a friend. It were inhumanity, and not virtue, not to be moved. In such cases, we cannot command ourselves: we cannot forbear weeping, and we ought not to forbear. We may accuse fate, but we cannot alter it: it is not to be removed either with reproaches or tears. They may carry us to the dead, but never bring them back again to us. To mourn without measure is folly and not to mourn at all is insensibility.

The comfort of having a friend may be taken away, but not that of having had one. In some respects, I have lost what I have had; in others, I still retain what I have lost. It is an ill construction of Providence to reflect only upon my friend being taken away, without any regard to the benefit of his being once given me.

Let us therefore make the best of our friends while we have them. He that has lost a friend has more cause of joy that he once had him, than of grief that he is taken away.

—Seneca (Hudson 1962)

§

Our greatest men bring in their life the message of man's future birth; for they dwell in the time to come, making it ready for ourselves. They reveal to us a life whose glory is not in the absence of suffering, but in the fact that its suffering had been made creative, transmuted into the stuff of life itself. It is like a tree which garners the sun's heat and light in its fiber and breaks out in beauty of fruitfulness. By extinguishing the fire of pain man may find his comfort, his period of slumber, which is the period of stagnant time, and imprisoned present; but by mastering this fire he lights his lamp of wisdom which gives illumination to the endless future.

There is suffering about which the question comes to our mind whether we deserve them. We must frankly acknowledge that explanations are not offered to us. So it does not help us in the least to complain; let us rather be worthy of the challenge thrown to us by them. That we have been wounded is a fact which can be ignored; but that we have been brave is a truth of the highest importance. For the former belongs to the outer world of cause and effect, while the latter belongs to the world of spirit.

—Rabindranath Tagore (Tagore 2006, 195)

§

O Father of all, we give back this life unto thee. In thy peace may we find our rest; in thy presence our sure trust. Teach us how to live, that we make of life and death alike a beauty filled with Thee.

So now, in the gentleness of springtime, and the evidence before us of the resurgence of life, and to the mercies of heaven and of all mankind, we commit the spirit of our brother and friend.

—Adapted from George C. Whitney (Hudson 1962)

§

So, the spirit separates itself from the body, passing like clouds over the valleys of sorrow and the mountains of happiness, and returns to its starting place, the endless ocean of love and beauty which is God. Amen.

—Anonymous (Hudson 1962)

§

Man that is born of a woman is of few days and full of trouble. He cometh forth like a flower, and is cut down: he fleeth also as a shadow, and continueth not.

In the midst of life, we are in death. Of whom may we seek for succor, but of thee, O Lord, in whom all souls rest and hope. . . . the night comes, in which no man can work. There the wicked cease from troubling and the weary are at rest. From henceforth, blessed are the dead, who die in the Lord; even so saith the Spirit; for they rest from their labors, and their works . . . follow them.

Forasmuch as it has pleased Almighty God to take unto himself this soul, we therefore commit the body to the ground, earth to earth, ashes to ashes, dust to dust, in the hope that as he has bourne the image of the earthly, so also may he bear the image of the heavenly.

—Adapted from Book of Common Prayer (Hudson 1962)

§

Infinite mystery of life, in whom is rest and peace for all who suffer, in whom life and death are as one; compassionate Father of all, giving life and receiving us again into thine arms when we are weary; we give Thee back the life of one beloved, who rests, deep-sheltered in thy peace.

There, too, we in our turn will find our rest and in the present comfort of thy presence we find strength to do the duties of the day. Grant us this day healing for our hearts as we now pray for all who face sorrow and bereavement. Lord, teach us how to live, that we may make of life and death alike a beauty filled with thee. And as we now say farewell to one we held dear, be thou our trust and confidence. Amen.

—Anonymous (Hudson 1962)

§

Let us believe that pure thoughts, brave words, and generous deeds can never die. . . . Let us believe that a noble self-denying life increases the moral wealth of man, and gives assurance that the future will be grander than the past. . . .

By the grave of man stands the angel of Silence.

No one can tell which is better—Life with its gleams and shadows, its thrills and pangs, its ecstasy and tears, its wreaths and thorns, its crowns, its glories and Golgothas; or death with its peace, its rest, its cool and placid brow that has no memory of fear of grief or pain.

Farewell, dear friend. The world is better for your life—the world is braver for your death.

Farewell! We loved you living, and we love you now.

—Robert G. Ingersoll (Ingersoll 1888)

§

This brave and tender man in every storm of life was oak and rock; but in the sunshine he was vine and flower. He was the friend of all heroic souls. He climbed the heights, and left all superstitions far below, while on his forehead fell the golden dawning of the grander day.

He loved the beautiful, and was with color, form, and music touched to tears. He sided with the weak, the poor, and wronged, and lovingly gave alms. With loyal heart and with the purest hands he faithfully discharged all public trusts.

He was a worshipper of liberty, a friend of the oppressed. A thousand times I have heard him quote these words: "For justice all place a temple, and all season, summer!" He believed that happiness was the only good, reason the only torch, justice the only worship, humanity the only religion, and love the only priest. He added to the sum of human joy; and were everyone to whom he did some loving service to bring a blossom to his grave, he would sleep to-night beneath a wilderness of flowers.

—"Eulogy at His Brother's Grave" by Robert G. Ingersoll (Ingersoll 1903, 132–33)

§

My Friends, I know how vain it is to gild a grief with words; and yet I wish to take from every grave its fear. Here in this world, where life and death are equal kings, all should be brave enough to meet what all the dead have met. The future has been filled with fear, stained and polluted by a heartless past. From the wondrous tree of life, the buds and blossoms fall with ripened fruit, and in the common bed of earth the patriarchs and babes sleep side by side. Why should we fear that which will come to all that is? We cannot tell, we do not know, which is the greater blessing—life or death. We cannot say that death is not a good. We do not know the grave is the end of this life or the door of another, whether the night here is not somewhere else a dawn. Neither can we tell which is the more fortunate—the child dying in his mother's arms, before its lips have learned to form a word, or he who journeys all the length of life's uneven road, painfully taking the last slow steps with staff and crutch.

Every cradle asks us, "Whence?" and every coffin, "Wither?" The poor barbarian, weeping above his dead, can answer these questions as intelligently and satisfactorily as the robed priest of the most authentic creed. The tearful ignorance of the one is just as consoling as the learned and unmeaning words of the other. No man standing where the horizon of life has touched a grave, has any right to prophecy a future filled with pain and tears. It may be that death gives all there is of worth to life. If those we press and strain against our hearts could never die, perhaps that love would wither from the earth. Maybe this common fate treads from out the paths between our hearts the weeds of selfishness and hate; and I had rather live and love where death is king than have eternal life where love is not. Another life is naught, unless we know and love again the ones who love us here.

They who stand with breaking hearts around this little grave need have no fear. The larger and nobler faith in all that is and is to be tells us that death, even at its worst, is only perfect rest. We know that through the common wants of life, the needs and duties of each hour, their grief will lessen day by day, until at last this grave will be to them a place of rest and peace, almost of joy. There is for them this consolation: The dead do not suffer. If they live again, their life will surely be as good as ours.

We have no fear. We are all children of the same mother, and the same fate awaits us all. We, too, have our religion, and it is this—help for the living, hope for the dead.

—Robert G. Ingersoll (Ingersoll n.d.)

§

Foreasmuch as the spirit of our brother/sister dwells no more in mortal form, we commit his/her body to the purifying flame, and return his/her ashes to the cradle of all life, the ocean, in the sure knowledge that his/her life continues in us and his/her words abide upon the earth. As he/she has borne the image of the earthly, so now he/she bears the image of the heavenly. Amen.

—Anonymous (Hudson 1962)

§

The Lord bless you and keep you;
The Lord make His face shine upon you,
And be gracious to you;
The Lord lift up His countenance upon you,
And give you peace, this day and forevermore.

—Adapted from Numbers 6:24–26 RSV

§

Sail forth—steer for the deep waters only,
Reckless O soul, exploring, I with thee, and thou with me,
For we are bound where mariner has not yet dared to go,
And we will risk the ship, ourselves and all.

O my brave soul!
O farther farther sail!
O daring joy, but safe! are they not all the seas of God?
O farther, farther, farther sail!

—Walt Whitman (Whitman 1919)

§

"The Lord giveth," and with tears we must declare, "And the Lord taketh away." Someday may we be able to add, "Blessed be the name of the Lord."

—Adapted from Job 1:21 KJV

§

Peace, my heart, let the time for
The parting be sweet.
Let it not be a death but completeness.
Let love melt into memory and pain
Into songs.
Let the flight through the sky end
In the folding of the wings over the nest.
Let the last touch of your hands be

Gentle like the flower of the night.
Stand still, O Beautiful End, for a
Moment, and say your last words in
Silence.
I bow to you and hold up my lamp
To light you on your way.

—Rabindranath Tagore (Tagore 2004, 111–12)

— 58 —

Albert Schweitzer Service[1]

PRELUDE "Cathedral (Little E Minor) Prelude & Fugue" Bach

HYMN "From Age to Age" Hosmer

PROLOGUE: THE PROBLEM

Narrator: One day near the turn-of-the-century in the market square at Colmar, in Upper Alsace, a gypsy-looking traveler with shaggy mustaches stood frowning at a statue of a naked Negro, that was at once a monument to and an indictment of colonial power.

"Can it be true, as I have heard," the traveler mused, "that we exploit these people and do not even give them doctors or medicine?"

On the way home to Strasburg, the dark image gave him no peace. "Why should my conscious be troubled?" he fumed. "I am a university professor, not a missionary." He might have added that before thirty this man had achieved fame in three other fields: as a concert organist, he was the favorite of European audiences; he was a world-renowned biblical scholar; and he had written an unforgettable life of Johann Sebastian Bach.

The man was Albert Schweitzer.

One evening, on his return from Colmar, Schweitzer found on his "writing table in the college one of the green-covered magazines in which the Paris Missionary Society reported every month on its activities. . . .

---

[1]. This service was written by the author and presented at the Church of the Reconciliation Unitarian Universalist, Utica, New York, on March 11, 1962. Subsequently, it was published and distributed in the 12 Celebrations Packet on Albert Schweitzer by the Department of Adult Education of the Unitarian Universalist Association.

In the very act of putting it aside" that he might go on with his work, Schweitzer mechanically opened the journal. As he did so his eye caught the title of an article, "Les Besoins de la Mission du Congo"—"The Needs of the Congo Mission" (Schweitzer 1949, 72).

1st Reader: The article said, "While we are preaching to these people about religion, they are suffering and dying before our eyes from physical maladies" (McGinnis 1985, 90).

Narrator: The conclusion ran:

2nd Reader: "Men and women who can reply simply to the Master's call, 'Lord, I am coming,' those are the people whom the church needs."

Narrator: "Having finished the article," Schweitzer reports, "I quietly began my work. My search was over" (Schweitzer 1949, 72).

So, at 30 years of age, Schweitzer took up the study of medicine, beginning yet another career. Ten years later, his preparations complete, he departed for Equatorial Africa and the jungle hospital at Lamberene where, except for occasional absences, he was to spend the rest of his life.

No sooner were his intentions known, however, when a cry was raised as if by a single voice from his friends and relatives to reconsider:

1st Reader (Angrily): Just when you have so much to offer the world, why bury your talents in an unknown jungle?

Narrator: To which Schweitzer replied simply:

3rd Reader (Slowly): "I wanted to be a doctor that I might be able to work without having to talk" (Schweitzer 1949, 77).

Narrator: Was this no more than a rationalization? Was Albert Schweitzer driven by a compulsion to escape the perplexities of Europe, or was he motivated by a religious commitment that has significance for the entire world? Was this to be the downfall of a great man at the height of his powers, or the fulfillment of his destiny through an example that would speak more eloquently than his words or books ever could? What was the nature of this man?

THE CHILD

Narrator: To answer these questions we must re-trace the steps of Schweitzer's life, beginning with his childhood. Born at Kayserberg in Upper Alsace on January 14, 1875, he spent his youth in Gunsbach, Munster, and later in Mulhausen. Although he was raised in the tradition of strict discipline and rigorous academic standards that were typical of the time, Schweitzer seems always to have been grateful to those who entered into his early years, as for example in this statement which is a tribute to the power of influence that we all have:

3rd Reader: "One thing stirs me when I look back at my youthful days, viz. the fact that so many people gave me something or were something to me without knowing it. Such people, with whom I have, perhaps, never exchanged a word, Yes, and others about whom I have merely heard things by report, have had a decisive influence upon me; they entered into my life and became powers within me. Much that I should otherwise not have felt so clearly or done so effectively was felt or done as it was, because I stand, as it were, under the sway of these people. Hence I always think that we all live, spiritually, by what others have given us in the significant hours of our life" (Schweitzer 1947, 151).

Narrator: Exacting as his upbringing was, it is clear the young Schweitzer also grew in sensitivity and the capacity to care. Hence, we find some of the first traces of his conception of "Reverence for Life":

2nd Reader: "It was quite incomprehensible to me . . . why in my evening prayers I should pray for human beings only. So, when my mother had prayed with me and had kissed me good night, I used to add silently a prayer that I had composed myself for all living creatures. It ran thus: 'O, heavenly Father, protect and bless all things that have breath; guard them from all evil, and let them sleep in peace'" (Schweitzer 1947, 274).

Narrator: Nor were such prayers the idle whims of an innocent and impressionable child. One of the things that stands out strongest in Schweitzer's early life was the determination that as he entered manhood, he would retain the convictions of his youth:

3rd Reader: "I listened, in my youth, to conversations between grown-up people through which there breathed a tone of sorrowful regret which oppressed the heart. The speakers looked back at the idealism and capacity for enthusiasm of their youth as something precious to which they ought to have held fast, and yet at the same time they regarded it as almost a law of nature that no one should be able to do so. This woke in me a dread of having ever, even once, to look back on my own past with such a feeling; I resolved never to let myself become subject to this tragic domination of mere reason, and what I thus vowed in almost boyish defiance I have tried to carry out" (Schweitzer 1947, 130).

THE SCHOLAR AND MINISTER

Narrator: So, from the child, Schweitzer became a man. He entered the University of Strasburg in 1893, had a brief tour of military duty in the infantry, and confirming his interest in the ministry he advanced in his theological studies and was ordained at St. Nicholas in the Fall of 1900. From there he was appointed Principal of the Protestant Theological Seminary.

Through his theological education Schweitzer became thoroughly versed in the Christian tradition. It was from this perspective that he challenged the effectiveness of ethical and rational religion, such as much of Unitarianism and Universalism of the late 1800's:

1st Reader: "The ethical religion of the philosophers of the second half of the nineteenth century is not firmly grounded. Its idea of God is quite incomplete. What is ethical in such teaching has no force. It lacks compulsive power and enthusiasm, and so this fine philosophical religion has had no significance for the thinking of the world in general. It is something which cannot be placed in the center of things; it is too delicate, too cautious, it utters no commands" (Schweitzer 1947, 216).

Narrator: From his initial theological interest and training Schweitzer was to become distinguished for his Biblical scholarship, which culminated in his classic work, *The Quest for the Historical Jesus*. In this great study Schweitzer reviews all the attempts that have been made to consider Jesus as a historical figure, rather than as an object of doctrine or worship. He concludes that the historical personality is so far removed, and that the tendency is so great for even the most objective scholars to project themselves and their times into the effort, that it is never fully possible to sketch the man of Nazareth as he was:

2nd Reader: "It was not only each epoch that found its reflection in Jesus; each individual created Him in accordance with his own character. There is no historical task which so reveals a man's true self as the writing of a life of Jesus" (Schweitzer 1947, 77).

1st Reader: "The study of the Life of Jesus has had a curious history. It set out in quest of the historical Jesus, believing that when it had found Him it could bring Him straight into our time as a teacher and Savior. It loosed the bands by which He had been riveted for centuries to the stony rocks of ecclesiastical doctrine, and rejoiced to see life and movement coming into the figure once more, and the historical Jesus advancing, as it seemed, to meet it. But he does not stay; He passes by our time and returns to His own" (Schweitzer 1947, 81).

Narrator: For liberals who look upon Jesus as a religious leader whose significance lies in what he was and said, Schweitzer's insights have implications that are just beginning to become clear:

3rd Reader (Quietly): "But the truth is it is not Jesus as historically known, but Jesus spiritually arisen within men, who is significant for our time and can help it" (Schweitzer 1947, 82).

3rd Reader (With reverence): "He comes to us as One unknown, without a name, as of old, by the lake side, he came to those men who knew him not. He speaks to us the same word: 'Follow thou me!' And sets us to the tasks which He has to fulfill for our time. He commands. And to those who obey Him, whether they be wise or simple, He will reveal Himself in the toils, the conflicts, the sufferings which they shall pass through in His fellowship, and, as an ineffable mystery, they shall learn in their own experience Who He is" (Schweitzer 1947, 88).

THE MUSICIAN

(This section is optional)

Narrator: One aspect of Schweitzer's comparatively early life which we have not touched upon is his career as a musician and his prominence as an authority on Bach. Almost as soon as he learned to read, young Schweitzer learned to play. As he said, "At eight, when my legs were hardly long enough to reach the pedals, I began to play the organ" (Schweitzer

1949, 7). His interest continued and throughout his life he took time from his busy schedule to give concerts in the music halls of Europe.

One of his greatest achievements was his biography of Bach, published in 1905. Of him, Schweitzer wrote:

2nd Reader: "Bach is clearly not a single but a universal personality. He profited by the musical development of three or four generations. . . . Bach is a terminal point. Nothing comes from him; everything merely leads up to him. To give his true biography is to exhibit the nature and the unfolding of German art that comes to completion in him and is exhausted in him—to comprehend it in all its strivings and its failures" (Schweitzer 1947, 51).

3rd Reader: "The unique thing about him is precisely the fact that he made no effort to win recognition for his greatest works, and did not summon the world to make acquaintance with them. Hence the kind of consecration that rests upon his works. We feel an unaffected charm in his cantatas such as we do not meet with in other art works" (Schweitzer 1947, 53–54).

Narrator: Nor was Schweitzer's interest in Bach unrelated to his primary concern for religion:

1st Reader: "Music is an act of worship with Bach. His artistic activity and his personality are both based on his piety. If he is to be understood from any standpoint of all, it is from this. For him, art was religion, and so it had no concern with the world or with worldly success. It was an end in itself" (Schweitzer 1947, 56).

Narrator: But perhaps the best way we can let Schweitzer tell you about Bach is to listen to him play some of his works. (Play music)[2]

(Music ends)

---

2. The music you may secure of Schweitzer playing Bach is the Columbia LP record "Albert Schweitzer playing Bach on the Organ" No. ML-5042, Vol. VI. This is one of a set. A good amplifying system is recommended; ordering this record is one of the few things that should be done well in advance of the service. The record should be played for a while, then tapered off where it says (music ends) and started again as background for the reading where (begin music) is denoted. On (music stops) volume should be cut off abruptly, and on (start music) the music played at good volume for a reasonable period. This would be shorter or longer depending on whether there is to be an offering. The recorded music could be played as background for the offering.

"Swiftly as it does the year round on the equator the blazing tropical day turned to night. A soft night. With a round cool-glowing moon. A night with a thousand voices. Soft voices. The voices of the . . . forest.

"A visitor from far-distant Oregon sat writing at a small work table in his room: a room in one of the long, low wooden buildings that made up the . . . hospital on the banks of the smooth, deep-surging Ogowe.

"Suddenly in the night a new voice: [Begin music] there could be no mistake: the voice of Johann Sebastian Bach: incisive, firmly reverent. . . .

"The visitor laid down his pen, quietly opened the door of his room, and crossed the clearing with the moon to guide him 'round the thick-waisted trees to a second of the long low buildings under the palms. Bach continued to speak. The visitor sat on the ground and listened.

(Music stops) "The voice of Bach stopped. A half-minute later a stocky, slightly-bowed figure came to the screen door and summoned the visitor in. And then into a little room to one side. A room with two antelope fawns in a pen and the piano with a long bench and under the bench rows of wooden pedals of the kind that organs have. A dark room. The figure slid itself onto the bench and tugged the visitor to sit beside. . . . And then Bach spoke again and the African night was music" (Arnold 1947, 327).

OFFERTORY "The Magnificat" Bach

"LE GRAND DOCTEUR" (PHYSICAN AND PHILOSOPHER)

Narrator: It was on March 26, 1913, that Albert Schweitzer, having completed almost ten years of medical training, first came to Africa. Moving up the Ogowe River, he arrived at the clearing at Lambarene and built his hospital, often working side by side with the natives doing construction work and even moving large timbers.

The story is told of how one afternoon Schweitzer was rolling heavy logs onto the riverbank. As he paused to wipe the perspiration from his forehead, he caught sight of a Negro in a white suit sitting by a patient whom he had come to visit. "Won't you give us a hand?" The great philosopher asked. "Oh, I couldn't do that," the native replied disdainfully, "I'm an intellectual!" To which Schweitzer mused, "You're lucky. I, too, wanted to be an intellectual but I didn't succeed."

Albert Schweitzer Service

It was here in Lambarene that Schweitzer made his home. It was here that he was to live with the natives, ministering to their bodies as well as their souls. It was here that he was to receive international acclaim through two world wars for his unswerving devotion to the cause of peace and humanitarianism; it was here that he came to be known affectionately as "le grande docteur"; it was here that in 1953 he received the Nobel Peace Prize.

It was here that Schweitzer had come to stand aside from the vortex of Europe to view the world with perspective and purpose:

2nd Reader: "We Westerners dream of a theory of the universe which corresponds to our impulse to action and the same time clarifies it. We have not been able to formulate such a theory definitely. At present we are in the state of possessing merely an impulse without any definite orientation. The spirit of the age drives us into action without allowing us to attain any clear view of the objective world and of life" (Schweitzer 1947, 239).

1st Reader (Angrily): "With the spirit of the age I am in complete disagreement, because it is filled with disdain for thinking. . . . But today in addition to that neglect of thought there is also prevalent mistrust of it. The organized political, social, and religious associations of our time are at work to induce the individual man not to arrive at his convictions by his own thinking but to make his own such convictions as they keep ready-made for him. Any man who thinks for himself and at the same time is spiritually free, is to them something inconvenient and even uncanny. He does not offer sufficient guarantee that he will merge himself in their organization in the way they wish. All corporate bodies look today for their strengths not so much to the spiritual worth of the ideas which they represent and to that of the people who belong to them, as to the attainment of the highest possible degree of unity and exclusiveness. . . . Thus, his whole life long, the man of today is exposed to influences which are bent on robbing him of all confidence in his own thinking. . . . By the spirit of the age, then, the man of today is forced into skepticism about his own thinking, in order to make him receptive to truth which comes to him from authority" (Schweitzer 1949, 170–71).

3rd Reader: (Shifting tone) "Renunciation of thinking is a declaration of spiritual bankruptcy" (Schweitzer 1949, 172).

1st Reader: "The city of truth cannot be built on the swampy ground of skepticism" (Schweitzer 1949, 173).

Narrator: So, it was from here in Africa Schweitzer's philosophy of "Reverence for Life," which prompted his decision to go to Lambarene and directed the course of his entire life, emerged into consciousness and came to fruition. For months Schweitzer had been struggling to find the core of his philosophy. Then, one day, he was called some distance up the Ogowe River for an emergency:

3rd Reader: "Slowly we crept upstream . . . Laboriously feeling—it was the dry season—for the channels between the sandbanks. Lost in thought I sat on the deck of the barge, struggling to find the elementary and universal conception of the ethical which I had not discovered in any philosophy. Sheet after sheet I covered with disconnected sentences, really to keep myself concentrated on the problem. Late on the third day, at the very moment when, at sunset, we were making our way through a herd of hippopotamuses, there flashed upon my mind, unforeseen and unsought, the phrase, 'Reverence for Life'" (Schweitzer 1947, 259).

2nd Reader (Slowing): "The iron door had yielded: the path in the thicket had become visible" (Schweitzer 1947, 259).

1st Reader: "The stream which had been flowing for a long distance underground comes again to the surface" (Schweitzer 1949, 177).

Narrator: What is "Reverence for Life?"

2nd Reader: (Deliberately) "Reverence for Life contains in itself resignation, an affirmative attitude toward the world, and ethics—the three essential elements in a philosophy of life, as mutually interrelated results of thinking" (Schweitzer 1949, 180).

Narrator: How is such an ethic related to Christianity?

1st Reader: "With the appearance of the philosophy of Reverence for Life, Christianity is now summoned to face once more the question whether it will or will not join hands with thought which is both ethical and religious in character" (Schweitzer 1949, 183).

3rd Reader: (Quickly) "Christianity cannot take the place of thinking, but it must be founded on it" (Schweitzer 1949, 184).

2nd Reader: (Slowly) "The ethic of Reverence for Life is the ethic of Love widened into universality. It is the ethic of Jesus, now recognized as a logical consequence of thought" (Schweitzer 1949, 180).

EPILOGUE: AN EVALUATION

Narrator: This, then, is Albert Schweitzer: as child, scholar, minister, musician, physician, and philosopher. Was his decision to spend most of his later life in Africa his downfall or fulfillment? Was he evading the claims of Europe or meeting the responsibilities implicit in his philosophy? I think most of us have reached our own conclusions at this point, but in retrospect consider the judgments of some of his contemporaries. Adlai Stevenson:

2nd Reader: "A large part of (this) impact arises from the fact that Dr. Schweitzer has devoted a lifetime to the pursuit of universals that know no national or continental limits: knowledge, truth, beauty, and spirit of compassion for fellow man" (Schweitzer 1955, 102).

Narrator: Albert Einstein:

1st Reader: "He has not preached and he has not warned and he did not dream of it that his example would become an ideal and a solace to innumerable others. He simply acts out of inner necessity" (Schweitzer 1955, 38).

Narrator: Norman Cousins:

3rd Reader: "It is not so much what he has done for others, but what others have done because of him and the power of his example. This is the measure of the man" (Schweitzer 1955, 33).

HYMN—"Forward Through the Ages"—Hosmer

CLOSING WORDS

Narrator: "Truth has no special time of its own. Its hour is now—always, and indeed then most truly when it seems most unsuitable to actual circumstances" (Schweitzer 1947, 30).

POSTLUDE—"Wedge Fugue"—Bach

Part V: Special Services

NOTES AND PRODUCTION SUGGESTIONS

To use this service in entirety, you must order in advance the Columbia LP record "Albert Schweitzer Playing Bach on the Organ" No. ML-5042, Vol. VI.

As this script is arranged, there are four participants: the narrator and three readers. The third reader may most effectively be a man; the first and second do not matter. As the service was used, the narrator stood to one side (in the pulpit), and the three readers stood to the other side at the front (by the reading stand); it was felt that the three readers should be together since they read certain passages in close relationship to each other: sometimes establishing rhythm, sometimes dissonance. Experimentation and variation in production, however, is to be encouraged. It is a script which will benefit from rehearsing. It is good to get a feel in advance of how the four participants will be related and respond to each other, how things should be paced (where pauses are good and where quickness is best), and in general how the readers can best convey that they are speaking for Schweitzer and not just reading, and how the narrator can best perform his function which is one of providing continuity and as the name says "narrating" from a perspective which provides opportunities for relief after especially intense sections.

Perhaps one of the most obvious areas of experimentation and adaptation for the script is in the direction of drama: the extent to which the readers may wish to do their parts more as "dramatic readings," change position or otherwise engage in movement, and act out various parts.

– Appendix A –
Online Videos of Sermons
Given in Key Largo, Florida

Sermon Title	URL
"A Better Love"	https://youtu.be/fnXT8gG7yc4
"Dark Night of the Soul"	https://youtu.be/sAwsQI_wzF0
"Earth's the Right Place for Love"	https://youtu.be/WA_RiEzP4Bs
"Feeding of the 5,000"	https://youtu.be/-0euPMkEPrg
"God Is Nigh"	https://youtu.be/tUdb4kNRuSM
"Happiness in an Imperfect World"	https://youtu.be/KHxsYf-R0dE
"Hospitality: The Mission of the Church"	https://youtu.be/DEkCguCjZWw
"The Keys of the Kingdom"	https://youtu.be/am9d6zlDEXU
"The Kingdom of God"	https://youtu.be/19Bh-9MbNrs
"The Meaning of Pain"	https://youtu.be/t04YscgL1-Q
"Prayer"	https://youtu.be/jqG-KfFwfOs

Appendix A

Sermon Title	URL
"The Sun Also Rises"	https://youtu.be/SBoV-kgxtkg
"Where Is God?"	https://youtu.be/j3kg6_Qiw5w
"This Side of Eden"	https://youtu.be/IqNw4wGnskg
"Endings and Beginnings"	https://youtu.be/Rt9CzHd89n0

– Appendix B –

List of Unitarian Universalist Meditation Manuals

Date	Title	Author
1993	*Life Tides*	Elizabeth Tarbox
1992	*Noisy Stones*	Robert R. Walsh
1991	*Been in the Storm So Long*	Mark Morrison-Reed and Jacqui James
1990	*Into the Wilderness*	Sara Moores Campbell
1989	*A Small Heaven*	Jane Ranney Rzepka
1988	*The Numbering of Our Days*	Anthony Friess Perrino
1987	*Exaltation*	David B. Parke, Editor
1986	*Quest*	Kathy Fuson Hurtt
1985	*The Gift of the Ordinary*	Charles S. Stephen, Jr., Editor
1984	*To Meet the Asking Years*	Gordon B. McKeeman, Editor
1983	*Tree and Jubilee*	Greta W. Crosby

Appendix B

Date	Title	Author
1981	Outstretched Wings of the Spirit	Donald S. Harrington
1980	Longing of the Heart	Paul N. Carnes
1979	Portraits from the Cross	David Rankin
1978	Songs of Simple Thanksgiving	Kenneth L. Patton
1977	The Promise of Spring	Clinton Lee Scott
1976	The Strangeness of This Business	Clarke D. Wells
1975	In Unbroken Line	Chris Raible, Editor
1974	Stopping Places	Mary Lou Thompson
1973	The Tides of Spring	Charles W. Grady
1972	73 Voices	Chris Raible and Ed Darling, Editors
1971	Bhakti, Santi, Love, Peace	Jacob Trapp
1970	Beginning Now	J. Donald Johnston
1969	Answers in the Wind	Charles W. McGehee
1968	The Trying Out	Richard Kellaway
1967	Moments of Springtime	Rudolf Nemser
1966	Across the Abyss	Walter D. Kring
1965	The Sound of Silence	Raymond Baughan
1964	Impassioned Clay	Ralph Helverson
1963	Seasons of the Soul	Robert T. Weston
1962	The Un-carven Image	Phillip Hewett

List of Unitarian Universalist Meditation Manuals

Date	Title	Author
1961	Parts and Proportions	Arthur Graham

Council of Liberal Churches

Date	Title	Author
1960	Imprints of the Divine	Raymond Hopkins
1959	Indictments and Invitations	Robert B. Cope
1958	Strange Beauty	Vincent Silliman
1957	Greatly To Be	Francis Anderson, Jr.
1956	My Heart Leaps Up	Frank O. Holmes

Unitarian

Date	Title	Author
1955	The Task is Peace	Harry Scholefield
1954	Taking Down the Defenses	Arthur Foote
1953	My Ample Creed	Palfrey Perkins
1952	This Man Jesus	Harry C. Meserve
1951	The Tangent of Eternity	John Wallace Laws
1950	Deep Sources and Great Becoming	Edwin C. Palmer
1949	To Take Life Strivingly	Robert Killian
1948	Come Up Higher	Hurley Begun
1947	Untitled	Richard Steiner
1946	The Pattern on the Mountain (Reissue)	E. Burdette Backus
1945	The Expendable Life	Charles G. Girelius
1944	The Disciplines of Freedom	Leslie T. Pennington

Date	Title	Author
1943	*Faith Forbids Fear*	Frederick May Eliot
1942	*Forward into the Light*	Frederick W. Griffin
1941	*Victorious Living*	W. W. W. Argow
1940	*Address to the Living*	Herbert Hitchen
1939	*The Pattern on the Mountain*	E. Burdette Backus
1938	*Gaining a Radiant Faith*	Henry H. Saunderson

Universalist

Date	Title	Author
1955	*Heritages*	Harmon M. Gehr
1954	*Words of Life*	Albert F. Ziegler
1953	*Wisdom About Life*	Tracy M. Pullman
1952	*Spiritual Embers*	John E. Wood
1951	*The Breaking of Bread*	Raymond John Baughan
1950	*Add to Your Faith*	Roger F. Etz
1949	*To Take Life Strivingly*	Robert Killam
1948	*Of One Flame*	Robert Cummins
1947	*Using Our Spiritual Resources*	Roger F. Etz
1946	*A New Day Dawns*	Walter Henry Macpherson
1945	*Beauty for Ashes*	Robert and Elsie Barber
1944	*The Price of Freedom*	Edson R. Miles
1943	*The Ladder of Excellence*	Frank D. Adams

List of Unitarian Universalist Meditation Manuals

Date	Title	Author
1942	*The Whole Armor of God*	Donald B. F. Hoyt
1941	*Earth's Common Things*	Max A. Kapp
1940	*The Interpreter*	Frederic W. Perkins
1939	*The Great Avowal*	Horace Westwood
1938	*Add to Your Faith*	Roger F. Etz

Bibliography

A.A. Grapevine. 2013. "Preamble." https://www.aa.org/assets/en_US/smf-127_en.pdf (accessed October 12, 2019).

Adams, T. Conley. 1963. Archives. Church of the Reconciliation Unitarian Universalist, Utica, New York.

Agler, Richard. 2018. *The Tragedy Test*. Eugene, OR: Resource.

Alcoholics Anonymous World Services. 1955. *Alcoholics Anonymous: The Story of How Many Thousands of Men and Women Have Recovered from Alcoholism*. 2nd ed. New York: Alcoholics Anonymous World Services.

———. 1957. *Alcoholics Anonymous Comes of Age: A Brief History of A.A*. New York: Alcoholics Anonymous World Services.

———. 1984. *"Pass It On:" The Story of Bill Wilson and How the A.A. Message Reached the World*. New York: Alcoholics Anonymous World Services.

———. 2011. *Twelve Steps and Twelve Traditions*. New York: Alcoholics Anonymous World Services.

Alexander, Cecil Frances. n.d. "All Things Bright and Beautiful." https://www.google.com/search?q=all+things+bright+and+beautiful+lyrics&rlz=1C1AWFC_enUS835US835&oq=all+thi&aqs=chrome.0.69i59j69i57j0j69i60l3.1455j0j4&sourceid=chrome&ie=UTF-8 (accessed October 9, 2019).

Amazing Real Life Experiences. 2014. "Truth is Stranger than Fiction: The Story of William Waldorf and George C. Boldt." http://amazingreallifeinfo.blogspot.com/2014/03/truth-is-stranger-than-fiction-story-of.html (accessed October 7, 2019).

Anderson, Maxwell. 1973. "Winterset." New York: Dramatists Play Service. https://books.google.com/books?id=6P8jBxOKYacC&pg=PA90&lpg=PA90&dq=maxwell+anderson+AND+%22this+is+the+glory+of+earth-born+men+and+women%22&source=bl&ots=p9jfWGQwi8&sig=ACfU3U1CYwte7JZtCTp8Wo8ShQMyXgxVug&hl=en&sa=X&ved=2ahUKEwj93p3Mo7DlAhVjrlkKHZijDL0Q6AEwAXoECAgQAQ#v=onepage&q=maxwell%20anderson%20AND%20%22this%20is%20the%20glory%20of%20earth-born%20men%20and%20women%22&f=false (accessed October 22, 2019).

Angoff, Charles. 1927. "Theodore Parker." *American Mercury* 10 (January) 85.

Apache Wedding Prayer Blessing. 2019. https://www.tripsavvy.com/apache-wedding-prayer-blessing-1861037 (accessed January 21, 2020).

Arnold, Melvin. 1947. "The Greatest Soul in Christendom." Translated by Charles R. Joy. *The Christian Register* 126, no. 8 (September) 324–27. https://iiif.lib.harvard.edu/manifests/view/drs:446916183$327i (accessed December 31, 2019).

Ashworth, Andi. n.d. https://thedrewpatch.blogspot.com/2008/01/ (accessed October 9, 2019).

Auden, W.H. n.d. "Christmas Oratorio." https://southerncrossreview.org/44/auden-oratio.htm (accessed October 18, 2019).

Augustine. 1961. *Confessions.* Translated by R.S. Pine Coffin. New York: Penguin.

Aurelius, Marcus. 2019. "Meditations." https://www.goodreads.com/quotes/7574143-nothing-happens-to-any-man-that-he-is-not-formed (accessed October 20, 2019).

B., Dick. 1992. *Dr. Bob and His Library.* Kihei, Maui, Hawaii: Paradise Research. https://books.google.com/books?id=aPVv5r77AVkC&pg=PA65&dq=fosdick+AND+%22life+consists+not+simply+in+what+heredity%22&hl=en&sa=X&ved=2ahUKEwj63aDHv57lAhVJvFkKHVwKB_cQ6AEwAHoECAQQAg#v=onepage&q=fosdick%20AND%20%22life%20consists%20not%20simply%20in%20what%20heredity%22&f=false (accessed October 15, 2019).

Babbit, Irving. 1936. *The Dhammapada.* New York: Oxford.

Baum, L. Frank. 2019. *The Wizard of Oz.* Orinda, CA: Sea Wolf.

Beecher, Henry Ward. 2018. https://debbiewaldenlewis.blogspot.com/2018/04/draw-near-from-ruins.html (accessed October 21, 2019).

Borg, Marcus. 1989. *Evolution of the Word.* New York: Harper Collins.

———. 2014. *Convictions: A Manifesto for Progressive Christians.* New York: Harper Collins.

———. 2016. *Convictions: How I Learned What Matters Most.* New York: Harper Collins.

Brightman, Sarah. 2019. "Time to Say Goodbye." https://genius.com/Sarah-brightman-time-to-say-goodbye-english-version-lyrics (accessed October 22, 2019).

Brother Lawrence. 1982. *The Practice of the Presence of God.* New Kensington, PA: Whitaker House. https://www.academia.edu/35528549/The_Practice_of_the_Presence_of_God_-_Brother_Lawrence (accessed October 9, 2019).

Browning, Elizabeth Barrett. 1908. *Sonnets from the Portuguese.* Rowenscourt Square: Cradock. https://books.google.com/books?id=U4Zczkvr_iQC&printsec=frontcover&dq=elizabeth+barret+browning+AND+how+do+i+love+thee?&hl=en&newbks=1&newbks_redir=0&sa=X&ved=2ahUKEwiox5OGgKrlAhWip1kKHbfqAEgQ6AEwAHoECAYQAg#v=onepage&q=elizabeth%20barret%20browning%20AND%20how%20do%20i%20love%20thee%3F&f=false (accessed October 20, 2019).

Buber, Martin. 1958. *I and Thou.* Translated by Ronald Gregor Smith. New York: Charles Scribner's Sons.

Buddha. 1894. *The Gospel of Buddha,* edited by Paul Carus. Chicago: Open Court. https://books.google.com/books?id=XZ8QAAAAYAAJ&pg=PA180&dq=buddha+AND+marriage+feast+in+jambunada&hl=en&newbks=1&newbks_redir=0&sa=X&ved=2ahUKEwjYhNPU_anlAhVMx1kKHYYfD_wQ6AEwAHoECAIQAg#v=onepage&q=buddha%20AND%20marriage%20feast%20in%20jambunada&f=false (accessed October 20, 2019).

Bultmann, Rudolf Karl. 1958. *Jesus and the Word.* New York: Charles Scribner's Sons.

Byron, George Gordon. n.d. https://www.goodreads.com/quotes/346426-there-is-a-pleasure-in-the-pathless-woods-there-is (accessed October 7, 2019).

———. n.d. Epitaph to a Dog. https://poets.org/poem/epitaph-dog (accessed October 9, 2019).

Carus, Paul. 1894. *The Gospel of Buddha.* Chicago: Open Court.

Bibliography

Celtic Blessing. n.d. https://www.darlington.gov.uk/media/3450/namingceremony readings.pdf (accessed October 19, 2019).

Chadwick, John White. 1900. *Theodore Parker: Preacher and Reformer.* Boston: Houghton, Mifflin.

Channing, William Ellery. 1894. *The Works of William E. Channing.* Boston: American Unitarian Association. https://books.google.com/books?id=_Y4kDuUoguYC&pg=PA420&dq=Channing+AND+%22Let+not+this+house+be+desecrated%22&hl=en&sa=X&ved=2ahUKEwj-9cv36Z_lAhWGq1kKHffnCB0Q6AEwAHoECAIQAg#v=onepage&q=Channing%20AND%20%22Let%20not%20this%20house%20be%20desecrated%22&f=false (accessed October 15, 2019).

Chapin, E.H. and J.G. Adams. 1856. *Hymns for Christian Devotion.* Boston: Abel Tompkins. https://www.goodreads.com/author/quotes/8183.Edward_Everett_Hale (accessed October 14, 2019).

Commager, Henry Steele. 1936. *Theodore Parker.* Boston: Beacon.

———. 1951. "Henry Steele Commager." *New Outlook* 4, no. 1 (January) 42. https://books.google.com/books?id=S3UQAAAAIAAJ&pg=PA42&lpg=PA42&dq=henry+steele+commager+AND+%22when+we+come+to+realize+the+nature+of+the+conflict%22&source=bl&ots=p8CyLmt1I5&sig=ACfU3U3AlmqtrIcsKjUGhDegNnkDOhlfKQ&hl=en&sa=X&ved=2ahUKEwiAn_S3_qjlAhUHXKoKHc_yDtcQ6AEwAHoECAAQAQ#v=onepage&q=henry%20steele%20commager%20AND%20%22when%20we%20come%20to%20realize%20the%20nature%20of%20the%20conflict%22&f=false (accessed October 19, 2019).

Conkling, Grace Hazard. 2019. "After Sunset." https://www.poemhunter.com/poem/after-sunset-2/ (accessed October 21, 2019).

De Benneville, George. 2012. "A Universalist Christian Meditation." https://andrewjbrown.blogspot.com/2012/10/a-universalist-christian-meditation-for.html (accessed October 15, 2019).

De Long, Juanita. n.d. "My Hereafter." https://dippingintolight.com/delong-juanita_hereafter/ (accessed October 22, 2019).

De Saint-Exupery, Antoine. 1943. *The Little Prince.* Translated by Katherine Woods. New York: Harcourt, Brace.

Dodge, Mary Mapes. 2015. "The Two Mysteries." https://www.bartleby.com/248/718.html (accessed October 22, 2019).

Donne, John. n.d. Meditations. Vol. 17. https://web.cs.dal.ca/~johnston/poetry/island.html (accessed October 8, 2019).

Donson, Naomi. 2004. "Players 'Fantasticks' is More Than the Sum of its Parts." https://www.heraldtribune.com/article/LK/20040410/news/605210152/SH/ (accessed October 8, 2019).

Douglas, Loyd C. 1929. *Magnificent Obsession.* Boston: Houghton Mifflin.

Driver, S.R. 1957. *An Introduction to the Literature of the Old Testament.* New York: Meridian.

Dunham, Barrows. 1947. "A World Awaited and a World Attained Dept." https://www.genjipress.com/2016/12/a-world-awaited-and-a-world-attained-dept.html (accessed October 19, 2019).

Durant, Will. 1926. *The Story of Philosophy.* New York: Pocket Book. https://books.google.com/books?id=suLI7RoaBEEC&pg=PR25&dq=life+has+meaning.+to+find+its+meaning+is+my+meat+and+drink&hl=en&sa=X&ved=2ahUKEwjojqOO4YrlAhUCw1kKHV-zCAMQ6AEwAnoECAUQAg#v=onepage&q=life%20

has%20meaning.%20to%20find%20its%20meaning%20is%20my%20meat%20 and%20drink&f=false (accessed October 7, 2019).

Dylan, Bob. n.d. "Naming Ceremony—Poems and Readings." https://www.calderdale.gov.uk/v2/sites/default/files/Naming-Ceremony-Poems-and-Readings.pdf (accessed October 19, 2019).

Ehrmann, Max. 1952. "Desiderata." https://mwkworks.com/desiderata.html (accessed October 14, 2019).

Einstein, Albert. 2014. *The World as I See It*. n.p.: Snowball. https://www.goodreads.com/quotes/1353503-each-of-us-is-here-for-a-brief-sojourn-for (accessed October 7, 2019).

———. 2019. "Goodreads." https://www.bartleby.com/90/0811.html (accessed October 20, 2019).

Eliot, Christopher. 1919. *Christian Register* 17 (March 6) 233. https://books.google.com/books?id=z5MCAAAAQAAJ&newbks=1&newbks_redir=0&printsec=frontcover&source=gbs_ge_summary_r&cad=0#v=onepage&q&f=false (accessed October 21, 2019).

Eliot, George. 1895. *Poems by George Eliot*. Vol. 2. Boston: Estes and Lauriat. https://books.google.com/books?id=4Wr86Xsb1OYC&pg=PA217&dq=GEORGE+ELIOT+AND+%22Oh,+may+I+join+the+choir+invisible+of+those+immortal+dead%22&hl=en&newbks=1&newbks_redir=0&sa=X&ved=2ahUKEwj7s-HU8K3lAhUIo1kKHa5uCZEQ6AEwAXoECAQQAg#v=onepage&q=GEORGE%20ELIOT%20AND%20%22Oh%2C%20may%20I%20join%20the%20choir%20invisible%20of%20those%20immortal%20dead%22&f=false (accessed October 21, 2019).

———. 1900. *Works of George Eliot*. Vol. 3: Adam Bebe. Boston: Little Brown. https://books.google.com/books?id=wr9-hcynVQUC&pg=PA492&dq=GEORGE+ELIOT+AND+Adam+Bebe+%22had+not+outlived+his+sorrow%22&hl=en&newbks=1&newbks_redir=0&sa=X&ved=2ahUKEwjyj8Wf7K3lAhXBtlkKHbRFCRIQ6AEwAXoECAAQAg#v=onepage&q=GEORGE%20ELIOT%20AND%20Adam%20Bebe%20%22had%20not%20outlived%20his%20sorrow%22&f=false (accessed October 21, 2019).

Eliot, T.S. n.d. "Little Gidding." http://www.columbia.edu/itc/history/winter/w3206/edit/tseliotlittlegidding.html (accessed October 11, 2019).

Ellis, Havelock. 1910. *Studies in the Psychology of Sex*. Vol. 6. Philadelphia: F.A. Davis. https://books.google.com/books?id=-S81AAAAIAAJ&pg=PA641&dq=havelock+ellis+AND+%22There+is+never+a+moment+when+the+new+dawn%22&hl=en&newbks=1&newbks_redir=0&sa=X&ved=2ahUKEwirstSb2q7lAhWps1kKHWDkAYcQ6AEwBnoECAMQAg#v=onepage&q=havelock%20ellis%20AND%20%22There%20is%20never%20a%20moment%20when%20the%20new%20dawn%22&f=false (accessed October 21, 2019).

Emerald Heritage. n.d. "9 Irish Blessings We Love." https://emerald-heritage.com/blog/2017/9-irish-blessings-we-love (accessed October 19, 2019).

Emerson, Ralph Waldo. n.d. "Transcendentalism." http://www.mesacc.edu/~barmd97231/Transcendentalism.html (accessed October 15, 2019).

———. 1860. *Tributes to Theodore Parker*. Boston: The Fraternity.

———. 1910. *Journals of Ralph Waldo Emerson*. Boston: Houghton Mifflin.

———. 1987. *The Essays of Ralph Waldo Emerson*. Cambridge: Harvard University Press. https://books.google.com/books?id=eipTa9ftjFEC&pg=PA31&dq=emerson+

AND+"perfect+sweetness+the+independence+of+solitude"&hl=en&sa=X&ved=2ahUKEwiIh7aYwp_lAhUkuVkKHW8ZB9oQ6AEwA3oECAIQAg#v=onepage&q=emerson%20AND%20"perfect%20sweetness%20the%20independence%20of%20solitude"&f=false (accessed October 18, 2019).

———. 2015. "Immortality." https://www.bartleby.com/90/0811.html (accessed October 20, 2019).

———. 2019. "Goodreads." https://www.goodreads.com/quotes/7331276-to-laugh-often-and-love-much-to-win-the-respect (accessed October 21, 2019).

Ericson, Edward L. 2009. "Live Journal." https://jheaton.livejournal.com/958677.html (accessed October 16, 2019).

Evans, F. Barton III. 1996. *Harry Stack Sullivan: Interpersonal Theory and Psychotherapy.* New York: Routledge.

Fairless, Michael. 1905. *The Roadmender.* Portland, ME: Thomas B. Mosher.

Ferlinghetti, Lawrence. 1958. *Coney Island of the Mind.* New York: New Directions. https://nationalismproject2015.weebly.com/christ-climbed-down.html (accessed January 6, 2020)

Fewkes, R.M. 1999. "All Souls Circle of Remembrance." https://www.firstparishnorwell.org/sermons/circle.html (accessed October 19, 2019).

Foote, Arthur II. n.d. "Unity Church-Unitarian." https://www.unityunitarian.org/about.html (accessed October 19, 2019).

Fosdick, Harry Emerson. n.d. "Harry Emerson Fosdick Quotes About Life." https://www.azquotes.com/author/5034-Harry_Emerson_Fosdick/tag/life (accessed October 7, 2019).

Foster, Richard J. 1992. *Prayer: Finding the Heart's New Home.* New York: Harper Collins.

Francis of Assisi. n.d. "Prayer." https://www.google.com/search?rlz=1C1AWFC_enUS835US835&ei=H-eqXZGdL-bs_Qa8o6qIBQ&q=saint+francis+of+assisi+prayer&oq=saint+fran&gs_l=psy-ab.1.3.0i67l6j0l2j0i67l2.92978.95087..105794...0.0..1.219.1202.6j3j1......0....1..gws-wiz.......0i10i67.DicjX9irn9I (accessed October 19, 2019).

Fromm, Erich. 1947. *Man for Himself: An Inquiry Into the Psychology of Ethics.* New York: Rinehart.

Frost, Robert. 1969. *The Poetry of Robert Frost,* edited by Edward Connery Latham. New York: Henry Holt.

Frothingham, Octavius Brooks. 1874. *Theodore Parker: A Biography.* Boston: James R. Osgood.

Gandhi, Mahatma. 1947. *Teachings of Mahatma Gandhi.* Mumbai: Indian Printing Works.

Gangulee, N. 1957. *The Buddha and His Message.* Mumbai: Popular Book Depot.

Garrison, Winfred Ernest. 1965. "Thy Sea is So Great—And Who am I." https://medium.com/@sismith89/thy-sea-so-great-and-who-am-i-667b036fa7aa (accessed October 14, 2019).

Gassner, John. 1952. "Billy Budd." *Best American Plays, Third Series 1945-1951,* edited by John Gassner, 365–94. New York: Crown.

Ghiselin, Brewster. 1954. *The Creative Process.* Berkeley: University of California Press.

Gibran, Kahlil. n.d. https://www.azquotes.com/quote/1032256 (accessed October 12, 2019).

———. 1942. *The Prophet.* New York: Alfred A. Knopf.

———. 2008. *Sand and Foam*. Delhi: Rajpal.

Gilbert, Richard S. n.d. "Gentleness in Living." https://www.uua.org/worship/words/meditation/gentleness-living (accessed October 15, 2019).

———. 2019a. "Universalist Quotations." http://nyscu.org/quotes.shtml (accessed October 15, 2019).

———. 2019b. "We are All More Human Than Otherwise." https://www.uua.org/worship/words/reading/we-are-all-more-human (accessed October 15, 2019).

Goodman, Ellen and Patricia O'Brien. 2001. *I Know Just What You Mean*. New York: Simon and Schuster.

Graves, Robert. 1989. *Conversations with Robert Graves,* edited by Frank L. Kersnowski. Jackson: University of Mississippi Press.

Gross, Ronald. 2002. *Socrates Way: Seven Master Keys to Using Your Mind to the Utmost*. New York: Penguin. https://books.google.com/books?id=vG3voShLdRoC&pg=PT218&dq=socrates+AND+%22Men+of+Athens,+I+am+your+friend%22&hl=en&sa=X&ved=2ahUKEwj81IPM14blAhUnrVkKHTXYCQMQ6AEwAHoECAEQAg#v=onepage&q=socrates%20AND%20%22Men%20of%20Athens%2C%20I%20am%20your%20friend%22&f=false (accessed October 5, 2019).

Grudem, Wayne. 1994. *Systematic Theology*. Grand Rapids: Zondervan.

Guthrie, Donald C. n.d. "Cultivating Gospel Healthy Systems." https://www.edcomm.org.au/assets/General-PDFs/EdComm-Conferences/2018/Anglican-EdComm-Resilient-Teaching-Conference-Donald-Guthrie-Slides-2.-Gospel-Healthy-Systems-May-5-2018.pdf (accessed October 9, 2019).

Hale, Edward Everett. 2019. "Quotes." https://www.goodreads.com/author/quotes/8183.Edward_Everett_Hale (accessed October 14, 2019).

Hamlet. n.d. "Chapter & Verse." *Harvard Magazine*. https://www.harvardmagazine.com/1998/03/browse.cv.html (accessed October 21, 2019).

Hardin, Michael. 1994. "The Twelve Step Program and Christian Spirituality." *Journal of Ministry in Addiction & Recovery* 1, no. 1 (October), 47–68.

Hardy, Elizabeth Clark. 1965. "Some Time at Eve." *Poems that Live Forever,* edited by Hazel Felleman. New York: Doubleday. https://books.google.com/books?id=8G8Eco22PrMC&pg=PR17&dq=elizabeth+clark+hardy+AND+Sometime+at+eve&hl=en&newbks=1&newbks_redir=0&sa=X&ved=2ahUKEwiBrMO3563lAhXRjFkKHQc5A9MQ6AEwAHoECAIQAg#v=onepage&q=elizabeth%20clark%20hardy%20AND%20Sometime%20at%20eve&f=false (accessed October 21, 2019).

Hedge, Frederic Henry. 1866. *Reason in Religion*. Boston: Walker, Fuller. https://books.google.com/books?id=-g8qAAAAYAAJ&pg=PA149&dq=frederick+henry+hedge+AND+welcome,+sister+death%22&hl=en&newbks=1&newbks_redir=0&sa=X&ved=2ahUKEwiSopWc6a3lAhURxVkKHYxsBWsQ6AEwAHoECAUQAg#v=onepage&q=frederick%20henry%20hedge%20AND%20welcome%2C%20sister%20death%22&f=false (accessed October 21, 2019).

Heifetz, Ronald A., et al. 2002. *Leadership on the Line: Staying Alive Through the Dangers of Leading*. Cambridge: Harvard Business School. https://books.google.com/books?id=jgo96rH_418C&pg=PT143&lpg=PT143&dq=%22the+human+enterprise+is+an+experiment+in+love+and+connection%22&source=bl&ots=kyokr5d3RC&sig=ACfU3U2TCw_VjnXfbFRoEy3cYSycxd_xWg&hl=en&sa=X&ved=2ahUKEwims4Sr_o_lAhXD1lkKHURuBRAQ6AEwAHoECAAQAQ#v=onepage&q=%

22the%20human%20enterprise%20is%20an%20experiment%20in%20love%20 and%20connection%22&f=false (accessed October 9, 2019).

Higginson, Thomas Wentworth. 1899. "Theodore Parker." *Contemporaries.* Boston: Houghton, Mifflin.

Hoenig, Sidney B. and Samuel H. Rosenberg. 1942. *A Guide to the Prophets.* New York: Bloch.

Hopper, Grace Murray. 2013. "A Ship in Harbor is Safe." https://quoteinvestigator.com/2013/12/09/safe-harbor/ (accessed October 8, 2019).

Howe, Charles A. 2001. "Albert Ziegler." http://uudb.org/articles/albertziegler.html (accessed October 14, 2019).

Hudson, Herbert E., IV. 1959. "The Paradox of Theodore Parker." *The Crane Review* 1, no. 3 (Spring) 111–20.

———. 1960. "Recent Interpretations of Parker: An Evaluation of the Literature Since 1936." *The Proceedings of the Unitarian Historical Society* 13, no. 1, 1–38.

———. 1961. "The Quest for the Historical Parker." *The Proceedings of the Unitarian Historical Society* 13, no. 2, 45–61.

———. 1962. Unpublished loose-leaf notebook.

———. 1965. "Billy Budd: Adam or Christ?" *The Crane Review* 7, no. 2, 62–67.

———. 1967. "The Speaking of Theodore Parker in the Anthony Burns Slave Incident." M.A. thesis, University of Illinois.

———. 1968. "Billy Budd: Adam or Christ?" In *Literature in Critical Perspectives,* edited by Walter K. Gordon, 753–57. New York: Appleton-Century-Crofts.

———. 2016. "Developing a Syllabus for Pastors and Those in Ministerial Training on Addiction Recovery Through Twelve Step Philosophy." DMin dissertation, Trinity Evangelical and Divinity School. Proquest (10257687).

———. 2017. *Anonymous Christians: Support by Clergy of Addiction Recovery Through Twelve Step Programs.* Eugene, OR: Resource.

Hughes, Olga Raevsky. 1974. *The Poetic World of Boris Pasternak.* Princeton: Princeton University Press. https://books.google.com/books?id=cXx9BgAAQBAJ&pg=PA117&dq=boris+pasternak+AND+your+soul+is+that+part+of+you+which+is+in+others&hl=en&sa=X&ved=2ahUKEwj1nb-ToJrlAhUDY6wKHWd4CcEQ6AEwAHoECAUQAg#v=onepage&q=boris%20pasternak%20AND%20your%20soul%20is%20that%20part%20of%20you%20which%20is%20in%20others&f=false (accessed October 13, 2019).

Humanists UK. 2019. "Immanuel Kant." https://humanism.org.uk/humanism/the-humanist-tradition/enlightenment/kant/ (accessed October 15, 2019).

Hunter, W. Bingham. 1986. *The God Who Hears.* Downers Grove, IL: Intervarsity. https://books.google.com/books?id=oNGVq9zNWYgC&pg=PA42&lpg=PA42&dq=%22What+can+you+tell+God+if+he+knows+everything%22&source=bl&ots=yS2ALzQcWA&sig=ACfU3U36-cB_mPyadP36_IHZ8oF64AcQQA&hl=en&sa=X&ved=2ahUKEwih1cDzsJLlAhUCMqwKHaq_DqwQ6AEwAHoECAIQAQ#v=onepage&q=%22What%20can%20you%20tell%20God%20if%20he%20knows%20everything%22&f=false (accessed October 10, 2019),

Ibrahim, Clene (ed.). 2019. *One Nation, Indivisible.* Eugene, OR: Wipf & Stock. https://wipfandstock.com/one-nation-indivisible.html (accessed November 9, 2019).

Ingersoll, Robert. n.d. "At the Grave of a Friend's Child." https://www.theingersolltimes.com/at-the-grave-of-a-friends-child/ (accessed October 22, 2018).

———. 1888. "A Tribute to Courtlandt Palmer." https://infidels.org/library/historical/robert_ingersoll/tribute-palmer.html (accessed October 22, 2019).

———. 1900. *The Works of Robert G. Ingersoll*. Vol. 12. New York: Cosimo.

———. 1903. *Great Speeches R.G. Ingersoll,* edited by J.B. McClure. Chicago: Rhodes and McClure. https://books.google.com/books?id=5b1NAQAAMAAJ&pg=PA253&dq=eulogy+at+his+brother%27s+grave+AND+robert+g.+ingersoll&hl=en&newbks=1&newbks_redir=0&sa=X&ved=2ahUKEwjE7vPSy7DlAhUGyFkKHS1wCqkQ6AEwAHoECAAQAg#v=onepage&q=this%20brave%20and%20tender%20man&f=false (accessed October 22, 2019).

———. 1911. *The Works of Robert G. Ingersoll*. Vol. 13. New York: Dresden. https://books.google.com/books?id=UAugAAAAMAAJ&pg=PA116&dq=robert+g.+ingersoll+AND+"why+should+we+fear"&hl=en&sa=X&ved=2ahUKEwjc_sHHzJrlAhWSmOAKHfARA0EQuwUwAHoECAYQBQ#v=onepage&q=robert%20g.%20ingersoll%20AND%20"why%20should%20we%20fear"&f=false (accessed October 13, 2019).

Irish Blessing. n.d. http://links2love.com/poetry_91.htm (accessed October 19, 2019).

Jacob Marries. n.d. http://jacobmarries.com/109Blessings.html (accessed October 19, 2019).

John of the Cross. 2003. *Dark Night of the Soul*. Translated by E. Allison Peers. Mineola, NY: Dover.

Joy, Charles R. (ed.). 1947. *Albert Schweitzer: An Anthology*. Boston: Beacon.

Keats, John. 2015. "Endymion." https://www.bartleby.com/360/6/154.html (accessed October 22, 2019).

Kepler, Johannes. 2014. "Thinking God's Thoughts." https://faith-seeking-understanding.org/tag/thinking-gods-thoughts-after-him/ (accessed October 10, 2019).

Kurtz, Ernest and Katherine Ketcham. 2002. *The Spirituality of Imperfection*. New York: Bantam.

Kushner, Harold S. 1981. *When Bad Things Happen to Good People*. New York: Schocken.

Lancaster, Evelyn. 1958. *The Final Face of Eve*. New York: McGraw Hill.

Lao-Tse. 2018. *How to Live in the World*. https://twitter.com/how2livein?lang=en (accessed October 8, 2019).

Lee, Hak Joon. 2018. "Kingdom and Kenosis: The Mind of Christ in Paul's Ethics." https://fullerstudio.fuller.edu/kingdom-and-kenosis-the-mind-of-christ-in-pauls-ethics/ (accessed October 8, 2019).

Liberator. July 18, 1856.

Lincoln, Abraham. n.d. https://www.goodreads.com/quotes/69-folks-are-usually-about-as-happy-as-they-make-their (accessed October 9, 2019).

Longfellow, Henry Wadsworth. n.d. "The Day is Done." https://www.poetryfoundation.org/poems/45896/the-day-is-done (accessed October 7, 2019).

———. 2019. "A Psalm of Life." Poetry Foundation. https://www.poetryfoundation.org/poems/44644/a-psalm-of-life (accessed October 21, 2019)

Lounsbury, Charles. n.d. "The Last Will and Testament." http://user.xmission.com/~emailbox/will.htm (accessed October 16, 2019).

Lugo, Sara. 2019. "If Tears." https://www.jah-lyrics.com/song/sara-lugo-if-tears (accessed December 27, 2019).

Bibliography

Maden, R.R. 1868. *The Life and Times of Robert Emmet.* New York: Haverty. https://spinnet.humanities.uva.nl/images/2014-05/emmet1803.pdf (accessed October 22, 2019).

Marquet, Albert. 1972. *Albert Camus: The Invincible Summer.* New York: Humanities. https://books.google.com/books?id=diHxAAAAMAAJ&q=camus+AND+%22there+was+in+me+an+invincible+summer%22&dq=camus+AND+%22there+was+in+me+an+invincible+summer%22&hl=en&sa=X&ved=2ahUKEwj20Y-YopzlAhVsw1kKHYvyA5UQ6AEwAHoECAQQAg (accessed October 14, 2019).

Mason, Ronald. 1951. *The Spirit Above the Dust.* London: Lehmann.

May, Gerald G. 1991. *Addiction and Grace: Love and Spirituality in the Healing of Addictions.* New York: Harper Collins.

McCall, Roy Clyde. 1936. "The Public Speaking Principles and Practice of Theodore Parker." PhD diss., University of Iowa.

McGinnis, Alan Loy. 1985. *Binging Out the Best in People: How to Enjoy Helping Others Excel.* Minneapolis: Augsburg. https://books.google.com/books?id=XVY4j1T6CqQC&pg=PA90&dq=Schweitzer+AND+they+are+suffering+and+dying+before+our+very+eyes+from+physical+maladies&hl=en&newbks=1&newbks_redir=0&sa=X&ved=2ahUKEwj-976jvcPlAhXJwVkKHWlWAOQQ6AEwAHoECAAQAg#v=onepage&q=Schweitzer%20AND%20they%20are%20suffering%20and%20dying%20before%20our%20very%20eyes%20from%20physical%20maladies&f=false (accessed October 30, 2019).

Melville, Herman. 1952. "Billy Budd." In *Selected Writings of Herman Melville.* New York: Modern Library.

Mercadante, Linda A. 1997. "Sin, Gender, and Addiction." *Journal of Ministry in Addiction & Recovery* 4, no. 1 (January) 37–45.

Milton, John. 1853. *The Poetical Works of John Milton,* edited by Egerton Brydges. London: Watson and Hazell. https://www.google.com/books/edition/The_Poetical_Works_of_John_Milton_Illust/_oIOAAAAQAAJ?hl=en&gbpv=1&dq=john+milton+AND+%22nothing+is+here+for+tears%22&pg=PA521&printsec=frontcover (accessed October 20, 2019).

Montgomery, Kathleen (ed.). 2001. *Day of Promise: Collected Meditations.* Vol 1. Boston: Skinner House. https://books.google.com/books?id=hoCMgxR19_cC&pg=PA15&dq=The+unexpected+stairway+AND+Barbara+Rohde&hl=en&sa=X&ved=2ahUKEwiujKu67J_lAhUQrVkKHfcgCFcQ6AEwAHoECAYQAg#v=onepage&q=The%20unexpected%20stairway%20AND%20Barbara%20Rohde&f=false (accessed October 15, 2019).

Morrison, J.H. 1875. "Theodore Parker as an Example to Young Ministers." *Unitarian Review* 3 (March) 250–56.

Mullin, Rita Thievon. 2007. *Harry Houdini: Death Defying Showman.* New York: Sterling.

Murray, Andrew. 2011. "Spiritview." https://spiritview.net/thoughts-on-humility/#comments (accessed October 17, 2019).

Naming Indian Children. 2018. http://www.apples4theteacher.com/native-american/names/giving-the-child-a-name.html (accessed October 19, 2019).

Niebuhr, Reinhold. 2010. "Serenity Prayer." http://www.prayerfoundation.org/dailyoffice/serenity_prayer_full_version.htm (accessed October 10, 2019).

Nouwen, Henri J.M. 1971. *Creative Ministry.* New York: Doubleday.

———. 1972. *The Wounded Healer: Ministry in Contemporary Society.* New York: Doubleday. https://books.google.com/books?id=6bC6AQAAQBAJ&pg=PA65&dq=Nouwen+AND+the+emptiness+of+the+past+and+future+can+never+be+filled+by+words&hl=en&sa=X&ved=2ahUKEwjoo4HcppnlAhUhWN8KHWJDDTsQ6AEwAnoECAYQAg#v=onepage&q=Nouwen%20AND%20the%20emptiness%20of%20the%20past%20and%20future%20can%20never%20be%20filled%20by%20words&f=false (accessed October 13, 2019).

———. 1992. *Life of the Beloved: Spiritual Living in a Secular World.* New York: Crossroad.

O'Donnell, Daniel. 2019. "The Church in the Wildwood." https://www.google.com/search?rlz=1C1AWFC_enUS835US835&ei=8uyjXcjtGeiv_QaG9L2QBw&q=the+church+in+the+wildwood+lyrics+AND+daniel+o%27donnell&oq=the+church+in+the+wildwood+lyrics+AND+daniel+o%27donnell&gs_l=psy-ab.3...12412.19349..19685...0.2..0.153.2174.7j14......0....1..gws-wiz.......0i71j0j0i22i30j0i22i10i3oj33i22i29i30j33i160.Sg1sLt9MVGs&ved=0ahUKEwjIrpjy6JrlAhXoV98KHQZ6D3IQ4dUDCAs&uact=5 (accessed October 13, 2019).

Old English Blessing. n.d. "Finest Quotes." http://www.finestquotes.com/quote-id-11147.htm (accessed October 20, 2019).

Oppenheim, James. 1907. "The Child." *Cosmopolitan* 44, 538. https://books.google.com/books?id=DE9OAQAAMAAJ&pg=PA538&dq=James+Oppenheim+AND+%22you+may+be+Christ+or+Shakespeare%22&hl=en&newbks=1&newbks_redir=0&sa=X&ved=2ahUKEwjSorDH66rlAhVNx1kKHSP2Bv8Q6AEwAnoECAQQAg#v=onepage&q=James%20Oppenheim%20AND%20%22you%20may%20be%20Christ%20or%20Shakespeare%22&f=false (accessed October 20, 2019).

O'Reilly, John Boyle. n.d. "Forever." https://www.poemhunter.com/poem/forever-329/ (accessed October 22, 2019).

Owen-Towle, Tom. 1993. *The Gospel of Universalism.* Boston: Skinner House. https://books.google.com/books?id=C4VcBTiTY6MC&pg=PA43&dq=quillen+hamilton+shinn+AND+%22there+is+no+hell%22&hl=en&sa=X&ved=2ahUKEwjv35SMs5_lAhUkUt8KHQO4DpIQ6AEwAHoECAQQAg#v=onepage&q=quillen%20hamilton%20shinn%20AND%20%22there%20is%20no%20hell%22&f=false (accessed October 15, 2019).

Parke, David B. 1957. *The Epic of Unitarianism: Original Writings from the History of Liberal Religion.* Boston: Skinner. https://books.google.com/books?id=9V7M7m8KitUC&pg=PA6&dq=%22may+this+blasphemous+and+philosophical+distinction+of+three+beings+in+one+God+be+rooted+out%22&hl=en&sa=X&ved=2ahUKEwiR8_P7qorlAhVEiFkKHalNDgUQ6AEwAHoECAAQAg#v=onepage&q=%22may%20this%20blasphemous%20and%20philosophical%20distinction%20of%20three%20beings%20in%20one%20God%20be%20rooted%20out%22&f=false (accessed October 7, 2019).

Parker, Theodore. 1867. "The New Crime Against Humanity." *Additional Speeches.* Vol. 2. Boston: Horace B. Fuller.

———. 2019. "Be Ours a Religion." Unitarian Universalist Association. https://www.uua.org/worship/words/reading/21514.shtml (accessed October 15, 2019).

Parrington, Vernon L. 1927. "Theodore Parker." In *Main Currents in American Thought.* Vol. 2. New York: Harcourt, Brace.

Pasternak, Boris. 1991. *Dr. Zhivago.* New York: Random House. https://books.google.com/books?id=a517KSzYoEwC&pg=PA68&lpg=PA68&dq=%22you+are+an

Bibliography 353

xious+about+whether+you+will+rise+from+the+dead%22+AND+Pasternak&source=bl&ots=MRKzoEzrFS&sig=ACfU3U3eVzRYBm19dEH8vom_Jq332zvEUQ&hl=en&sa=X&ved=2ahUKEwjE5MO7_6zlAhWjwFkKHSeIBAgQ6AEwAnoECAgQAQ#v=onepage&q=%22you%20are%20anxious%20about%20whether%20you%20will%20rise%20from%20the%20dead%22%20AND%20Pasternak&f=false (accessed October 21, 2019).

Patheos. 2017. https://www.patheos.com/blogs/monkeymind/2012/01/a-letter-to-a-twentieth-century-minister-from-a-twenty-first-century-minister.html (accessed October 19, 2019).

Patton, Kenneth L. n.d. "Let Us Worship." http://www.yorku.ca/jmason/Patton.htm (accessed October 15, 2019).

———. 1944. "Ours, O Men, Has Been Yesterday." *Journal of Liberal Religion* 6, no. 1, 233. https://books.google.com/books?id=hsoSAAAAIAAJ&q="Ours,+O+Men,+has+been+yesterday"&dq="Ours,+O+Men,+has+been+yesterday"&hl=en&sa=X&ved=2ahUKEwin4KyFkp_lAhVGmeAKHehsBywQ6AEwAHoECAAQAQ (accessed October 15, 2019).

———. 2015. University Unitarian Church. http://www.uuchurch.org/worship/awe-mystery/ (accessed October 5, 2019).

Paul, S.K. 2006. *The Complete Poems of Rabindranath Tagore's Gitanjali*. New Delhi: Sarnp & Sons. https://books.google.com/books?id=IproIa_rIv8C&printsec=frontcover&dq=tagore+and+%22where+the+mind+is+without+fear%22&hl=en&sa=X&ved=2ahUKEwj48u6jtJ_lAhWFiOAKHcKQDOgQ6AEwAXoECAUQAg#v=onepage&q=%22where%20the%20mind%20is%20without%20fear%22&f=false (accessed October 15, 2019).

Peck, Scott. 1978. *The Road Less Traveled*. New York: Touchstone.

Phillips, William J. 2009. *One World at a Time*. Bloomington, IN: Xlibris.

Pohl, Christine. 1999. *Making Room: Recovering Hospitality as a Christian Tradition*. Grand Rapids: William B. Eerdmans. https://books.google.com/books?id=3uCAShDkca8C&printsec=frontcover&dq=pohl+AND+making+room&hl=en&sa=X&ved=2ahUKEwio9NzF1Y_lAhXIwVkKHZqpCDkQ6AEwAHoECAEQAg#v=onepage&q=pohl%20AND%20making%20room&f=false (accessed October 9, 2019).

Popik, Barry. 2014. "Courage is Fear That Has Said Its Prayers." https://www.barrypopik.com/index.php/new_york_city/entry/courage_is_fear_that_has_said_its_prayers (accessed October 8, 2019).

Prince, Morton. 1906. *The Dissociation of a Personality: A Biographical Study in Abnormal Psychology*. New York: Longmans, Green.

Quarles, Frances. 1881. *Complete Works of Prose and Verse*. Edinburgh: University Press. https://books.google.com/books?id=pLsxAQAAMAAJ&pg=PA188&lpg=PA188&dq=%22why+dost+thou+wonder,+O+man%22&source=bl&ots=5_6Ddgi-vH&sig=ACfU3UofB3ftW91lx_eYz4iBx851lJI-6w&hl=en&sa=X&ved=2ahUKEwiLnN3S7YrlAhWkpFkKHbnRB_sQ6AEwAHoECAUQAQ#v=onepage&q=%22why%20dost%20thou%20wonder%2C%20O%20man%22&f=false (accessed October 7, 2019).

Remembrances and Celebrations, edited by Jill Werman Harris. 1999. New York: Pantheon. https://books.google.com/books?id=wM3a45Fhu5EC&pg=PA254&dq="say+not+they+die,+those+splendid+souls"&hl=en&newbks=1&newbks_redir=0&sa=X&ved=2ahUKEwi1uvqM-

Bibliography

qzlAhUrrlkKHTgpDkoQ6AEwAHoECAMQAg#v=onepage&q="say%20not%20 they%20die%2C%20those%20splendid%20souls"&f=false (accessed October 21, 2019).

Robinson, H. Wheeler. 1937. *The Old Testament, Its Making and Meaning*. New York: Abington-Cokesbury.

Rose, Billy. n.d. "Pitching Horseshoes." *Reader's Digest*. http://www.thehealingsite.us/take%20time.html (accessed October 16, 2019).

Ross, Floyd D. and Tynette Wilson Hills. 1954. *Questions that Matter Most: Asked by the World's Religions*. Boston: Beacon. https://books.google.com/books?id=A6ErAQAAMAAJ&q=chuang-tse+AND+%22WAS+I+THEN+A+M AN+DREAMING+i+WAS+A+BUTTERFLY%22&dq=chuang-tse+AND+%22W AS+I+THEN+A+MAN+DREAMING+i+WAS+A+BUTTERFLY%22&hl=en&n ewbks=1&newbks_redir=0&sa=X&ved=2ahUKEwi4i-eM5a3lAhVOq1kKHQoI ClsQ6AEwAX0ECAAQAg (accessed October 21, 2019).

Russell, Bertrand. 1923. *A Free Man's Worship*. Portland, ME: Mosher. https://books.google.com/books?id=tH87AAAAYAAJ&printsec=frontcover&dq=bertrand+ russell+AND++a+free+man%27s+worship&hl=en&newbks=1&newbks_redi r=0&sa=X&ved=2ahUKEwi42prB2qblAhUELKwKHcJWDroQ6AEwAHoEC AUQAg#v=onepage&q=%22the%20life%20of%20man%20is%20a%20long%20 march%22&f=false (accessed October 18, 2019).

Sandburg, Carl. 1970. *Complete Poems of Carl Sandburg*. New York: Harcourt. https://books.google.com/books?id=bCSu8UHz9EUC&pg=PA588&dq=the+wheel+t urns+AND+sandburg&hl=en&newbks=1&newbks_redir=0&sa=X&ved=2ah UKEwjvuLb_4a3lAhUqrlkKHf5CBVEQ6AEwAHoECAAQAg#v=onepage&q =the%20wheel%20turns%20AND%20sandburg&f=false (accessed October 21, 2019).

———. 2016. "The Sea Moves Always." https://hemmingplay.com/2016/08/15/the-sea-moves-always/ (accessed October 14, 2019).

Santayana, George. 1998. *Prayers for the Classroom*, edited by Philip A. Verhalen. Collegeville, MN: Liturgical. https://books.google.com/books?id=Aymbj17_1pw C&pg=PA140&dq=%22with+you+a+part+of+me+hath+passed+away%22&hl= en&newbks=1&newbks_redir=0&sa=X&ved=2ahUKEwjX8M7gm67lAhXM1V kKHfJNDSMQ6AEwAX0ECAMQAg#v=onepage&q=%22with%20you%20a%20 part%20of%20me%20hath%20passed%20away%22&f=false (accessed October 21, 2019).

Sasson, Siegfried. n.d. "To My Son." https://www.poetrynook.com/poem/my-son-5 (accessed October 19, 2019).

———. 2000. *Seasons of Life: A Poetic Anthology*, edited by Nigel Collins. Amherst, New York: Prometheus.

Schweitzer, Albert. 1947. *An Anthology*, edited by Charles R. Joy. Boston: Beacon. https://books.google.com/books?id=G94HAAAAMAAJ&pg=PA133&source=g bs_toc_r&cad=3#v=onepage&q&f=false (accessed January 6, 2020).

———. 1949. *Out of my Life and Thought: An Autobiography*. Translated by C.T. Campion. New York: Mentor. https://books.google.com/books?id=X4t-BAA AQBAJ&pg=PT152&dq=out+of+my+life+and+thought&hl=en&newbks=1 &newbks_redir=0&sa=X&ved=2ahUKEwiD58eKn7HlAhXFtlkKHaW4A08 Q6AEwAHoECAAQAg#v=onepage&q=out%20of%20my%20life%20and%20 thought&f=false (accessed October 22, 2019).

———. 1955. *To Dr. Albert Schweitzer on His 80th Birthday*, edited by Homer A. Jack. New York: Profile.

Seaburg, Carl. 1998. *Great Occasions*. Boston: Skinner House. https://books.google.com/books?id=1_20xsHU4QUC&pg=PA309&lpg=PA309&dq=%22here+we+are,+you+and+I,+and+the+millions+of+men+and+animals%22&source=bl&ots=46LlEWUx93&sig=ACfU3U3EWQV3F0DAlq-9dQxHIMEZ86suGQ&hl=en&sa=X&ved=2ahUKEwji-7qO1J3lAhXRxlkKHVF_CP8Q6AEwAX0ECAMQAQ#v=onepage&q=%22here%20we%20are%2C%20you%20and%20I%2C%20and%20the%20millions%20of%20men%20and%20animals%22&f=false (accessed October 15, 2019).

Seredy, Kate. 1990. *The Singing Tree*. New York: Puffin.

Shakespeare, William. 1992. *Julius Caesar*. New York: Washington Square.

Shapiro, Stephen. 2005. "Innovation Insights." https://stephenshapiro.com/salutation-to-the-dawn/ (accessed October 15, 2019).

Shoemaker, Samuel. 2008. *The Conversion of the Church: The Genius of Fellowship*. N.p.: Tuchy Palmieri.

Socrates. 1880. *The Trial and Death of Socrates*. Translated by F.J. Church. London: MacMillan. https://books.google.com/books?id=z5MCAAAAQAAJ&newbks=1&newbks_redir=0&printsec=frontcover&source=gbs_ge_summary_r&cad=0#v=onepage&q&f=false (accessed October 21, 2019).

St. Francis of Assisi. n.d. "Prayer." https://www.google.com/search?q=st.+francis+prayer&rlz=1C1AWFC_enUS835US835&oq=st.+francis+&aqs=chrome.2.69i57j0l5.10151j0j4&sourceid=chrome&ie=UTF-8 (accessed October 8, 2019).

Stern, Chaim, ed. 1998. *Day by Day Reflections*. Boston: Beacon. https://books.google.com/books?id=nq9k1jOeO8MC&pg=PA112&dq=karl+jaspers+AND+%22this+is+the+vision+of+a+great%22&hl=en&sa=X&ved=2ahUKEwjm8ojQ8p7lAhXDVN8KHeqiCp8Q6AEwAHoECAYQAg#v=onepage&q=karl%20jaspers%20AND%20%22this%20is%20the%20vision%20of%20a%20great%22&f=false (accessed October 15, 2019).

Stern, Milton R. 1957. *The Fine Hammered Steel of Herman Melville*. Urbana: University of Illinois Press.

Stevenson, Robert Louis. n.d. "We Thank Thee." http://www.appleseeds.org/we-thank-rls.htm (accessed October 19, 2019).

———. 1886. *The Strange Case of Dr. Jekyll and Mr. Hyde*. New York: Charles Scribner's Sons.

Stewardson, Clara H. and Roslyn Weiss. 1998. *Socrates Dissatisfied: An Analysis of Plato's Crito*. New York: Oxford. https://books.google.com/books?id=vG3voShLdRoC&pg=PT218&dq=socrates+AND+%22Men+of+Athens,+I+am+your+friend%22&hl=en&sa=X&ved=2ahUKEwj81IPM14blAhUnrVkKHTXYCQMQ6AEwAHoECAEQAg#v=onepage&q=socrates%20AND%20%22Men%20of%20Athens%2C%20I%20am%20your%20friend%22&f=false (accessed October 7, 2019).

Stowe, Harriet Beecher. n.d. "When I Awake, I Am Still With Thee." https://books.google.com/books?id=p9coAAAAYAAJ&pg=PA356&dq=harriet+beecher+stowe+and+%22still,+still+with+thee%22&hl=en&sa=X&ved=2ahUKEwiD_afq4prlAhWEg-AKHRnbCSEQ6AEwAXoECAgQAg#v=onepage&q=harriet%20beecher%20stowe%20and%20%22still%2C%20still%20with%20thee%22&f=false (accessed October 13, 2019).

———. 1856. *Religious Studies, Sketches and Poems.* New York: Houghton Mifflin. https://books.google.com/books?id=p9c0AAAAYAAJ&pg=PA356&dq=harriet+beecher+stowe+AND+still,+still+with+thee&hl=en&newbks=1&newbks_redir=0&sa=X&ved=2ahUKEwjA7_ih2K7lAhUBm1kKHe5dA_0Q6AEwAHoECAAQAg#v=onepage&q=harriet%20beecher%20stowe%20AND%20still%2C%20still%20with%20thee&f=false (accessed October 21, 2019).

Tachibana, S. n.d. *The Ethics of Buddhism.* Surrey, UK: Curzon.

Tagore, Rabindranath. n.d. http://www.eastkentquakers.org.uk/favershammeeting.html (accessed October 7, 2019).

———. n.d. "My Song." https://allpoetry.com/My-Song (accessed October 22, 2019).

———. April 28, 1943. *Christian Advocate* 22–23. https://books.google.com/books?id=2LTrOHskhMgC&q=Our+true+life+lies+in+a+great+depth+within+us+AND+Tagore&dq=Our+true+life+lies+in+a+great+depth+within+us+AND+Tagore&hl=en&sa=X&ved=2ahUKEwj9iredooblAhVsrlkKHcsXDAkQ6AEwBHoECAEQAg (accessed October 5, 2019).

———. 1996. *The English Writings of Rabinranath Tagore.* Delhi: Wellwish.

———. 2004. *The English Writings of Rabinranath Tagore,* edited by Sisir Kumar Das. Delhi: Wellwish. https://books.google.com/books?id=bsTNd7_Jt4EC&pg=PA111&dq=tagore+AND+%22peace,+my+heart,+let+the+time%22&hl=en&newbks=1&newbks_redir=0&sa=X&ved=2ahUKEwjytNeiorDlAhVDwVkKHdU-DWoQ6AEwAXoECAEQAg#v=onepage&q=tagore%20AND%20%22peace%2C%20my%20heart%2C%20let%20the%20time%22&f=false (accessed October 22, 2019).

———. 2006. *The Complete Poems of Rabinranath Tagore,* edited by S.K. Paul. New Delhi: Sarup and Sons. https://books.google.com/books?id=IproIa_rIv8C&printsec=frontcover&source=gbs_ge_summary_r&cad=0#v=onepage&q&f=false (accessed October 22, 2019).

———. 2019. "My Song." https://www.goodreads.com/quotes/9097194-my-song-this-song-of-mine-will-wind-its-music (accessed October 22, 2019).

Taps. n.d. https://www.ausa.org/history-taps (accessed October 9, 2019).

Teasdale, Sara. 2019. "Barter." Poetry Foundation. https://www.poetryfoundation.org/poems/46006/barter-56d225c3374d8 (accessed October 5, 2019).

Tennyson, Alfred Lord. 2019. "In Memoriam A.H.H. Obiit MDCCCXXXIII:27." https://www.poetryfoundation.org/poems/45336/in-memoriam-a-h-h-obiit-mdcccxxxiii-27 (accessed December 27, 2019).

———. 2019. "Ulysses." Poetry Foundation. https://www.poetryfoundation.org/poems/45392/ulysses (accessed October 8, 2019).

Thigpen, Corbett and Hervey M. Cleckley. 1983. *The Three Faces of Eve.* New York: Popular Library.

Thomas. Mike. 2016. "Through the Looking Glass: Christian Reflections." http://aharvestofmiracles.blogspot.com/2009/07/theresa-of-avila-nada-te-turbe-let.html (accessed October 8, 2019).

Thompson, Lawrance. 1952. *Melville's Quarrel with God.* Princeton, NJ: Princeton University Press.

Thoreau, Henry David. n.d. https://www.azquotes.com/quote/769086 (accessed October 8, 2019).

———. 1992. *Walden and Other Writings.* New York: Modern Library.

———. 2012. *Walden.* https://althouse.blogspot.com/2012/04/i-did-not-wish-to-live-what-was-not.html (accessed October 8, 2019).

Tillich, Paul. 1952. *The Courage to Be*. New Haven: Yale University Press.
———. 1967. *Systematic Theology*. 3 vols. New York: Harper and Row.
Trine, Ralph Waldo. n.d. *The Higher Powers of Mind and Spirit*. New York: Lanval. https://books.google.com/books?id=Bx_I3s39ODAC&pg=PA102&dq=edwin+markham+AND+%22we+men+of+earth+have+here+the+stuff%22&hl=en&sa=X&ved=2ahUKEwia3prxq53lAhVMwlkKHdh6BPwQ6AEwAnoECAEQAg#v=onepage&q=edwin%20markham%20AND%20%22we%20men%20of%20earth%20have%20here%20the%20stuff%22&f=false (accessed October 14, 2019).
VanYperen, Jim. 2002. *Peace: A Guide to Overcoming Church Conflict*. Chicago: Moody.
Vogt, Von Ogden. 2011. "The Grapevine Newsletter." Pullman Memorial Universalist Church. Albion, New York. https://pullmanmemorial.files.wordpress.com/2011/05/june-2011-grapevine.pdf (accessed October 15, 2019).
Wedding in Paradise. n.d. "Charge and Benediction." https://a-wedding-in-paradise.com/charge-benediction/ (accessed October 19, 2019).
Weiss, John. 1864. *The Life and Correspondence of Theodore Parker*. 2 vols. New York: D. Appleton.
Whitford, Bradley. 2019. "Female Fitness Daily." https://femalefitnessdaily.com/bradley-whitford-infuse-your-life-with-action/ (accessed October 14, 2019).
Whitman, Walt. 1902. *Poems of Walt Whitman*. New York: Thomas V. Crowell. https://books.google.com/books?id=z_cHRbMRByYC&printsec=frontcover&dq=walt+whitman+AND+%22Whoever+you+are%22&hl=en&sa=X&ved=2ahUKEwiY-ZLp5Z_lAhXS1VkKHWa4AKwQ6AEwAXoECAMQAg#v=onepage&q=for%20none%20more%20than%20you%20is%20immortality&f=false (accessed October 15, 2019).
———. 1919. "Passage to More Than India." https://songofamerica.net/song/sail-forth/ (accessed October 22, 2019).
———. 2019. "On the Beach at Night." Poetry Foundation. https://www.poetryfoundation.org/poems/45475/on-the-beach-at-night (accessed October 20, 2019).
Wilbur, Earl Morse. 1952. *A History of Unitarianism: In Transylvania, England, and America*. 3 vols. Boston: Beacon Press. http://www.pacificuu.org/wilbur/ahu/book2/12.htm (accessed October 19, 2019).
Williams, L. Griswold. n.d. "Handout #1: Congregational Covenants." https://www.uua.org/re/tapestry/adults/river/workshop7/175905.shtml (accessed October 19, 2019).
Williams, Margery. 1997. *The Velveteen Rabbit: Or, How Toys Become Real*. Philadelphia: Running.
Williams, Sarah. 1936. *Best Loved Poems of the American People*, edited by Hazel Felleman. Garden City, NY: Garden City.
———. 2019. "Goodreads." https://www.goodreads.com/author/show/5438774.Sarah_Williams (accessed October 20, 2019).
Wing, Nell. 2009. "Origin of the Serenity Prayer: A Historical Paper." https://www.aa.org/assets/en_US/smf-129_en.pdf (accessed October 19, 2019).
Yagota, Ben. 2000. *Will Rogers: A Biography*. Norman: University of Oklahoma Press.
Zimmerman, Julie. 2002. "Sorting Out the Truth About St. Francis of Assisi." http://www.appleseeds.org/St-Fran_Preach-Gospel.htm (accessed October 19, 2019).

www.ingramcontent.com/pod-product-compliance
Lightning Source LLC
Chambersburg PA
CBHW050613300426
44112CB00012B/1483